THE

50 GREATEST PLAYERS

IN

CINCINNATI BENGALS

HISTORY

ALSO AVAILABLE IN THE 50 GREATEST PLAYERS SERIES

THE
50 GREATEST PLAYERS
IN
CINCINNATI BENGALS
HISTORY

ROBERT W. COHEN

LYONS
PRESS

ESSEX, CONNECTICUT

An imprint of The Globe Pequot Publishing Group, Inc.
64 South Main Street
Essex, CT 06426
www.globepequot.com

Distributed by NATIONAL BOOK NETWORK

British Library Cataloguing in Publication Information available

Library of Congress Cataloging-in-Publication Data available

ISBN 978-1-4930-7915-5 (paperback: alk. paper)
ISBN 978-1-4930-7916-2 (electronic)

♾ The paper used in this publication meets the minimum requirements of American National Standard for Information Sciences—Permanence of Paper for Printed Library Materials, ANSI/ NISO Z39.48-1992.

CONTENTS

ACKNOWLEDGMENTS

I wish to thank Kate Yeakley of RMYauctions.com, George A. Kitrinos, Keith Allison and All-Pro Reels Photography, Jeffrey Beall, Alexander Jonesi, Navin Rajagopalan, and Erik Drost, each of whom generously contributed to the photographic content of this work.

INTRODUCTION

THE BENGALS LEGACY

The Cincinnati Bengals came into being primarily through the efforts of Paul Brown, the legendary head coach who, from 1946 to 1962, led the Cleveland Browns to four All-America Football Conference (AAFC) and three National Football League (NFL) championships while serving as the team's part-owner, general manager, and head coach. Eager to get back into the game after being ousted by new Browns owner Art Modell following the conclusion of the 1962 campaign, Brown convinced Ohio governor Jim Rhodes during a meeting between the two men in 1965 that the state had the ability to accommodate a second pro football team. One year later, Cincinnati's city council approved the construction of 60,389-seat Riverfront Stadium, a multipurpose facility built on the dilapidated riverfront section of the city that served as home to both the Bengals and Reds from 1970 to 1999.

Awarded a franchise in the then nine-team American Football League (AFL) in 1967, a group headed by Brown officially named its new team the Bengals in recognition of previous Cincinnati pro football franchises with the same name that had competed during the 1930s and 1940s. Beginning play in 1968, the Bengals, who spent their first two seasons playing their home games at Nippert Stadium, the current home of the University of Cincinnati Bearcats, initially took up residence in the AFL West, which they shared with the Oakland Raiders, Kansas City Chiefs, San Diego Chargers, and Denver Broncos. Meanwhile, the New York Jets, Houston Oilers, Miami Dolphins, Boston Patriots, and Buffalo Bills comprised the league's Eastern Division.

The expansion Bengals did not fare particularly well at first, posting an overall record of 7-20-1 from 1968 to 1969 that earned them a pair of last-place finishes. However, their play improved dramatically following the NFL/AFL merger in 1970. With three former NFL teams (Cleveland Browns, Pittsburgh Steelers, and Baltimore Colts) agreeing to move to the newly constructed AFC, pro football adopted a new two-conference, three-division setup that placed the Bengals in the AFC Central Division, where they competed directly against the Browns, Steelers, and Houston Oilers. Finding the new alignment very much to their liking, the Bengals captured their first division title in 1970 by compiling a record of 8–6 during the regular season. But they subsequently suffered a 17–0 defeat at the hands of the eventual Super Bowl champion Baltimore Colts in the opening round of the postseason tournament.

Far less successful in 1971, the Bengals finished just 4–10, before going 8–6 the following year and laying claim to their second division title in 1973 by posting a mark of 10–4. However, they again came up short in the divisional round of the playoffs, this time losing to the defending Super Bowl champion Miami Dolphins by a score of 34–16. Following a mediocre 7–7 showing in 1974, the Bengals advanced to the playoffs as a wild card the following year by compiling a regular-season record of 11–3. But they again exited the postseason tournament quickly, losing to the Oakland Raiders by a score of 31–28 in the opening round.

Choosing to retire from coaching at the end of the year, 67-year-old Paul Brown, who had directed the Bengals from the sidelines since their inception, turned over the mantle of leadership to former offensive line coach Bill Johnson. In his eight years as head man in Cincinnati, Brown guided the Bengals to an overall record of 55-56-1, three playoff appearances, and two division titles. Meanwhile, during his time in the Queen City, Brown had the privilege of coaching standout performers such as quarterback Ken Anderson, wide receiver Isaac Curtis, center Bob Johnson, and tight end Bob Trumpy on offense, and lineman Mike Reid, linebacker Bill Bergey, and cornerbacks Ken Riley and Lemar Parrish on defense. Although Brown would never again coach in the NFL, he continued to serve as Bengals general manager until his death in 1991, when his son, Mike, assumed GM duties.

The Bengals compiled a winning record under Bill Johnson in each of the next two seasons, performing especially well in 1976, when they just missed making the playoffs with a mark of 10–4. However, Johnson received his walking papers after the Bengals lost their first five games in 1978, leading to the hiring of former Rice University head coach, Homer

Rice. Continuing to struggle under Rice, the Bengals posted identical 4–12 records in 1978 and 1979, prompting management to turn to Hall of Fame offensive lineman Forrest Gregg, who had previously served as head man in Cleveland from 1975 to 1977 and with Toronto of the Canadian Football League in 1979.

After going just 6–10 their first year under Gregg, the Bengals captured consecutive division titles in 1981 and 1982, advancing to the Super Bowl in the first of those campaigns by defeating the Buffalo Bills, 28–21, in the opening round of the playoffs and the San Diego Chargers, 27–7, in the AFC Championship Game, before losing to the San Francisco 49ers in Super Bowl XVI by a score of 26–21.

An extremely well-balanced team, the 1981 Bengals excelled on both offense and defense, outscoring their opponents by a combined margin of 421–304 during the regular season, en route to compiling a record of 12–4. Although quarterback Ken Anderson earned NFL MVP honors with his exceptional play behind center, he received a significant amount of help from running back Pete Johnson, wide receiver Cris Collinsworth, and standout offensive linemen Anthony Muñoz and Max Montoya. Meanwhile, linebackers Reggie Williams and Jim LeClair, ends Ross Browner and Eddie Edwards, and cornerbacks Louis Breeden and the ageless Ken Riley all starred for the Bengals on the defensive side of the ball.

After suffering a humiliating 44–17 defeat at the hands of the New York Jets in the wild card round of the 1982 AFC playoffs, the Bengals finished just 7–9 under Gregg the following year, causing management to replace him with former Indiana University head coach Sam Wyche, who had previously spent nearly a decade (including three years with the Bengals) serving as a backup quarterback in the NFL. Wyche subsequently led the Bengals to a pair of mediocre finishes in 1984 and 1985, before guiding them to a mark of 10–6 in 1986 and a record of 12–4 two years later that earned them their fifth division title.

Led by NFL MVP Boomer Esiason, running backs James Brooks and Ickey Woods, star wideout Eddie Brown, and the most dominant offensive lineman in the game, Anthony Muñoz, the Bengals boasted the NFL's most prolific offense in 1988, scoring a league-high 448 points during the regular season. Solid on defense as well, the Bengals featured linebacker Reggie Williams, run-stuffing nose tackle Tim Krumrie, and hard-hitting safety David Fulcher on that side of the ball, making them the AFC's most complete team, which they proved by defeating Seattle, 21–13, in the divisional round of the playoffs and Buffalo, 21–10, in the conference championship game. Once again, though, San Francisco prevented them from capturing the NFL championship, with Joe Montana's 10-yard touchdown pass to John Taylor with just 34 seconds left in regulation giving the 49ers a 20–16 victory over the Bengals in Super Bowl XXIII.

Not nearly as dominant in 1989, the Bengals concluded the campaign with a record of just 8–8, before winning their sixth division title the following year, despite posting a rather mediocre mark of 9–7 during the regular season. But after routing the Houston Oilers, 41–14, in the wild card round of the playoffs, the Bengals suffered a 20–10 defeat at the hands of the Los Angeles Raiders in the divisional round of the postseason tournament.

Having won four division titles and appeared in two Super Bowls the previous 10 years, the Bengals looked forward to more success heading into the 1991 campaign. However, following the passing of Paul Brown on August 5 of that year, the Bengals entered the darkest period in franchise history—one in which they posted a losing record in 11 of the next 12 seasons as Sam Wyche (1991), David Shula (1992–1996), Bruce Coslet (1996–2000), and Dick LeBeau (2000–2002) all took turns coaching the team.

After winning only three games under Wyche in 1991, the Bengals posted an overall record of just 19–52 under Shula, before management replaced him at the helm with Coslet midway through the 1996 campaign. The Bengals subsequently showed some improvement under Coslet in 1996 and 1997, going a combined 14–11. But they performed miserably with him in charge the next three seasons, posting a composite mark of just 7–28, before management handed him his walking papers. Faring no better under LeBeau the next three seasons, the Bengals went a combined 12–33, costing him his job as well.

Certainly, much of the blame for the Bengals' failures could be attributed to the many poor picks they made in the annual NFL Draft. While the team's brain trust showed sound judgment when it selected wide receiver Carl Pickens in the second round in 1992, fellow wideout Darnay Scott in the second round in 1994, offensive tackle Willie Anderson with the 10th overall pick in 1996, and running back Corey Dillon in the second round in 1997, it fumbled the ball when it selected quarterback David Klingler sixth overall in 1992, running back Ki-Jana Carter with the first overall pick in 1995, and quarterback Akili Smith third overall in 1999. And with both Klingler and Smith proving to be huge draft busts, the Bengals found themselves being hampered by poor quarterback play for much of the period, with only Jeff Blake performing well behind center for two or three seasons.

Meanwhile, with the NFL expanding to 30 teams in 1995, the Jacksonville Jaguars joined the Bengals, Browns, Steelers, and Oilers in the AFC Central Division. One year later, the Browns moved to Baltimore and renamed themselves the Ravens. Following suit in 1997, the Oilers relocated from Houston to Tennessee, although they retained their original moniker for two years until they became the Titans. Things remained status quo in the AFC Central until 1999, when a new expansion version of the Cleveland Browns entered the division, increasing the number of teams to six. Then, with the AFC adding the Houston Texans to its fraternity of ballclubs in 2002, each conference adopted a four-division setup, placing the Bengals in the newly formed AFC North, which they have since shared with the Steelers, Browns, and Ravens.

In addition to the changes within their division, the Bengals, who had called Riverfront Stadium (later renamed Cinergy Field in 1996) home since 1970, moved into newly constructed Paul Brown Stadium in 2000. Located on approximately 22 acres of land, Paul Brown Stadium, which has since been renamed Paycor Stadium in deference to its sponsor, has a listed seating capacity of 65,515. Nicknamed "The Jungle," Paycor Stadium has served as home to the Bengals for the last 24 seasons.

Things finally began to improve in Cincinnati after the Bengals hired former Baltimore Ravens and Washington Redskins defensive coordinator Marvin Lewis as their new head coach following an embarrassing 2–14 showing in 2002. Bringing stability to the organization for the first time in years, Lewis guided the Bengals to consecutive 8–8 finishes in his first two seasons, before leading them to an 11–5 record and their first division title in 15 years in 2005.

Featuring a talented roster that included former Heisman Trophy winning quarterback Carson Palmer, whom they had selected with the first overall pick in the 2003 NFL Draft, running back Rudi Johnson, receivers Chad Johnson and T. J. Houshmandzadeh, All-Pro tackle Willie Anderson, defensive lineman Justin Smith, and linebacker Brian Simmons, the Bengals entered the 2005 postseason tournament with high hopes. But their dreams of advancing to the Super Bowl for the third time in franchise history all but ended in the first quarter of their opening-round playoff loss to the eventual Super Bowl champion Pittsburgh Steelers, when Palmer suffered a broken leg that required reconstructive surgery during the following offseason.

Although Palmer returned to action in 2006, the Bengals failed to make the playoffs in any of the next three seasons, finishing well out of contention in 2008, when another serious injury to their starting quarterback and an off year by ailing wideout Chad Johnson relegated them to a mark of just 4-11-1. However, with both Palmer and Johnson fully healthy by the start of the 2009 campaign, the Bengals captured the AFC North title with a record of 10–6. Again, though, they exited the postseason tournament quickly, losing to the Jets, 24–14, in the opening round.

The Bengals subsequently finished just 4–12 in 2010, before beginning an extremely successful five-year run during which they won two division titles and made five consecutive playoff appearances with Andy Dalton starting for them behind center. Solid but unspectacular, Dalton went on to establish himself as one of the franchise's career leaders in every major passing category, with the help of star receiver A. J. Green, who ranks among the finest wideouts in team annals. Meanwhile, Geno Atkins and Carlos Dunlap excelled for the Bengals on defense, giving them one of the top defensive line tandems in the league.

But while the Bengals performed well during the regular season, they faltered in the playoffs each year, suffering five straight first-round losses in postseason play. After advancing to the playoffs as a wild card in both 2011 and 2012, the Bengals suffered consecutive first-round losses to the Houston Texans, losing to them, 31–10, in the first of those campaigns and, 19–13, in the second. A division winner in 2013, the Bengals compiled a record of 11–5 during the regular season. But this time they lost to the San Diego Chargers in the opening round by a score of 27–10. Advancing to the playoffs as a wild card for the third time in four years in 2014 after finishing the regular season with a mark of 10-5-1, the Bengals subsequently failed to mount a serious challenge to the Indianapolis Colts in the opening round of the postseason tournament, losing to them by a score of 26–10. Entering the 2015 playoffs with high hopes after winning the division title with a record of 12–4, the Bengals came up short in the opening round for the fifth straight time, this time suffering a heartbreaking 18–16 defeat at the hands of the division rival Pittsburgh Steelers.

While many football pundits began calling for the firing of Marvin Lewis due to the constant failures of his team once it reached the playoffs, he remained head coach in Cincinnati until the end of 2018, when he and the organization announced that they had mutually decided to part ways after the Bengals posted three straight losing records. In his 16 years as head coach of the Bengals, Lewis led them to an overall regular-season record of 131-122-3, seven playoff appearances, and four division titles. Named NFL Coach of the Year in 2009, Lewis won more games than any other head coach in franchise history. Unfortunately, he also failed to lead the Bengals to victory in any of the seven playoff games in which they appeared during his tenure.

Moving on from Lewis, the Bengals named longtime NFL assistant coach Zac Taylor their new head man prior to the start of the 2019 campaign. Taylor, who had previously worked with quarterbacks and wide receivers in Miami, Cincinnati, and Los Angeles (Rams), struggled in his first two seasons as head coach in Cincinnati, leading the Bengals to a total of just six victories in 2019 and 2020. But since selecting quarterback Joe Burrow and wide receiver Ja'Marr Chase in the first round of consecutive drafts, improving their offensive line, and adding some much-needed help on defense, the Bengals have thrived under Taylor the past three seasons.

After finishing first in the AFC North with a regular-season record of 10–7 in 2021, the Bengals posted victories over the Las Vegas Raiders (26–19), Tennessee Titans (19–16), and Kansas City Chiefs (27–24 in OT) in the playoffs that earned them a trip to the Super Bowl. However, they came up just a bit short against the Los Angeles Rams in Super Bowl LVI, losing to their NFC counterparts by a score of 23–20. The Bengals followed that up by laying claim to the division title again in 2022, finishing the regular season with a mark of 12–4, before defeating the Baltimore Ravens (24–17) and Buffalo Bills (27–10) in the first two rounds of the playoffs. But this time they lost to the Chiefs, 23–20, in the AFC Championship Game. Forced to play without an injured Joe Burrow for much of 2023, the Bengals failed to advance to the postseason tournament, concluding the campaign with a record of just 9–8.

Nevertheless, with a potent offense led by Burrow and Chase and a solid defense anchored by standout linemen Trey Hendrickson and Sam Hubbard, the Bengals figure to be perennial contenders for conference championship honors for years to come. Their next AFC title will be their fourth. They have also won 12 division titles. Featuring several outstanding performers through the years, the Bengals have inducted seven players into their Ring of Honor, two of whom are also in the Pro Football Hall of Fame.

FACTORS USED TO DETERMINE RANKINGS

It should come as no surprise that selecting the 50 greatest players ever to perform for a team with the rich history of the Cincinnati Bengals presented quite a challenge. Even after narrowing the field down to a mere 50 men, I still needed to devise a method of ranking the elite players that remained.

Certainly, the names of Anthony Muñoz, Ken Anderson, Ken Riley, Chad Johnson, Willie Anderson, Geno Atkins, and Joe Burrow would appear at, or near, the top of virtually everyone's list, although the order might vary somewhat from one person to the next. Several other outstanding performers have gained general recognition through the years as being among the greatest players in team annals, with Isaac Curtis, Tim Krumrie, Lemar Parrish, Reggie Williams, Jim LeClair, and A. J. Green heading the list of other Bengals icons. But how does one compare players who lined up on opposite sides of the ball with any degree of certainty? Furthermore, how does one differentiate between the pass-rushing and run-stopping skills of front-seven defenders Atkins and Krumrie and the ball-hawking skills of defensive backs Riley and Parrish? And, on the offensive end, how can a direct correlation be made between the contributions made by standout lineman Max Montoya and skill position players such as James Brooks and Corey Dillon? After initially deciding whom to include on my list, I then needed to determine what criteria I should use to formulate my final rankings.

The first thing I decided to examine was the level of dominance a player attained during his time with the Bengals. How often did he lead the league in a major statistical category? Did he ever capture league MVP honors? How many times did he earn a trip to the Pro Bowl or a spot on the All-Pro Team?

I also chose to assess the level of statistical compilation a player achieved while wearing a Bengals uniform. I reviewed where he ranks among the team's all-time leaders in those statistical categories most pertinent to his position. Of course, even the method of using statistics as a measuring stick has its inherent flaws. Although the level of success a team experiences rushing and passing the ball is impacted greatly by the performance of its offensive line, there really is no way to quantifiably measure the level of play reached by each individual offensive lineman. Conversely, the play of the offensive line affects tremendously the statistics compiled by a team's quarterback and running backs. Furthermore, the NFL did not keep an official record of defensive numbers such as tackles and quarterback sacks until the 1980s (although the Bengals kept their own records prior to that, and pro football researchers have tabulated "unofficial" sack totals in recent years). In addition, when examining the statistics compiled by offensive players, the era during which a quarterback, running back, or wide receiver competed must be factored into the equation.

To illustrate my last point, rules changes instituted by the league office have opened up the game considerably over the course of the last two decades. Quarterbacks are accorded far more protection than ever before, and officials have also been instructed to limit the amount of contact defensive backs are allowed to make with wide receivers. As a result, the game has experienced an offensive explosion, with quarterbacks and receivers posting numbers that players from prior generations rarely even approached. That being the case, one must place the numbers Joe Burrow has compiled to this point in his career in their proper context when comparing him to earlier Bengals quarterbacks Ken Anderson and Boomer Esiason. Similarly, the statistics posted by Ja'Marr Chase and Tee Higgins must be viewed in moderation when comparing them to previous Bengals wideouts Isaac Curtis and Carl Pickens.

Other important factors I needed to consider were the overall contributions a player made to the success of the team, the degree to which he improved the fortunes of the club during his time in Cincinnati, and the manner in which he impacted the team, both on and off the field. While the number of championships and division titles the Bengals won during a player's years with the team certainly factored into the equation, I chose not to deny a top performer his rightful place on the list if his years in the Queen City happened to coincide with a lack of overall success by the club. As a result, the names of players such as Jeff Blake and Darnay Scott will appear in these rankings.

One other thing I should mention is that I only considered a player's performance while playing for the Bengals when formulating my rankings. That being the case, the names of standout performers such as Bill Bergey and Coy Bacon, both of whom had many of their finest seasons for other teams, may appear lower on this list than one might expect. Meanwhile, the names of Hall of Famers Charlie Joiner and Terrell Owens are nowhere to be found.

Having established the guidelines to be used throughout this book, the time has come to reveal the 50 greatest players in Bengals history, starting with number 1 and working our way down to number 50.

1
ANTHONY MUÑOZ

Despite the important place that Ken Anderson holds in Bengals history, Anthony Muñoz represented the only possible choice for the top spot on this list. Referred to by former Bengals head coach Sam Wyche as "the greatest offensive tackle the game has ever known," Muñoz, who spent his entire 13-year career in Cincinnati, is widely regarded as the finest offensive lineman in NFL history. A member of teams that won four division titles and two AFC championships, Muñoz gained Pro Bowl and All-Pro recognition 11 times each, en route to earning spots on both the NFL 75th Anniversary All-Time Team and the NFL 100 All-Time Team. Named NFL Offensive Lineman of the Year on seven separate occasions, Muñoz later received the additional honors of gaining induction into the Pro Football Hall of Fame in his very first year of eligibility and being accorded a number 17 ranking on the *Sporting News'* 1999 list of the 100 Greatest Players in NFL History and a number 12 ranking on the NFL Network's 2010 list of the NFL's 100 Greatest Players. Here, Muñoz receives a number one ranking, finishing well ahead of his closest competitor, Ken Anderson.

Born in Ontario, California, on August 19, 1958, Michael Anthony Muñoz grew up some 40 miles northeast of Los Angeles, where his mother, Esther, raised him and his four siblings by herself after his father deserted the family. Praising his mom for her hard work and dedication to her children, Muñoz recalled, "She did it all. We didn't have a lot, but we had each other; and we were close to each other and happy enough."

Although his father lived nearby, Muñoz saw him just twice, later telling Jay Greenberg of *Sports Illustrated*, "I never had a father, so I never knew what I was missing. As I look back, I don't even know if I was poor. We were provided for, but we didn't have any extras."

Encouraged by his mother to pursue his athletic interests, Muñoz spent his early years focusing primarily on baseball since officials did not permit him to compete in Pop Warner Football because of his great size. A power-pitcher and power-hitter on the diamond, Muñoz excelled to such a

Anthony Muñoz is generally considered to be the greatest offensive lineman in NFL history.

degree that Jim Semon, the director of the summer recreation program in Ontario, remembered, "He was on so many teams that when they had to play each other, they would fight over him."

Although Muñoz continued to play baseball at Chaffey High School, he also excelled in football and basketball, proving to be especially proficient on the gridiron, where he starred as a two-way lineman. An outstanding student as well, Muñoz earned scholastic All-America honors. Heavily recruited by several major colleges as graduation neared, Muñoz ultimately chose to enroll at USC after the school agreed to allow him to skip spring football practice so that he could also play for the university's baseball team. However, a series of knee injuries sustained on the football field limited Muñoz to just one year of baseball competition.

Making a name for himself on the gridiron, Muñoz started for the Trojans at left offensive tackle for four years. But both his freshman and junior seasons ended prematurely due to injury, preventing him from taking part in the team's two Rose Bowl victories. Muñoz also missed virtually his entire senior year after tearing knee ligaments in the regular-season opener. However, after undergoing his third knee surgery in four years, Muñoz chose not to request a medical redshirt that would have enabled him to play as a fifth-year senior in 1980. Electing instead to play in the Rose Bowl, Muñoz, who said at the time, "I can't imagine missing that experience with my guys," helped running back Charles White gain 247 yards on the ground during USC's 17–16 win over the previously undefeated Ohio State Buckeyes. Commenting on his star left tackle's magnificent performance afterward, Trojans head coach John Robinson said, "To me, that's a perfect game. That's one of the greatest things I've ever seen happen. . . . He's potentially the most outstanding offensive lineman I ever saw anywhere. He's one of the greatest players at any position I ever saw."

With questions regarding the health of Muñoz's knees abounding heading into the annual NFL Draft, Bengals owner Paul Brown dispatched head coach Forrest Gregg to USC, where the Hall of Fame tackle conducted a one-on-one workout with the young lineman. After rushing directly at Muñoz a few times, Gregg decided to employ a different maneuver, recalling, "I rushed like I was going inside and then went outside on him. He reacted like a football player would. He jammed me on the chest with both hands and knocked me on my rear. He was very apologetic, and I said, 'No, no, no, you did what you were supposed to do.' I thought, 'We've got to have this guy.'" A few weeks later, the Bengals got their man when they selected Muñoz with the third overall pick of the 1980 NFL Draft.

Laying claim to the starting left tackle job immediately upon his arrival in Cincinnati, Muñoz performed well in his first pro season, earning a spot on the 1980 NFL All-Rookie Team, before beginning a string of 11 straight Pro Bowl and All-Pro nominations the following year. Putting to rest any concerns over his oft-injured knees, Muñoz missed just four non-strike games from 1980 to 1991, at one point starting 105 consecutive contests.

Establishing himself during that time as the league's finest player at his position, Muñoz excelled in every aspect of offensive line play, dominating his opponent as both a run-blocker and pass-protector. Standing 6'6" and weighing close to 280 pounds, Muñoz possessed good size, great strength, and tremendous quickness, with former Houston Oilers defensive end William Fuller saying, "I'll tell you that he was one great player. The man had the most unbelievably quick feet at the position that I ever saw. Nobody was even close. And when you combine that with his technique, it was a brutal assignment to try to get the best of him. He had the best feet, and his hands were just about at the same level. He was the best, and by a wide margin."

Also blessed with an extraordinary ability to change direction without losing his balance, Muñoz received raves for his excellence in that area from longtime Bengals offensive line coach Jim McNally, who stated, "I don't care who he was playing against, what the conditions were like, or what his assignment was. He never fell down. He had the most incredible balance I've ever seen. Even against the quickest pass-rushers, he would never leave his feet. He had incredible balance and anticipation. He was a great player to coach and just a tremendous student of the game."

In describing what it was like running behind Muñoz, speedy Bengals running back James Brooks said, "I didn't feel like I needed that much room to make a big play. I was quick, and I could get through a small crack. But, when you run behind Anthony, you don't get a small crack. He was so big, so powerful, and just so good that you got a whole lane to run through, and then you could cut off his back as he was finishing his block. He was like nobody I ever played with."

Never allowing himself to get caught up in the mind games played by others, Muñoz always remained focused on the task at hand, saying, "I enjoyed what I was doing, and I never really thought it was about me showing the other guy who was tougher. I wanted to create a hole for the running back or protect the quarterback. To me, that was all about technique. My technique against his technique. You want to turn it into some physical battle or some war, fine. But that's not going to change my objective. I want to open a hole. I want to create a running lane. I want to protect the quarterback. I'm not going to get drawn into your war."

Commenting on the mental approach her husband applied to his craft, Muñoz's wife, DeDe, told *Sports Illustrated*: "If you really watch the way he plays offensive line, it's different than any other player in the league. Instead of trying to intimidate someone or overpower them, all he wanted to do was show how his skill level was higher than his opponent's. It's artistic the way he plays. He makes it look easy."

In discussing Muñoz, NFL all-time sack leader Bruce Smith stated, "He never said anything when you played against him. No trash talking. No nothing. The only thing I ever heard from him was an apology when his fingers went inside my facemask. If that had happened with other players, you

Muñoz earned Pro Bowl and All-Pro honors 11 times each.
Courtesy of RMYAuctions.com

would have thought they had done it to get an edge. Not with Anthony. Not only didn't he need to get an edge, he would never have played dirty, not even for a second. . . . There are no comparisons between him and other tackles. He's proven it year after year that he's the best."

Always in tremendous physical condition, Muñoz employed a rigorous workout regimen year-round that included weightlifting and running three to four miles every day. Praised by his teammates for his extraordinary work ethic, Muñoz, said former Bengals offensive lineman Max Montoya, practiced and played like a man who had something to prove, with Montoya stating, "That's the way he played for 13 years, like he was trying to work his way into a starting slot."

When asked how he maintained such a high level of play for so long, Muñoz said, "It was year-round, staying consistent, staying in shape, working on my technique. One of the things a lot of people know is that I didn't take a whole lot of time after my last game to get back into training my body. . . . I had already achieved a high level of conditioning during the season; as you know, you get banged up a little bit, but I can adapt to the season, and I knew that I would go out and I'd lift, and I'd run, but I'd also work on my technique in the offseason."

Muñoz's exceptional athletic ability also allowed the Bengals to occasionally employ him as a receiver in short-yardage or goal-line situations, with four of his career receptions resulting in touchdowns.

After starting virtually every game the Bengals played the previous 12 seasons, Muñoz missed half of the 1992 campaign due to knee and shoulder problems, prompting him to announce his retirement at the end of the year. Muñoz, who ended his career having appeared in a total of 185 games, 184 of which he started, did not have to wait long to be voted into the Pro Football Hall of Fame, gaining induction the first time his name appeared on the ballot in 1998. Although the Bengals have not officially retired his #78, they have not reissued it since he left the team.

In addition to his many other honors, Muñoz earned the distinction of being named on 27 of the 50 ballots cast by a panel of experts, reporters, and analysts assembled by ESPN in 2022 to determine the greatest players at each position in NFL history. When asked about his selection of Muñoz at left tackle, Jacksonville Jaguars reporter Michael DiRocco replied, "It's pretty simple for me: He was as dominant a player at his position as there has been in the NFL. A mauler with the feet of a dancer, he could overpower guys or beat them with his mobility. Muñoz is the standard against which all offensive tackles are measured."

Following his playing days, Muñoz remained in Cincinnati, where he spent seven years doing color commentary for NFL games, before becoming a college football analyst. After temporarily leaving the booth when his eldest son began playing football at the University of Tennessee, Muñoz resumed his broadcasting career as an analyst for Bengals preseason games. Extremely active in the community as well, Muñoz, who, during his playing days, won the Cincinnati Bengals Man of the Year Award five times and the NFL Man of the Year Award once, runs the Anthony Muñoz Foundation, a nonprofit organization he established in 2002 that is dedicated to providing mental, physical, and spiritual assistance to youth in the Tri-State region.

Muñoz has also spoken to over 150 high school assemblies discouraging the use of drugs and alcohol; assisted in two football camps in Guadalajara, Mexico; spoken to military units all over the United States; co-chaired 12 Anthony Muñoz Cystic Fibrosis golf tournaments; served as a member of the Advisory Board of Citizens for Community Values; and, since 2022, has served as chief football relationship officer for the Pro Football Hall of Fame.

A devout Christian, Muñoz says, "My faith has been everything for me in my life, college, my 13 years playing in the NFL. Since I've been retired from the NFL, it continues to be the most important thing in my life."

CAREER HIGHLIGHTS

Best Season

Muñoz gained official NFL Offensive Lineman of the Year recognition from the Associated Press three times, being so honored in 1981, 1987, and 1988. The NFL Players Association accorded him that same honor in 1982, 1988, 1989, and 1990. Meanwhile, the NFL Alumni Association voted Muñoz NFL Offensive Lineman of the Year in 1987, 1989, 1990, and 1991. And Muñoz won the Seagram's Seven Crowns of Sports award for NFL Offensive Lineman of the Year in 1981 and 1986. With both Muñoz and former Bengals offensive line coach Jim McNally identifying the 1986 campaign as the finest of his career, who are we to argue?

Memorable Moments/Greatest Performances

Muñoz helped the Bengals amass 509 yards of total offense during a 34–33 win over the Baltimore Colts on December 7, 1980.

Muñoz scored the first of his four career touchdowns when he gathered in a 1-yard pass from Boomer Esiason during a 20–17 overtime victory over the Browns on December 2, 1984.

Muñoz's tremendous blocking up front helped the Bengals amass 555 yards of total offense during a 45–27 win over the Houston Oilers on December 1, 1985, with 231 of those yards coming on the ground and the other 324 through the air.

Although the Bengals lost to the Oilers, 32–28, on November 9, 1986, Muñoz scored his second career touchdown on a 5-yard pass from Boomer Esiason.

In addition to helping the Bengals amass 621 yards of total offense during a 52–21 bludgeoning of the Jets in the 1986 regular-season finale, Muñoz lit the scoreboard again when he gathered in a 2-yard TD pass from Esiason.

Muñoz combined with Esiason one last time during a 31–29 loss to the Oilers on November 1, 1987, with the quarterback hitting his left tackle with a 3-yard touchdown pass.

Muñoz acquitted himself extremely well against Bruce Smith in the 1988 AFC Championship Game, holding the Hall of Fame defensive end to no sacks during a 21–10 Bengals win.

Notable Achievements

- Scored four touchdowns.
- Missed just one non-strike game from 1980 to 1990, starting 164 of 165 contests.
- Ranks among Bengals career leaders with 13 seasons played (tied for 6th) and 185 games played (7th).
- Four-time division champion (1981, 1982, 1988, and 1990).
- Two-time AFC champion (1981 and 1988).
- Member of 1980 NFL All-Rookie Team.
- 1991 NFL Walter Payton Man of the Year.
- Seven-time NFL Offensive Lineman of the Year (1981, 1982, 1986, 1987, 1988, 1989, and 1990).
- 11-time Pro Bowl selection (1981, 1982, 1983, 1984, 1985, 1986, 1987, 1988, 1989, 1990, and 1991).
- Nine-time First-Team All-Pro selection (1981, 1982, 1983, 1985, 1986, 1987, 1988, 1989, and 1990).
- Two-time Second-Team All-Pro selection (1984 and 1991).
- 10-time First-Team All-AFC selection (1981, 1982, 1983, 1984, 1985, 1986, 1987, 1988, 1989, and 1990).
- Pro Football Reference All-1980s First Team.
- NFL 1980s All-Decade First Team.
- Named to Bengals 40th Anniversary All-Time Team in 2007.
- Named to Bengals 50th Anniversary All-Time Team in 2017.
- Named to NFL 75th Anniversary All-Time Team in 1994.
- Named to NFL 100 All-Time Team in 2019.
- Number 17 on the *Sporting News'* 1999 list of the 100 Greatest Players in NFL History.

- Number 12 on the NFL Network's 2010 list of the NFL's 100 Greatest Players.
- Inducted into Bengals Ring of Honor in 2021.
- Inducted into Pro Football Hall of Fame in 1998.

2

KEN ANDERSON

In expressing his admiration for Ken Anderson, longtime Bengals owner Mike Brown said of the quarterback who led his team to three division titles and its first AFC championship, "He was the heart and soul of our team. Without question, he was the most important player the Bengals ever had."

The first NFL quarterback to successfully run what later became known as the "West Coast Offense," Anderson spent his entire 16-year career in Cincinnati, making the Bengals viable contenders in the AFC Central Division much of that time. The franchise's all-time leader in passing yards, Anderson, who also ranks second in team annals in pass completions and touchdown passes, threw for more than 3,000 yards and 20 touchdowns twice each, en route to earning four Pro Bowl selections, two All-Pro nominations, and one league MVP trophy. One of the most accurate passers of his time, Anderson led the NFL in passing yards twice, pass-completion percentage three times, and passer rating on four separate occasions, with his superior passing skills and outstanding leadership ability landing him a spot on the Bengals 50th Anniversary All-Time Team and a place in the Bengals Ring of Honor.

Born in the tiny town of Batavia, Illinois, on February 15, 1949, Kenneth Allan Anderson grew up close friends with future NBA Hall of Famer Dan Issel, with whom he later co-owned a 782-acre farm in Kentucky. The son of a high school janitor whose job gave him access to the school's athletic equipment, Anderson competed in several sports during his formative years, before focusing primarily on football after he entered Batavia High School.

Although Anderson performed well on the gridiron at Batavia High, he failed to receive any scholarship offers, forcing him to enroll at Augustana College, a private Lutheran school in Rock Island, Illinois. A four-year starter at quarterback for the Vikings, Anderson garnered numerous individual accolades while competing at the NCAA Division III level, earning

Ken Anderson passed for more yards than any other quarterback in franchise history.

honorable mention All-America and First-Team All-Lutheran College honors his sophomore year, gaining College Conference of Illinois and Wisconsin (CCIW) All-Conference recognition three straight times, and being named MVP of the CCIW as a senior in 1970.

Impressed with Anderson's outstanding play at the collegiate level, the Bengals selected him in the third round of the 1971 NFL Draft, with the 67th overall pick. Arriving in Cincinnati prior to the start of training camp after fulfilling his commitment to the National Guard, Anderson spent most of his rookie year backing up Virgil Carter, starting just four games for a Bengals team that finished the regular season 4–10. Replacing Carter behind center the following year, Anderson posted modest numbers, concluding the campaign with just 1,918 yards passing and seven TD passes. Nevertheless, Anderson helped the Bengals improve their record to 8–6, before leading them to a 10–4 mark and the division title in 1973 by ranking among the league leaders with 2,428 passing yards and 18 touchdown passes. Although the Bengals failed to capture the division title in either of the next two seasons, they advanced to the playoffs once, with Anderson establishing himself as one of the league's top signal-callers by posting the following numbers:

YEAR	PASS YDS	TD PASSES	INTS	COMP. %	QBR*
1974	**2,667**	18	10	**64.9**	**95.7**
1975	**3,169**	21	11	60.5	**93.9**

* Please note that any numbers printed in bold throughout this book indicate that the player led the NFL in that statistical category that year.

In addition to leading the NFL in passing yards and quarterback rating both years, Anderson placed at, or near, the top of the league rankings in TD passes and pass-completion percentage both seasons, earning in the process one Pro Bowl selection and two All-AFC nominations. More important, the Bengals concluded the second of those campaigns with a record of 11–3 that earned them a trip to the playoffs as a wild card. However, they subsequently suffered a heartbreaking 31–28 defeat at the hands of the Oakland Raiders in the divisional round of the postseason tournament.

Developing into an elite quarterback with the help of then–Bengals offensive coordinator Bill Walsh, the 6'2", 212-pound Anderson did an expert job of running arguably the league's most intricate offense, with longtime Bengals center Bob Johnson saying, "Walsh's offense was very complex. Kenny was very smart, and he ran that offense to perfection."

An extremely wise decision-maker who rarely threw to the wrong receiver and moved well in the pocket, Anderson received words of praise from Steelers Hall of Fame linebacker Jack Lambert, who said, "He never throws into a crowd. If a receiver is well-covered, he always goes elsewhere. Not sometimes, but always. Now, that makes things tough."

Particularly effective at delivering the ball accurately to his receivers, the strong-armed Anderson earned high grades for his proficiency in that area from former Bengals offensive lineman Dave Lapham, who stated, "Precision passing. I mean, the most accurate I've ever seen. He could put it in the tightest spots. Beautiful mechanics. Just extremely intelligent. Attention to detail, an accounting-type personality, a computer-like mind."

Bengals tight end Bob Trumpy expressed similar sentiments when he said of his former teammate, "He was *insanely* accurate. . . . He had that math mind . . . the way you gotta' think to get things done."

Trumpy also spoke of Anderson's humility and unpretentious nature, saying, "He said nothing to anybody. All quarterbacks have an extra gene when it comes to ego. Anderson did not have that ego. He did not have that 'I'm the best, I'm here.' He was amazing. . . . Anderson wanted to be one of the guys his entire career. We used to call him 'Freddie Franchise.' He was it. We were gonna' ride him straight to the Super Bowl, and he never disappointed us as a player. We didn't measure up to him. . . . He was never loud in the huddle. He was never critical of anybody. He just did his job, and he expected you to do yours."

Former Bengals fullback Pete Johnson added, "Kenny didn't care about being famous. He was a football player."

Although the Bengals failed to return to the playoffs in 1976, Anderson helped lead them to a regular-season record of 10–4 by throwing for 2,367 yards and finishing third in the league with 19 touchdown passes, earning in the process his second consecutive Pro Bowl nomination. But, with the Bengals offensive line failing to protect him sufficiently, Anderson did not perform nearly as well from 1977 to 1980, throwing more TD passes than interceptions and posting a QBR above 70.0 just once each.

Aided by an influx of new talent in 1981, Anderson returned to top form, earning Pro Bowl, First-Team All-Pro, NFL MVP, and NFL Comeback Player of the Year honors by posting a league-best 98.4 quarterback rating and ranking among the leaders with 3,754 passing yards, 29 touchdown passes, and a 62.6 pass-completion percentage, with his exceptional play leading the Bengals to a regular-season record of 12–4, their third division title, and their first AFC championship. Continuing to perform well in the postseason, Anderson led the Bengals to victories over Buffalo (28–21) and San Diego (27–7) in the AFC playoffs, before completing 25-of-34 pass attempts for 300 yards and two touchdowns during a heartbreaking 26–21 loss to San Francisco in Super Bowl XVI.

Anderson followed that up by passing for 2,495 yards and leading the league with a quarterback rating of 95.3 and a pass-completion

Anderson's superb play in 1981 gained him recognition as the NFL's Most Valuable Player.
Courtesy of RMYAuctions.com

percentage of 70.6 during the strike-shortened 1982 campaign, earning in the process the last of his four Pro Bowl nominations. But after posting solid numbers again in 1983, Anderson began to experience a decline in productivity, forcing him to relinquish his starting job to Boomer Esiason early in 1985. After spending one more season in Cincinnati assuming a backup role, Anderson announced his retirement following the conclusion of the 1986 campaign having amassed career totals of 32,838 passing yards, 197 touchdown passes, 160 interceptions, 2,220 rushing yards, and

20 rushing touchdowns, completed 59.3 percent of his passes, and compiled a quarterback rating of 81.9. At the time of his retirement, Anderson, who posted an overall record of 91–81 as a starter, ranked seventh all-time in passing yards and held NFL records for consecutive pass completions (20), completion percentage for a single game (20-of-22, 90.9 percent, vs. Pittsburgh in 1974), and completion percentage for a season (70.6 percent in 1982).

Following his playing days, Anderson spent six seasons doing color commentary on Bengals radio broadcasts, before serving as a member of the team's coaching staff for the next 11 years—six as quarterbacks coach and five as offensive coordinator. Anderson later served as an assistant on the coaching staffs of the Jacksonville Jaguars and Pittsburgh Steelers, before retiring from football in 2010.

Ranked by the NFL Network in 2008 as the 10th best player yet to gain induction into the Pro Football Hall of Fame, Anderson continues to remain on the outside looking in, an omission that rankles many of his former teammates.

In addressing Anderson's exclusion, Bob Trumpy said, "I don't know what Hall of Fame balloters believe that Anderson is missing, but we couldn't beat Pittsburgh. Neither could anybody else. I don't know that you can hold that against Ken Anderson. We just didn't measure up to his performance. He never failed us. . . . Long ago, he should have been in the Hall of Fame."

Isaac Curtis said of his longtime teammate, "I think one of the all-time great quarterbacks. I mean, he's as intelligent a quarterback that there is at playing back then, and even today. I think his knowledge of the game, his passing, his timing—I don't even know why Kenny's not in the Hall of Fame. . . . I think his numbers are there when you look at his peers, and I think if we had won that Super Bowl, there wouldn't be any doubt that he would be in there. In my personal opinion, Kenny is certainly one of the top quarterbacks and top passers that's ever been in this league—and I've watched a lot of quarterbacks."

And former Bengals quarterback Greg Cook, whose once-promising career ended prematurely due to injury, commented, "Kenny proved that, when he had the talent around him, he wasn't just the best quarterback in the NFL. He was the best player in the NFL."

CAREER HIGHLIGHTS

Best Season

Although Anderson also performed exceptionally well in 1975 and 1982, he played his best ball for the Bengals during the AFC championship campaign of 1981 when, en route to earning NFL MVP, NFL Player of the Year, and NFL Offensive Player of the Year honors, he established career-high marks with 3,754 passing yards, 29 touchdown passes, 320 yards gained on the ground, and a QBR of 98.4.

Memorable Moments/Greatest Performances

Anderson led the Bengals to a 27–24 win over the Houston Oilers in the final game of the 1973 regular season by throwing for 293 yards and three touchdowns, with his two TD tosses to Isaac Curtis covering 77 and 67 yards.

Anderson helped lead the Bengals to a 34–24 victory over the Cleveland Browns on October 13, 1974, by running for one score and passing for three others, the longest of which came on a 65-yard connection with Charlie Joiner.

Anderson threw four touchdown passes in one game for the first time in his career during a 33–6 win over the Chiefs on November 24, 1974, connecting twice with Isaac Curtis and once each with Ed Williams and Chip Myers.

Anderson turned in an extremely efficient performance against the Bills on November 17, 1975, completing 30 of 46 passes for 447 yards and two touchdowns during a 33–24 Bengals win.

Anderson earned NFL Offensive Player of the Week honors for the first time by throwing for 346 yards and two touchdowns during a convincing 34–7 victory over the Steelers on October 18, 1981, with the longest of his TD passes going 73 yards to David Verser.

Anderson led the Bengals to a 38–21 win over the Denver Broncos on November 22, 1981, by running for one score and passing for 396 yards and three touchdowns, the longest of which came on a 65-yard connection with Charles Alexander.

Anderson starred in defeat on December 20, 1982, running for one score and throwing for 416 yards and two touchdowns during a 50–34 loss to the Chargers.

Anderson earned his second NFL Offensive Player of the Week nomination by completing 27 of 31 pass attempts for 323 yards and two touchdowns during a 35–27 win over the Houston Oilers in the 1982 regular-season finale, at one point completing 20 straight passes, which set a new NFL record (since broken).

Notable Achievements

- Passed for more than 3,000 yards twice, topping 3,500 yards once.
- Threw more than 20 touchdown passes twice, surpassing 25 TD passes once.
- Completed more than 60 percent of passes seven times, topping 70 percent once.
- Posted touchdown-to-interception ratio of better than 2–1 once.
- Posted passer rating above 90.0 four times.
- Led NFL in pass completions twice, passing yards twice, pass-completion percentage three times, and passer rating four times.
- Holds Bengals career records for most pass attempts (4,475), passing yards (32,838), and seasons played (16).
- Ranks among Bengals career leaders with 2,654 pass completions (2nd), 197 touchdown passes (2nd), and 192 games played (5th).
- Three-time division champion (1973, 1981, and 1982).
- 1981 AFC champion.
- Two-time NFL Offensive Player of the Week.
- Three-time Bengals team MVP (1974, 1975, and 1981).
- 1975 NFL Walter Payton Man of the Year.
- 1981 NFL MVP.
- 1981 NFL Player of the Year.
- 1981 NFL Offensive Player of the Year.
- 1981 NFL Comeback Player of the Year.
- Four-time Pro Bowl selection (1975, 1976, 1981, and 1982).
- 1981 First-Team All-Pro selection.
- 1975 Second-Team All-Pro selection.
- Two-time First-Team All-AFC selection (1975 and 1981).
- Two-time Second-Team All-AFC selection (1974 and 1982).
- Named to Bengals 50th Anniversary All-Time Team in 2017.
- Inducted into Bengals Ring of Honor in 2021.

3

KEN RILEY

A true shutdown corner before the term became a regular part of football parlance, Ken Riley spent his entire 15-year career in Cincinnati, recording more interceptions and amassing more interception-return yards than any other player in franchise history. An extraordinarily consistent player who went about his job in workmanlike fashion, Riley picked off at least five passes in a season seven times, in helping the Bengals win four division titles and one AFC championship. Extremely durable, Riley appeared in all but eight games the Bengals played from 1969 to 1983, at one point starting 86 consecutive contests. Along the way, Riley earned three All-Pro nominations and four All-AFC selections, before being further honored following the conclusion of his playing career by being named to the Bengals 50th Anniversary All-Time Team and gaining induction into both the team's Ring of Honor and the Pro Football Hall of Fame.

Born in Bartow, Florida, on August 6, 1947, Kenneth Jerome Riley grew up some 40 miles east of Tampa, where he got his start in organized football as a high school quarterback at the all-Black Union Academy. Performing well enough on the gridiron to earn an athletic scholarship to Florida A&M University, a historically Black college located in Tallahassee, Florida, Riley spent four years starting behind center for head coach Jake Gaither, leading the Rattlers to an overall record of 23–7 and three Southern Intercollegiate Athletic Conference titles. An excellent student as well, Riley earned his team's scholastic award and a Rhodes Scholar candidacy, before obtaining a master's degree from the University of South Florida while playing professionally.

Selected by the Bengals in the sixth round of the 1969 NFL/AFL Common Draft, with the 135th overall pick, Riley arrived in Cincinnati the same year as former University of Cincinnati quarterback Greg Cook, who head coach and general manager Paul Brown claimed five rounds earlier, with the fifth overall pick of the draft. Moved to cornerback shortly after he reported to training camp, Riley said years later, "We were stereotyped then.

Everything down the middle—the quarterback, the center, the middle linebacker—those positions required thinking, so they didn't put us there."

Despite being shifted to a position completely foreign to him, Riley's outstanding athleticism, superior intellect, and prior experience at quarterback enabled him to adapt quickly to his new post, with current Bengals owner Mike Brown (then the team's assistant general manager) recalling, "He had never played the position, and he took to it so quickly, and it was quite remarkable. He would have a feel by the pattern when the ball was

Ken Riley picked off more passes and amassed more interception-return yards than anyone else in team annals.

going to come. He would think like a quarterback. He would just sense what was going on in the quarterback's mind as he covered."

After earning the starting right-cornerback job during the early stages of the regular season, Riley acquitted himself extremely well as a rookie, recording four interceptions, which he returned for a total of 66 yards, while also recovering two fumbles and amassing 334 yards returning kick-offs. Continuing to perform well after the AFL merged with the NFL the following year, Riley helped the Bengals win their first two division titles by picking off a total of 19 passes over the course of the next five seasons.

Excelling in every phase of cornerback play, the 5'11", 185-pound Riley not only did an excellent job of sticking to his man and tracking the football, but he also tackled extremely well, with longtime teammate Bob Trumpy recalling, "Ken Riley upended some of the greatest receivers in the history of the league. . . . I saw him flip Lance Alworth right on the top of his head. In Pittsburgh, I saw him flip Lynn Swann and John Stallworth. He flipped Paul Warfield every time we played him. . . . He did it consistently. He was a complete cornerback. I've heard this stuff about shutdown corners. I don't know what that is. . . . Teams ran more than they do now, and Riley was a great tackler. He didn't try to block anybody. He tackled them."

A consummate team player, Riley also made the other players around him better, with former Bengals receiver Cris Collinsworth saying, "I probably learned more football from Kenny Riley than from anyone I played for or against. Everything I did that worked against everybody else never worked against him. But as soon as he would pick off a pass on my route or beat me to a spot, he'd tell me why, explain what I'd done wrong. He wanted me to be better because that made the team better."

Collinsworth added, "I don't know how you put a number on intelligence. And I don't know how many touchdowns he saved the Bengals because he knew what was coming."

Meanwhile, in discussing Riley, as both a player and a man, Mike Brown said, "Ken was a top cover-corner. He could play the ball at the point of reception so well that he became one of the top interceptors of all time. And he would tackle. Only 185 pounds, he hit hard. Receivers knew they would pay a price if they caught a ball in front of him. Most of all, Ken was a smart player. He didn't miss assignments. Ever. He was a wonderful person. He looked out for others. Everyone at all levels of the team respected him. He was a man that could be counted on."

Yet, despite everything Riley brought to the Bengals, he often found himself being overlooked for postseason honors, failing to gain Pro Bowl or All-Pro recognition in any of his first six seasons. Certainly, the Bengals' inability to make a deep playoff run and Riley's quiet demeanor contributed to his lack of notoriety, as he once admitted when he said, "I was very low-key. I always felt actions spoke louder than words."

Nevertheless, Riley never let his lack of recognition bother him, saying years later, "I never really spoke about it or made any big fuss about not being in a Pro Bowl. First of all, I didn't want to get hurt. I've seen some guys get hurt in the Pro Bowl, so it wasn't any big thing for me."

However, Riley admitted that more Pro Bowl nominations likely would have made his path to the Pro Football Hall of Fame an easier one, adding, "If I had known that was going to be such a big deal; I don't know if that would have helped. That and not winning the Super Bowl."

Riley finally began to garner attention from the media in 1975, when his six interceptions, two fumble recoveries, and one defensive touchdown helped the Bengals compile a regular-season record of 11–3 that earned them a spot in the playoffs as a wild card. Accorded Second-Team All-Pro honors by the Associated Press, Riley also garnered First-Team All-AFC recognition from both the AP and the *Sporting News*. Although the Bengals failed to return to the playoffs the following year despite finishing the season with a record of 10–4, Riley found himself being similarly honored after placing second in the league with nine interceptions, which he returned for a total of 141 yards and one touchdown.

Riley remained a fixture on the right side of the Bengals defense for seven more years, starting all but five games from 1977 to 1983—a period during which he recorded another 27 interceptions. Performing especially well in 1983, Riley earned his lone First-Team All-Pro nomination by registering eight interceptions, which he returned for 89 yards and two touchdowns, before announcing his retirement at the end of the year. Over 15 NFL seasons, Riley intercepted 65 passes, amassed 596 interception-return yards, recovered 18 fumbles, and scored five defensive touchdowns, with his 65 picks representing the fifth-highest total in league history.

Following his playing days, Riley, who occasionally worked as a substitute teacher at Raines High School in Jacksonville, Florida, during NFL offseasons, returned to his alma mater, Florida A&M, where he spent eight seasons serving as head football coach, before eventually becoming the school's athletic director. After fulfilling that role for 10 years, Riley retired to his hometown of Bartow, Florida, where he remained until June 7, 2020, when he died of a heart attack at the age of 72.

Unfortunately, Riley did not live long enough to see the Pro Football Hall of Fame open its doors to him. Posthumously inducted in 2023, Riley spent many years wondering why he continued to come up short in the

Riley finally gained admission to the Pro Football Hall of Fame in 2023—three years following his passing.

balloting, once saying, "I think my numbers are deserving of the Hall of Fame. I've always been a modest and low-key type guy. I've always thought your work would speak for you. It's like it's working against me now because the older you get and the longer you stay out of it, people forget who you are."

In expressing his thoughts on why Riley deserved to gain admittance to the Hall of Fame some years prior to his induction, longtime Bengals teammate Ken Anderson stated, "Number one, he was a great player. Number two, he was a great teammate. You talk to guys like Isaac Curtis and

Cris Collinsworth, who would go against him in practice; then, who, after the play was over, he would coach them up on what he saw that they were tipping off. He was all about team, trying to make the team better."

Anderson continued, "When you talk about 65 interceptions, playing in an era where you're only playing 14 games a year until the late '70s when they changed the pass-blocking rules . . . (where) offensive linemen had to keep their hands within the framework of their bodies. So, quarterbacks only threw the ball 18 times a game. . . . That was the era that he played in. So, for him to come up with 65 interceptions is just remarkable. If anybody deserves to be in the Hall of Fame, it's Kenny Riley."

Expressing the belief that Riley's induction came far too late, Bengals owner Mike Brown said in a statement, "Everyone at all levels with the team respected him. Ken looked out for others. He was known as someone who would help. Had he lived, Ken would have been delighted in being selected for the Hall of Fame. Now the Bengals family will have to do that for him. We miss him and we celebrate him."

Bengals radio analyst Dave Lapham also spoke on behalf of his former teammate, saying, "This is so deserved. Aside from his incredible talent, the other thing about him is he never got hurt. It was amazing. He never had any sort of significant injury, but that doesn't mean he didn't play hurt. Some guys don't play hurt, but he did all the time."

Lapham added, "He had the ball skills of an offensive skill player, and that's what he was, a former quarterback. He was so smart, and he was so solid, like when he picked off Joe Namath multiple times down the stretch of Joe's career. But he talked about how great Namath was, not how great Kenny Riley was. That was Kenny Riley in a nutshell. A great human being and player."

Meanwhile, Willie Anderson, who failed to gain admittance to the Hall of Fame in his 10th year of eligibility, said, "I'm in a good mood because Kenny Riley is in. Because I know what it meant for him. He mentioned it to me before he passed away. The only sad part about it is he's not here to see it, but I talk to his son. We text. They're excited. They've been pushing for me, pulling for me, and we've all been pulling for them. Tonight's a great feeling. I know what that man meant. I love it when the greats who came before me get honored."

CAREER HIGHLIGHTS

Best Season

Riley performed brilliantly in his final season, earning his only First-Team All-Pro nomination in 1983 by picking off eight passes, amassing 89 interception-return yards, and scoring two touchdowns. But the Bengals finished the regular season with a record of just 7–9. On the other hand, Riley helped the Bengals post a mark of 10–4 in 1976 by finishing second in the league with a career-high nine interceptions, placing fifth in the circuit with 141 interception-return yards, recovering two fumbles, and scoring a touchdown. All things considered, Riley made a slightly greater overall impact in 1976.

Memorable Moments/Greatest Performances

Although the Bengals lost to the Denver Broncos, 30–23, on October 19, 1969, Riley recorded his first career interception which he subsequently returned 66 yards.

Riley contributed to a 45–7 rout of the Patriots in the 1970 regular-season finale by picking off two passes in one game for the first time in his career.

Riley scored his first points as a pro when he returned an interception 30 yards for a touchdown during a 21–14 win over the Atlanta Falcons on October 26, 1975.

Riley helped lead the Bengals to a 28–7 victory over the Packers on September 26, 1976, by recording two interceptions, one of which he returned 53 yards for a touchdown.

Riley contributed to a 42–3 pasting of the Jets in the final game of the 1976 regular season by picking off three passes.

Riley earned NFL Defensive Player of the Week honors by intercepting Jim Plunkett three times during a 31–17 win over the Los Angeles Raiders on November 28, 1982, returning one of his picks 56 yards for a touchdown.

Riley lit the scoreboard again on September 25, 1983, when he returned his interception of a Jack Thompson pass 34 yards for a touchdown during a 23–17 win over Tampa Bay.

Riley scored what proved to be the game-winning touchdown of a 28–21 victory over the Browns on October 23, 1983, when he ran 42 yards to paydirt after picking off a Brian Sipe pass in the fourth quarter.

Although the Bengals lost to the Vikings, 20–14, in the 1983 regular-season finale, Riley intercepted Wade Wilson twice in the final game of his career.

Notable Achievements

- Missed just eight games in 15 seasons, starting 86 consecutive contests from 1973 to 1978.
- Scored five defensive touchdowns.
- Recorded at least five interceptions seven times, picking off at least eight passes twice.
- Amassed 141 interception-return yards in 1976.
- Finished second in NFL in interceptions three times.
- Led Bengals in interceptions seven times.
- Holds Bengals career records for most interceptions (65), interception-return yards (596), and touchdown interceptions (5).
- Ranks second in franchise history in fumble recoveries (18), seasons played (15), and games played (207).
- Tied for fifth in NFL history with 65 career interceptions.
- Four-time division champion (1970, 1973, 1981, and 1982).
- 1981 AFC champion.
- 1982 Week 12 NFL Defensive Player of the Week.
- 1983 First-Team All-Pro selection.
- Two-time Second-Team All-Pro selection (1975 and 1976).
- Three-time First-Team All-AFC selection (1975, 1976, and 1983).
- 1981 Second-Team All-AFC selection.
- Pro Football Reference All-1970s Second Team.
- Named to Bengals 40th Anniversary All-Time Team in 2007.
- Named to Bengals 50th Anniversary All-Time Team in 2017.
- Inducted into Bengals Ring of Honor in 2021.
- Inducted into Pro Football Hall of Fame in 2023.

4

WILLIE ANDERSON

Widely recognized as the finest right tackle of his generation, Willie Anderson spent 12 seasons in Cincinnati, proving to be one of the few bright spots on mostly losing teams. Anchoring the Bengals' offensive line for more than a decade, Anderson excelled as both a run-blocker and pass-protector, at one point going three seasons without surrendering a sack. The only right tackle since Rams Hall of Famer Jackie Slater to garner Pro Bowl recognition four straight times, Anderson also earned four All-Pro nominations and two All-AFC selections, before being further honored by being named to the Bengals 50th Anniversary All-Time Team and inducted into the Bengals Ring of Honor.

Born in Prichard, Alabama, on July 11, 1975, Willie Aaron Anderson grew up in the suburban neighborhood of Whistler, where he attended Vigor High School. A star on the gridiron at Vigor High, Anderson established himself as one of the nation's top prospects by his senior year. Expected to remain close to home and continue his football career at the University of Alabama, Anderson surprised everyone by accepting an athletic scholarship to Auburn University, where he spent three seasons playing for the Crimson Tide's fiercest rival.

A three-year starter at Auburn under head coach Terry Bowden, Anderson played guard as a freshman, before moving to tackle the following year. Performing brilliantly at both posts, Anderson helped lead the Tigers to an overall record of 28-5-1, with his exceptional play his junior year earning him Second-Team All-America honors. Choosing to forgo his final year of college, Anderson declared himself eligible for the 1996 NFL Draft, where the Bengals selected him in the first round, with the 10th overall pick.

Following his arrival in Cincinnati, Anderson spent most of his first pro season starting at left tackle, performing well enough at that post to earn a spot on the NFL All-Rookie Team. Moved to the right side of the Bengals' offensive line prior to the start of the 1997 campaign, Anderson began a

10-year stint as the team's starting right tackle, a period during which he emerged as the league's finest player at his position.

Although the Bengals' failures as a team prevented Anderson from gaining the recognition he deserved his first few years in the league, the massive tackle proved to be a tremendous force up front, providing ample protection for a slew of quarterbacks that started behind center, while also creating huge holes for the team's corps of running backs. Standing 6'5" and weighing 340 pounds, Anderson, who made a lasting impression on his teammates as a rookie by bench-pressing 675 pounds, possessed tremendous strength, making him extremely effective as a straight-ahead blocker. Surprisingly quick for a man his size, Anderson also did an outstanding job of helping Bengals runners turn the corner and guiding them

Willie Anderson anchored the Bengals' offensive line from his right tackle position for more than a decade.

downfield, with his superior blocking enabling Corey Dillon to establish new NFL single-game rushing records (since broken) for most yards gained by a rookie (246) and most yards gained (278). Anderson also helped Rudi Johnson rush for a franchise-record 1,458 yards in 2005.

Crediting Anderson for much of his success, Dillon stated, "I made my living running to the right. One cut and go. I knew Will would always give me a crease. There was always room, always space."

Equally dominant in pass protection, Anderson surrendered just 16 sacks over the course of his career, yielding no sacks and just one pressure from 1999 to 2001, despite going up against some of the greatest pass-rushers the game has seen. In his 12 years with the Bengals, Anderson faced nine men who currently rank among the NFL's 11 all-time leading sackers. And only one of them (Bruce Smith) ever recorded a sack against him.

In discussing Anderson, whom he faced twice, New York Giants Hall of Fame defensive end Michael Strahan told Bengals.com, "He's one of the best tackles of our time. . . . I consider him to be right there as the best right tackle of his generation. When I found out Willie wasn't in the Hall of Fame, I was surprised. Unbeatable."

Describing the strategy he used to dominate his opponent at the point of attack, Anderson said, "The thing I focus on just before the snap is the inside half of the guy across from me. Coaches call it having 'big eyes.' You keep those big eyes focused on his inside number, the number that's right across from you, because that's the part of him that tells you where he's going to go. Whether he's going to make a move outside or try to bull-rush you."

Extremely durable as well, Anderson appeared in all but two games the Bengals played from 1996 to 2006, at one point starting 112 consecutive contests.

After Anderson, who served as offensive captain most of his time in Cincinnati, made Dr. Z's *Sports Illustrated* All-Pro team in 1999 and was named a first alternate to the Pro Bowl in 2001 and 2002, the Bengals' rise from the depths of the NFL the next few seasons allowed him to garner the individual accolades that had previously eluded him. Accorded Pro Bowl and All-Pro honors four straight times from 2003 to 2006, Anderson, in addition to becoming the first right tackle to be named to the Pro Bowl in four consecutive seasons since Jackie Slater accomplished the feat from 1987 to 1990, also became the first player at that post in nearly three decades to earn First-Team All-Pro honors three straight times. Meanwhile, with the Bengals capturing the division title in 2005, Anderson also gained First-Team All-AFC recognition for the first time in his career.

Anderson continued to start for the Bengals at right tackle until the early stages of the 2007 campaign, when he sustained an injury to his back that forced him to miss the season's final nine games. Anderson's lengthy stay in Cincinnati ended somewhat acrimoniously the following year when the Bengals released him on August 30, 2008, after he refused to take a pay cut. Anderson subsequently signed with the Baltimore Ravens, with whom he appeared in 14 games, 11 of which he started, before announcing his retirement at the end of the year.

After mending fences with the Bengals, Anderson, who appeared in a total of 181 contests as a member of the team, received the honor of gaining induction into their Ring of Honor in 2022, at which time owner Mike Brown stated, "Willie was as good a right offensive tackle as you could draw up. He had it all—strength, movement, and attitude."

Since retiring as an active player, Anderson has remained close to the game through the Willie Anderson Sports Academy, an Atlanta-based sports program that specializes in training young athletes in football and basketball. Anderson, whom the Bengals nominated as their Man of the Year five times during his playing days, focuses most of his individual attention on further developing the skills of young offensive linemen, saying, "I just want 32 (NFL) line coaches to trust me that I can teach their guys, and at the same time, I want high school kids to learn life through me. To teach everybody is a little different, but we can all get to the same goals."

BENGALS CAREER HIGHLIGHTS

Best Season

Anderson performed magnificently in both 2004 and 2006, surrendering just one sack and being called for only two penalties in the first of those campaigns, before allowing just 11 quarterback pressures in the second. But with the Bengals winning the division title and Anderson gaining consensus First-Team All-Pro recognition in 2005, we'll identify that as the most impactful season of his career.

Anderson went three seasons without surrendering a single sack.

Memorable Moments/Greatest Performances

Anderson helped the Bengals amass 463 yards of total offense during a 41–31 win over the Falcons on November 24, 1996, by holding his man, defensive end Chuck Smith, to no sacks and just one tackle.

Anderson's superior blocking at the point of attack helped the Bengals gain 407 yards on the ground during a 31–21 win over the Denver Broncos on October 22, 2000.

Anderson helped the Bengals amass 544 yards of total offense during a 26–23 overtime win over the Steelers on December 30, 2001, with 403 of those yards coming through the air.

Anderson's tremendous blocking up front helped the Bengals rush for 253 yards and gain another 251 yards through the air during a 58–48 win over the Browns on November 28, 2004, with Cleveland's defense failing to register a single sack of Carson Palmer.

Notable Achievements

- Missed just two games from 1996 to 2006, appearing in 174 of 176 contests.
- Ranks eighth in franchise history in games played (181).
- 2005 division champion.
- Member of 1996 NFL All-Rookie Team.
- Five-time Bengals Man of the Year.
- Four-time Pro Bowl selection (2003, 2004, 2005, and 2006).
- Three-time First-Team All-Pro selection (2004, 2005, and 2006).
- 2003 Second-Team All-Pro selection.
- Two-time First-Team All-AFC selection (2005 and 2006).
- Pro Football Reference All-2000s Second Team.
- Named to Bengals 40th Anniversary All-Time Team in 2007.
- Named to Bengals 50th Anniversary All-Time Team in 2017.
- Inducted into Bengals Ring of Honor in 2022.

5

GENO ATKINS

A n elite defender who spent his entire professional career in Cincinnati, Geno Atkins overcame early questions about his size, or lack thereof, to establish himself as one of the finest interior defensive linemen of his era. Anchoring the Bengals defense from his post at right tackle, Atkins did an exceptional job of clogging up the middle against the run and applying inside pressure to opposing quarterbacks, ending his 11-year stint in the Queen City with the third-most sacks of any player in franchise history. A major contributor to Bengals teams that made five consecutive playoff appearances and won two division titles, Atkins earned eight Pro Bowl selections and three All-Pro nominations, before being further honored by being named to the NFL 2010s All-Decade Team.

Born in Pembroke Pines, Florida, on March 28, 1988, Geno Renard Atkins Jr. grew up in nearby Fort Lauderdale, where he learned how to play football at an early age from his father, Gene Atkins, a former safety with the New Orleans Saints and Miami Dolphins. Developing into a star on the gridiron at St. Thomas Aquinas High School, Atkins helped lead the Raiders to consecutive runner-up finishes in the Florida Class 5A championship tournament, recording 70 tackles and four fumble recoveries as a junior in 2004, before registering 117 tackles, 7 1/2 sacks, four forced fumbles, and two fumble recoveries the following season, with his exceptional play his senior year earning him First-Team Class 5A and Florida Class 5A Defensive Player of the Year honors. Excelling in track and field as well, Atkins placed second in the 2006 FHSAA 3A-4A Outdoor State Finals with a throw of 48.35 meters in the discus and tied for first in the shotput with a top throw of 18.01 meters.

Offered an athletic scholarship to the University of Georgia, Atkins spent four years playing defensive tackle for the Bulldogs, gaining All-SEC recognition twice by recording a total of 33 1/2 sacks, including 15 as a sophomore and 10 1/2 as a senior.

Geno Atkins ranks third in franchise history with 75 1/2 career sacks.
Courtesy of Navin Rajagopalan

Despite Atkins's outstanding play in college and powerful 6'1",
300-pound frame, many pro scouts considered him too short to succeed
at the next level, causing him to fall to the fourth round of the 2010 NFL
Draft, where the Bengals selected him with the 120th overall pick. Atkins
subsequently spent his first year in Cincinnati assuming a backup role, registering three sacks and 16 tackles, before laying claim to the starting right
tackle job in 2011, when he helped the Bengals advance to the playoffs
for the first of five straight times by recording 7 1/2 sacks, 47 tackles, two
forced fumbles, and two fumble recoveries, earning in the process Pro Bowl

and Second-Team All-Pro honors. Atkins followed that up with an even stronger performance in 2012, gaining Pro Bowl, First-Team All-Pro, and First-Team All-AFC recognition by registering 12 1/2 sacks, forcing four fumbles, and making 54 tackles, 17 of which resulted in a loss.

Commenting on Atkins's exceptional play, Khaled Elsayed, the chief operating officer for *Pro Football Focus*, said, "You notice him so often, and you don't normally see that with a defensive tackle. He's just so explosive."

After suffering a torn ACL that limited him to just nine games in 2013, Atkins returned to action the following year to begin a string of six straight seasons in which he started every game the Bengals played. Performing at an extremely high level throughout the period, Atkins earned Pro Bowl honors each season, recording at least nine sacks on four separate occasions.

Atkins's consistently excellent play made a believer out of Bengals defensive line coach Jay Hayes, who, after once saying of his protégé, "He's short. He's not the prototype (defensive tackle)," commented, "He is the type of guy that makes plays. He's not flashy. He just plays his technique and plays it well—and he's disruptive. He's the best player I've ever coached."

Surprisingly quick for a man his size, Atkins also possessed great strength, with Bengals offensive lineman Andrew Whitworth saying of his teammate, "It feels like you're blocking someone that's a hundred pounds heavier than he is. He's just got extreme power and strength, and he uses it. It's really hard to stop him from going where he's going, and you know already that you're in a lot of trouble. . . . Geno's one of those guys that you can get in front of and feel like you've got the block handled, but he's so powerful he's just gonna' keep moving you backwards. He's bulling you, he's running smack into you, and then the one time you lean on him, he tosses you to the side and goes around you. He's got rare strength and power for a guy his stature."

Cleveland Browns guard Joel Bitonio discussed the problems Atkins presented to him in pass protection, saying, "He's a pretty relentless pass-rusher. He picks and chooses when he goes, but, when he wants to come, he's one of the toughest bull-rushers in the league."

In assessing Atkins's varied skill set, Bill Belichick stated, "There's been a few guys like him at that position. They're very hard to handle in there—their quickness. He has very good playing strength and leverage. He's more of a compact guy, but he has great leverage. Good quickness, good motor, and like a lot of those guys, he's very smart and instinctive."

Belichick continued, "He just can anticipate who's going to block him or what the combination is going to be up front, and then he anticipates and uses his quickness, and his power, and his length, or I'd say leverage, to gain an advantage. And once he gains an advantage, it's very hard for those blockers—the guards, the centers, sometimes the tackles on those doubles—just to regain it. . . . He's just too quick and too explosive to . . . once he has that gap, or he has that little bit of a position advantage, then he capitalizes on it and gains it, and a lot of times he gets held. He causes a lot of penalties, and that's another way he's disruptive is some first-and-20s, and second-and-20s off penalties on those plays."

A quiet man who didn't take part in elaborate in-game celebrations and went about his job in workmanlike fashion, Atkins rarely drew attention to himself, prompting teammate Carlos Dunlap to say, "That's just how Geno is. He lets his pads do the talking."

In describing the approach that he took to his profession, Atkins stated, "I mean honestly, you do it the right way, show up, go to OTAs, training camp, do all the stuff. Don't make big hoopla or talk to the media about it."

Displaying his admiration for Atkins, Bengals head coach Marvin Lewis said, "I think Geno—his production, everything he's done—has warranted the reputation that he's garnered. He's one of the best defensive players in the league. Anytime we draft a player, we're hoping he continues to ascend. It hasn't surprised me how effective Geno has been."

Extremely loyal, Atkins, who never tested free agency, expressed his desire to finish his career with the Bengals prior to the start of the 2018 campaign, saying, "They were the team that drafted me. I love it here. I love the city. I love the organization. It's something to cement my legacy here, and I think that it's important to finish where I started."

After earning his sixth consecutive Pro Bowl selection the previous season, Atkins barely played in 2020, making just one tackle and no sacks after sustaining a shoulder injury during training camp. Released by the Bengals on March 19, 2021, Atkins subsequently announced his retirement, ending his career with 75 1/2 sacks, 384 tackles (228 solo), 100 tackles for loss, eight forced fumbles, two fumble recoveries, and one touchdown. Since retiring from football, Atkins has spent most of his time with his two young children and spreading awareness of sickle cell disease, a blood disorder he learned that he had during his freshman year at Georgia.

Atkins earned eight Pro Bowl selections and three All-Pro nominations during his time in Cincinnati.
Courtesy of Jeffrey Beall

CAREER HIGHLIGHTS

Best Season

Atkins had an exceptional year for the Bengals in 2015, earning one of his two First-Team All-Pro nominations by recording 11 sacks, 42 tackles, and 21 hits on opposing quarterbacks. But he performed even better three years earlier, when, en route to gaining consensus First-Team All-Pro recognition, he established career-high marks with 12 1/2 sacks, 54 tackles, 39 solo stops, and four forced fumbles, prompting *Pro Football Focus* to identify his 2012 campaign as the best ever turned in by a defensive tackle since the site began tracking league-wide performance in 2008.

Memorable Moments/Greatest Performances

Atkins scored the only touchdown of his career on the final play of a 30–20 win over the Jaguars on October 9, 2011, when he ran the ball into the end zone after recovering a fumble on the Jacksonville 10 yard line.

Atkins contributed to a 28–6 win over the Chiefs on November 18, 2012, by recording a sack, forcing two fumbles, and registering six solo tackles.

Atkins earned AFC and NFL Defensive Player of the Week honors by recording two sacks, one forced fumble, and six tackles during a 13–10 win over the Steelers on December 23, 2012.

Atkins again gained recognition as AFC Defensive Player of the Week by registering two sacks, four hits on the opposing quarterback, and five tackles during a 23–10 win over the Browns on December 11, 2016.

Atkins helped lead the Bengals to a 30–16 win over the Oakland Raiders on December 16, 2018, by sacking Derek Carr three times and recording six tackles, four of which resulted in a loss.

Notable Achievements

- Scored one defensive touchdown.
- Finished in double digits in sacks three times.
- Led Bengals in sacks five times.
- Ranks among Bengals career leaders with 75 1/2 sacks (3rd) and eight forced fumbles (8th).
- Two-time division champion (2013 and 2015).
- Two-time AFC Defensive Player of the Week.
- 2012 Week 16 NFL Defensive Player of the Week.
- Eight-time Pro Bowl selection (2011, 2012, 2014, 2015, 2016, 2017, 2018, and 2019).
- Two-time First-Team All-Pro selection (2012 and 2015).
- 2011 Second-Team All-Pro selection.
- Five-time First-Team All-AFC selection (2012, 2015, 2016, 2017, and 2018).
- NFL 2010s All-Decade Team.
- Pro Football Reference All-2010s Second Team.

6

CHAD (OCHOCINCO) JOHNSON

One of the NFL's most unpredictable and entertaining players throughout his career, Chad Johnson spent 10 seasons in Cincinnati, often drawing attention to himself with his flamboyant personality and elaborate touchdown celebrations. Yet, at the same time, Johnson proved to be one of the league's most productive wideouts, surpassing 90 receptions four times and 1,000 receiving yards on seven separate occasions. The franchise's career leader in each of those categories, Johnson also ranks first in team annals in touchdown catches, yards from scrimmage, and all-purpose yards, with his outstanding play earning him six Pro Bowl selections, three All-Pro nominations, and a spot on the Bengals 50th Anniversary All-Time Team.

Born in Miami, Florida, on January 9, 1978, Chad Javon Johnson grew up in the city's Liberty City section, where he got his start in organized football at Miami Beach Senior High School. Following his graduation, Johnson briefly attended Langston University in Langston, Oklahoma, before transferring to Santa Monica College, a community college located in Santa Monica, California. After three years at Santa Monica, Johnson received an athletic scholarship to Oregon State University, where he spent his senior year playing alongside future Bengals teammate T. J. Houshmandzadeh, helping the Beavers compile an 11–1 record by making 37 receptions for 806 yards and eight touchdowns.

Selected by the Bengals in the second round of the 2001 NFL Draft, with the 36th overall pick, Johnson saw a limited amount of action as a rookie, making just 28 receptions for 329 yards and one touchdown. Emerging as an offensive weapon after he joined the starting unit the following year, Johnson scored five touchdowns and led the team with 69 catches and 1,166 receiving yards, doing so while living under rather unusual conditions.

Revealing during a 2023 appearance on *Club Shay Shay* that he spent his first two seasons in Cincinnati living inside Paul Brown Stadium, Johnson told host Shannon Sharpe, "You gotta remember, I stayed at the

Chad Johnson ranks first in team annals in five different offensive categories, including receptions, receiving yards, and touchdown catches.
Courtesy of Keith Allison

stadium the first two years because I didn't want to spend no money. What's the point? Why are you telling me to go rent a house, go buy a house, or go rent a condo when everything I need is right here in the facility? Showers, cafeteria, TV, couch, gaming system. What's the point? I was so locked in. It wasn't about having my own space."

Recalling that he finally found his own place prior to the start of his third season, Johnson added, "That's when Marvin (Lewis) came in and said, 'It's time for you to be responsible. Spread your wings. Get your own place'. . . . I moved right down the street. One little bedroom."

Taking his game up a notch after finding a place of his own, Johnson posted the following numbers over the course of the next five seasons:

YEAR	RECS	REC YDS	TD RECS
2003	90	1,355	10
2004	95	1,274	9
2005	97	1,432	9
2006	87	**1,369**	7
2007	93	1,440	8

After setting a new single-season franchise record for most receiving yards in the first of those campaigns, Johnson broke his own mark two years later, before eclipsing it again in 2007. In addition to leading the NFL in receiving yards in 2006, Johnson gained more yards through the air than any other AFC receiver in four of those five seasons. Johnson also placed in the league's top five in receptions twice and TD catches once, earning in the process three All-Pro selections and five consecutive Pro Bowl nominations. Meanwhile, after winning just two games in 2002, the Bengals posted a losing record in just one of those five seasons, capturing the division title in 2005 with a mark of 11–5.

Johnson, who stood 6'1" and weighed close to 190 pounds, possessed excellent moves and outstanding speed, which he used to separate himself from his defender. Praising his former teammate for his proficiency in that area, Carson Palmer stated, "I don't know if there's a receiver that's played this game that could create more separation than Chad could."

Palmer added, "He was the most dominant receiver for I don't know how many years. I could see at the line of scrimmage; you would look across the ball and I could see there were guys that were scared to death that he was out there."

In assessing his own skill set, Johnson said, "My biggest asset is my combination of size and speed. . . . I'm a physical receiver, yet I can run and move like someone who is 5–8 or 5–9."

But as Johnson's reputation continued to grow, so, too, did his ego and sense of self-importance, which he exhibited in any number of ways. Never one to feign modesty, Johnson stated on one occasion, "Stopping me? That's impossible. There's not anything that can really stop me."

Other notable quotes included, "There's three things in life that's certain: death, taxes, and 85 [his uniform number] will always be open," "They've got a better chance of finding Osama than stopping me tonight," and, "You can't be humble and be great."

Displaying his arrogance and narcissistic nature at one point during the 2005 season, Johnson announced that he intended to keep a checklist called "Who Covered 85 in '05," that would evaluate the defensive backs who successfully managed to cover him.

Constantly seeking to draw attention to himself, Johnson also invented several creative touchdown celebrations, one of which involved him giving CPR to a football. On another occasion, Johnson dropped to one knee and "proposed" to a cheerleader.

Although Bengals head coach Marvin Lewis objected to Johnson's theatrics, he chose not to censor him, saying, "It goes against everything coaches stand for, particularly myself. We don't need to bring attention to ourselves, but that's what got him up and excited to go play."

Despite Johnson's strong performance in 2007, the Bengals finished the season with a losing record, prompting some within the organization and several members of the local media to blame the team's failures on what they claimed to be his selfish behavior. Objecting to the treatment he received over the course of the campaign, Johnson, who once said, "You have to have some type of selfishness to you in anything that you do to be successful at it," stated during a January 13, 2008, interview on ESPN's *Mike & Mike* radio show, "I was labeled selfish and a cancer, and it hurt. . . . Fingers were pointed at me this year. If the team and the organization wants to further itself (make the playoffs), I think you need to get rid of the problem. . . . It hurt me. To do me that way and not to have my back. Things were said, and nobody came to my defense."

Although Johnson subsequently asked to be traded, the team refused to part ways with him, with Marvin Lewis saying at the time, "He is a Cincinnati Bengal for quite a while."

Several months later, just prior to the start of the 2008 regular season, Johnson legally changed his last name to "Ochocinco," which means "85" in Spanish.

Hampered by injuries for much of 2008, Johnson made just 53 receptions for 540 yards and four touchdowns, before rebounding the following year to earn his sixth Pro Bowl nomination by catching 72 passes, amassing 1,047 receiving yards, and scoring nine touchdowns. But, after Johnson

Johnson surpassed 90 receptions four times and 1,000 receiving yards seven times.
Courtesy of Navin Rajagopalan

posted less impressive numbers in 2010, finishing the season with 67 receptions, 831 receiving yards, and four TDs, the Bengals traded him to the Patriots for two draft picks on July 28, 2011.

Johnson, who left Cincinnati with career totals of 751 receptions, 10,783 receiving yards, 10,958 yards from scrimmage, and 66 touchdown catches, ended up spending just one season in New England, making only 15 receptions for 276 yards and one touchdown in a backup role, before being released by the Patriots the following offseason. After legally changing his last name from Ochocinco back to Johnson on July 24, 2012, Johnson signed with the Miami Dolphins. But he never appeared in a game with them since they released him following his arrest for domestic violence prior to the start of the regular season.

After sitting out the 2012 and 2013 campaigns, Johnson spent one season playing for the Montreal Alouettes of the Canadian Football League, before announcing his retirement after the Alouettes suspended him for failing to report for mandatory training camp in the spring of 2015. Following his career in football, Johnson tried his hand at soccer, serving as a member of Boca Raton FC of the United Premier Soccer League for two seasons, before joining Florida A&M University's Athletics Department as an athletics ambassador and consultant in March 2023.

BENGALS CAREER HIGHLIGHTS

Best Season

Johnson performed exceptionally well for the Bengals in 2007, when, in addition to catching 93 passes and scoring eight touchdowns, he established career-high marks with 1,440 receiving yards and 1,487 yards from scrimmage. But the Bengals finished the regular season with a record of just 7–9. On the other hand, when Johnson earned First-Team All-Pro honors in 2005 by making 97 receptions, scoring nine touchdowns, and amassing 1,432 receiving yards and 1,465 yards from scrimmage, the Bengals won the division title, making that the most impactful season of his career.

Memorable Moments/Greatest Performances

Johnson helped lead the Bengals to a 34–26 win over the Baltimore Ravens on October 19, 2003, by making five receptions for 130 yards and one touchdown, which came on a career-long 82-yard connection with Jon Kitna.

Johnson proved to be a huge factor during a 34–27 win over the San Diego Chargers on November 23, 2003, catching 10 passes for 107 yards and three touchdowns.

Johnson contributed to a 23–10 victory over Denver on October 25, 2004, by making seven receptions for 149 yards and one TD, which came on a 50-yard hookup with Carson Palmer.

Johnson helped lead the Bengals to a 27–26 win over Baltimore on December 5, 2004, by making 10 receptions for 161 yards and two touchdowns.

Johnson gave the Bengals a 23–22 win over the Giants on December 26, 2004, by gathering in a 4-yard touchdown pass from Jon Kitna with just 44 seconds left in the game.

Although the Bengals lost to the Indianapolis Colts, 45–37, on November 20, 2005, Johnson had a big game, making eight receptions for 189 yards and one touchdown, which came on a 68-yard connection with Carson Palmer.

Johnson starred in defeat again on November 12, 2006, when he made 11 receptions for a career-high 260 yards and two touchdowns during a 49–41 loss to the Chargers.

Johnson followed that up by making six receptions for 190 yards and three touchdowns during a 31–16 win over New Orleans one week later, scoring on plays that covered 41, 60, and 4 yards.

Although the Bengals suffered a 51–45 defeat at the hands of the Browns on September 16, 2007, Johnson caught 11 passes for 209 yards and two touchdowns.

Johnson earned AFC Offensive Player of the Week honors by making 12 receptions for 103 yards and three touchdowns during a 35–6 win over the Tennessee Titans on November 25, 2007.

Notable Achievements

- Surpassed 90 receptions four times.
- Surpassed 1,000 receiving yards seven times.
- Scored 10 touchdowns in 2003.
- Led NFL with 1,369 receiving yards in 2006.
- Finished third in NFL in receptions once and receiving yards twice.
- Led Bengals in receptions five times and receiving yards nine times.
- Holds Bengals career records for most receptions (751), receiving yards (10,783), yards from scrimmage (10,958), all-purpose yards (10,958), and touchdown receptions (66).
- Ranks among Bengals career leaders with 66 touchdowns (2nd) and 396 points (7th).
- Two-time division champion (2005 and 2009).
- 2007 Week 12 AFC Offensive Player of the Week.
- Six-time Pro Bowl selection (2003, 2004, 2005, 2006, 2007, and 2009).

- Two-time First-Team All-Pro selection (2005 and 2006).
- 2003 Second-Team All-Pro selection.
- Four-time First-Team All-AFC selection (2003, 2004, 2005, and 2006).
- Named to Bengals 40th Anniversary All-Time Team in 2007.
- Named to Bengals 50th Anniversary All-Time Team in 2017.
- Inducted into Bengals Ring of Honor in 2023.

7
A. J. GREEN

Rivaling Chad Johnson as the greatest receiver in franchise history, A. J. Green spent a decade in Cincinnati, recording the second-most receptions and amassing the second-most receiving yards of any player in team annals. A prototype number one wideout who had the ability to both move the chains and beat his man deep downfield, Green possessed a rare combination of size and speed that made him one of the most unstoppable receivers in the NFL from 2011 to 2017. A member of Bengals teams that made five consecutive playoff appearances and won two division titles, Green surpassed 80 receptions three times and 1,000 receiving yards on six separate occasions, leading the team in both categories seven straight times. A seven-time Pro Bowler, Green also earned two All-Pro nominations, before departing for Arizona, where he ended his playing career.

Born in Summerville, South Carolina, on July 31, 1988, Adriel Jeremiah Green experienced tragedy early in life, when, at the age of four, he lost his only sibling, older brother Avionce, who died in a car wreck on the way to a school carnival. The son of a steelworker and a clerk at Walmart, Green grew up in the nearby blue-collar town of Ridgeville, recalling, "Growing up in Ridgeville, South Carolina, pretty much all I saw was people working hard. . . . In my neighborhood, people were truckers and teachers and store clerks and bus drivers and everything else under the sun. But what they all had in common was that everyone was dependable and worked really hard. We all got what we needed, but it didn't always come easy."

Revealing that he didn't participate much in sports until he reached middle school, Green stated, "In elementary school, I didn't even play sports. I was just straight up on the juggling team. I started out with floating scarves. Then I went to tennis balls and all that. Then, by like the fourth grade, I was doing the Chinese yo-yo. And I was good, man. I was like a master Chinese yo-yo person. I was top-five Dead or Alive in South Carolina."

A. J. Green ranks second in franchise history only to Chad Johnson in receptions
and receiving yards.
Courtesy of Alexander Jonesi

Having developed excellent hand-eye coordination with his juggling,
Green emerged as a star in multiple sports at Summerville High School,
excelling as a wide receiver in football, a forward in basketball, and a long
jumper and triple jumper in track and field. Particularly outstanding on the
gridiron, Green earned All-State honors four times by making 279 receptions and amassing 5,373 receiving yards, finishing his career with the
fourth most catches and second most receiving yards in the history of the
National Federation of High Schools. Continuing to perform at an elite

level after he accepted an athletic scholarship to the University of Georgia, Green spent three seasons playing under head coach Mark Richt, gaining All-SEC First-Team recognition twice by making 166 receptions for 2,619 yards and 23 touchdowns, before declaring himself eligible for the 2011 NFL Draft after his junior year.

Selected by the Bengals in the first round, with the fourth overall pick, Green lived up to the lofty expectations set for him his first year in the league, earning Pro Bowl honors and a spot on the 2011 NFL All-Rookie Team by making 65 receptions for 1,057 yards and seven touchdowns, with his outstanding play, and that of fellow rookie, Andy Dalton, helping the Bengals advance to the playoffs for the first of five straight times. Reaching truly elite status in his second season, Green began an exceptional four-year run during which he posted the following numbers:

YEAR	RECS	REC YDS	TD RECS
2012	97	1,350	11
2013	98	1,426	11
2014	69	1,041	6
2015	86	1,297	10

Although slowed somewhat in 2014 by a toe injury that forced him to miss three games, Green ranked among the league leaders in every major pass-receiving category in each of the other three seasons, earning in the process four straight Pro Bowl selections and two All-Pro nominations. And by amassing 1,297 receiving yards in 2015, Green became just the second player in NFL history to reach the magical 1,000-yard mark in each of his first five seasons, joining Randy Moss on an extremely exclusive list. More importantly, the Bengals continued their string of consecutive playoff appearances, winning the division title in both 2013 and 2015, although they failed to advance beyond the wild card round of the postseason tournament.

Generally ranked among the top five receivers in the game throughout the period, the 6'4", 207-pound Green possessed a wide catch radius that made him an excellent third-down target. Blessed with outstanding speed as well, Green, who ran a sub-4.5-second 40-yard dash at the NFL scouting combine, also possessed the ability to beat his man deep or outrun him once he gathered in the football, recording 13 scoring plays of 50 or more yards over the course of his career, including seven that covered at least

70 yards. Meanwhile, Green's strong work ethic, low-key personality, and humility made him extremely popular with his teammates.

Driven by his fear of failure, Green said, "I think what pushes me every day is that I'm so afraid to fail. I think it comes from what I went through in school growing up and not being great in the classroom and having to work harder than everybody else."

Humble by nature, Green proved to be the polar opposite of his immediate predecessor on this list, Chad Johnson, saying after he had already attained elite status, "I've been the same guy since day one. No matter how successful I am in life, I'm going to stay true to myself and stay humble and grounded. I feel like that's where your success comes from. Once you get that big head, it's over. You feel like you can't be stopped. Staying humble is the only way you can be great."

Despite missing the final six games of the 2016 campaign with a torn hamstring, Green earned his sixth consecutive Pro Bowl nomination by making 66 receptions for 964 yards and four touchdowns. Although Green again gained Pro Bowl recognition the following year by catching 75 passes, amassing 1,078 receiving yards, and scoring eight touchdowns, he appeared a step slower. Nevertheless, he remained unconcerned, stating, "I don't have to rely on my athletic abilities to get by. I actually understand the game. I know the game of football. I know how to read DBs, I know how to read defenses—little stuff like that, that I didn't have in 2011."

However, Green posted far less impressive numbers in 2018, when, limited to just nine games by a badly injured toe, he made 46 receptions for 694 yards and six touchdowns. Green subsequently missed the entire 2019 campaign after tearing ligaments in his ankle during training camp. Upon his return to action the following year, Green caught just 47 passes, amassed only 523 receiving yards, and scored just two touchdowns.

Yet, even in his somewhat diminished state, Green made an extremely favorable impression on Bengals second-year offensive coordinator Brian Callahan. In discussing everything Green brought to the team, Callahan said, "Great players are hard to come by. I think A.J. will be regarded as the best Bengal receiver of all-time. . . . He's been a really great player in the NFL for a lot of years now, and he's been productive every time he's stepped out there. His leadership is invaluable. His professionalism helps all of our guys on offense, and everything he does, he does with a purpose. When he gets a chance to go out there, he contributes. There's just an energy that he's got about him, and those guys all feed off him."

Green helped lead the Bengals to two division titles and five playoff appearances.
Courtesy of Keith Allison and All-Pro Reels Photography

Further elaborating on Green's Bengals legacy, Callahan added, "Some of the games that he's played against Baltimore, and some of the moments that he's had that he's kind of answered the bell and made a great play, that's the kind of thing that fanbases in cities don't forget. So, you tie in all the things that he's done on the field, all the big moments he's had, and then all the things he does behind the scenes that people don't get to see, you can see why he is what he means to the Bengals and what he means to the city of Cincinnati."

But, with Green having experienced a precipitous decline in offensive production, the Bengals chose not to actively pursue him when he became a free agent at the end of the year, prompting him to sign with the Arizona Cardinals prior to the start of the 2021 season. Before leaving Cincinnati, though, Green, who, in his 10 years with the Bengals, caught 649 passes, amassed 9,430 receiving yards and 9,523 yards from scrimmage, and scored 65 touchdowns, thanked the organization and the fans who had supported him via a message on Instagram that read:

> Wow. My time with the Cincinnati Bengals has come to an end. What an amazing journey it's been! I'd like to thank the Bengals organization for believing in me and giving me an opportunity to live out my dreams. It was truly an honor to wear those stripes. Thank you to the Brown family. I'm forever grateful.
>
> To the fans—it's been 10 incredible years! You've been such an inspiration to me. Thank you for the continuous support and motivation. Seeing the stadium filled with fans rocking my jersey each game meant more to me than one can imagine. I was proud to represent y'all! It's luv for life!
>
> This community has been so good to my family. THANK YOU for the beautiful memories. Wishing you all the best!

Green ended up spending two seasons in Arizona, making another 78 receptions for 1,084 yards and five touchdowns, before announcing his retirement on February 6, 2023, stating in an Instagram post: "I've never been a man of many words, so I'll keep this short. Thank you. Thank you to all who have supported, encouraged, and inspired me throughout my career. Special thank you to the University of Georgia, Cincinnati Bengals, and Arizona Cardinals for the opportunity to pursue my dreams. I've stayed true to the game, and it owes me nothing. Be blessed. Love y'all! The next chapter begins . . . "

Since retiring from football, Green has continued the work he began during his time in Cincinnati that helps empower youth by providing educational opportunities to those in underserved communities. In addition to giving to numerous nonprofit organizations to help them build youth community centers and scholarship funds for teens in his hometown of Summerville, Green remains involved with his high school, where he has donated money for the purchase of new computers and athletic equipment. Green also provides an annual athletic scholarship to the University of

Georgia through the AJ Green Family Football Scholarship and funds the AJ Green Skills Camp, a football skills camp for high school aged kids in Summerville.

BENGALS CAREER HIGHLIGHTS

Best Season

Although Green also earned Second-Team All-Pro honors the previous year, he had his finest all-around season for the Bengals in 2013, when he helped them capture the division title by establishing career-high marks with 98 receptions, 1,426 receiving yards, and 11 touchdowns.

Memorable Moments/Greatest Performances

Green scored the first touchdown of his career in his first game as a pro when he gathered in a 41-yard TD pass from Bruce Gradkowski during a 27–17 win over the Browns in the 2011 regular-season opener.

Green helped lead the Bengals to a 38–31 win over Washington on September 23, 2012, by making nine receptions for 183 yards and one touchdown, which covered 73 yards.

Green starred in defeat in the 2013 regular-season opener, making nine receptions for 162 yards and two touchdowns during a 24–21 loss to the Bears.

Green had a big day against Detroit on October 20, 2013, making six receptions for 155 yards and one touchdown during a 27–24 Bengals win, with his TD coming on a career-long 82-yard connection with Andy Dalton.

Although the Bengals eventually lost to Baltimore in overtime by a score of 20–17 on November 10, 2013, Green made a huge play when he gathered in a game-tying 51-yard touchdown pass from Andy Dalton as time expired in regulation. He finished the contest with eight receptions for 151 yards and that one TD.

Green helped the Bengals begin the 2014 campaign on a positive note by making six receptions for 131 yards and one touchdown during a 23–16 win over the Ravens in the opening game of the regular season, hooking up with Andy Dalton on a 77-yard scoring play with just under five minutes left in regulation that provided the margin of victory.

Green turned in one of his greatest performances in a losing effort on December 7, 2014, making 11 receptions for 224 yards and one touchdown during a 42–21 loss to Pittsburgh, with his TD coming on an 81-yard connection with Andy Dalton.

Green earned his lone AFC Offensive Player of the Week nomination by making 10 receptions for 227 yards and two touchdowns during a 28–24 win over Baltimore on September 27, 2015, connecting with Andy Dalton on scoring plays of 80 and 7 yards, with his 7-yard TD grab late in the final period providing the winning margin.

Green helped lead the Bengals to a 23–22 victory over the Jets in the 2016 regular-season opener by making 12 receptions for 180 yards and one touchdown, which came on a 54-yard connection with Andy Dalton.

Green contributed to a 22–7 win over Miami on September 29, 2016, by catching 10 passes for 173 yards and one touchdown.

Green proved to be a huge factor in a 31–17 victory over the Browns on October 23, 2016, making eight receptions for 169 yards and one touchdown, which came on a 48-yard hookup with Andy Dalton on the final play of the first half.

Green helped lead the Bengals to a 20–16 win over the Bills on October 8, 2017, by making seven receptions for 189 yards and one touchdown, which came on a 77-yard connection with Andy Dalton.

Green gave the Bengals a 37–36 victory over the Atlanta Falcons on September 30, 2018, by gathering in a 13-yard TD pass from Andy Dalton with just seven seconds left in the game.

Notable Achievements

- Surpassed 80 receptions three times, topping 90 catches twice.
- Surpassed 1,000 receiving yards six times.
- Scored at least 10 touchdowns three times.
- Led Bengals in receptions and receiving yards seven times each.
- Ranks among Bengals career leaders with 649 receptions (2nd), 9,430 receiving yards (2nd), 9,523 yards from scrimmage (3rd), 9,523 all-purpose yards (4th), 65 touchdown receptions (2nd), 65 touchdowns (3rd), and 390 points (9th).
- Two-time division champion (2013 and 2015).
- Member of 2011 NFL All-Rookie Team.
- 2015 Week 3 AFC Offensive Player of the Week.
- September 2012 AFC Offensive Player of the Month.

- Seven-time Pro Bowl selection (2011, 2012, 2013, 2014, 2015, 2016, and 2017).
- Two-time Second-Team All-Pro selection (2012 and 2013).
- 2012 First-Team All-AFC selection.
- Pro Football Reference All-2010s Second Team.

8

MAX MONTOYA

The greatest interior offensive lineman in franchise history, Max Montoya spent 11 seasons in Cincinnati, starting at right guard for the Bengals in 10 of those. Combining with Anthony Muñoz to form what became known as "The Mexican Connection," Montoya gave the Bengals consistently excellent play on the right side of their offensive line, providing outstanding pass protection and superior run-blocking, while missing a total of just four non-strike games from 1980 to 1989. A key contributor to teams that won three division titles and two AFC championships, Montoya earned three Pro Bowl selections and one All-Pro nomination, before departing for Los Angeles, where he continued to perform at an elite level for the Raiders for five more years. Named to the Bengals 50th Anniversary All-Time Team, Montoya accomplished all he did after having to wait until the seventh round of the 1979 NFL Draft to hear his name called.

Born in Montebello, California, on May 12, 1956, Max Montoya Jr. grew up in nearby La Puente, where he played football and basketball his first two years at La Puente High School, before missing his final season after being diagnosed with a heart murmur. Failing to receive any college scholarship offers as a result, Montoya enrolled at Mt. San Antonio Community College in the Los Angeles suburb of Walnut, California, where, after being cleared for football, he performed so well as a sophomore that UCLA offered him an athletic scholarship.

After redshirting his first year at UCLA, Montoya spent the next two seasons starting for the Bruins at offensive tackle, helping them post a record of 7–4 in 1977 and a mark of 8-3-1 in 1978, with his outstanding play in the second of those campaigns earning him All–Pac-10 honors. Yet, despite Montoya's strong performance, concerns over his long-term health caused him to fall to the seventh round of the 1979 NFL Draft, where the Bengals finally selected him with the 168th overall pick.

Assuming the role of a backup his first year in Cincinnati, Montoya garnered very little playing time, starting only one game for a Bengals team

Max Montoya started for the Bengals at right guard for 10 seasons.

that compiled a record of just 4–12. But, after being tutored by new head coach and Hall of Fame offensive lineman Forrest Gregg prior to the start of the ensuing campaign, Montoya started almost every non-strike game the Bengals played over the course of the next 10 seasons, at one point starting 105 consecutive contests at right guard. And with Montoya and Anthony Muñoz anchoring their offensive line, the Bengals grew increasingly effective at running the football, with the athleticism of both men allowing them to employ elements of what is now called the zone run-blocking scheme.

Standing 6'5" and weighing some 285 pounds, Montoya possessed the size and strength to excel as a straight-ahead blocker on inside running plays. Extremely quick as well, Montoya also did a superb job of protecting his quarterback and leading Bengals runners to the outside, with fellow guard Dave Lapham saying of his former teammate, "In the era we played in, he was, from a pass protector and as a pulling guard, as good as there was. Big, barrel-chested upper body. Just stoned guys. He was phenomenal in that regard. In a 10- and 20-yard area, he was cat-quick. He was quick as hell. Always ran great pass courses when he was a pulling guard. Max would get nasty when he had to get nasty. He definitely wasn't taking anything from anybody."

Meanwhile, Anthony Muñoz said of his longtime line-mate, "Max Montoya, to me, was one of the best guards I ever watched play. You get him on the football field, you better be ready for war. Max Montoya came every Sunday to battle. He is probably the one guy who has not gotten enough credit out of all the guys that are constantly mentioned (for the Pro Football Hall of Fame)."

One of the league's most durable players, Montoya not only started almost every game the Bengals played his last 10 years in Cincinnati, but he played some of the best ball of his career after turning 30 years of age, earning Pro Bowl and All-AFC honors three times each from 1986 to 1989, while also garnering his only All-Pro nomination in the last of those campaigns.

In discussing his longevity and ability to compete at an extremely high level well into his 30s, Montoya said, "I stayed pretty much serious-injury free for most of my career. I really only had one serious knee injury, a couple of broken fingers—not a whole bunch. I was pretty fortunate."

Even though Montoya earned All-Pro honors in 1989, the Bengals chose not to protect him on their roster the following offseason, making him a Plan B free agent who had the ability to negotiate with other teams. Electing to sign with the Los Angeles Raiders, Montoya, who owned two restaurants in Cincinnati, told the *Los Angeles Times* after inking his deal with the Raiders, "I think they [the Bengals] were taking a calculated risk, knowing that I had a lot of ties in Cincinnati and had been there for a lot of years and was very comfortable with the situation. They figured, and I figured, that I wasn't going to go anywhere. . . . But I didn't think as many teams would come after me like they did and start swaying me with money."

Commenting on Montoya's decision to leave Cincinnati, Mike Brown, then the Bengals assistant general manager, said, "He was a fine player for the Cincinnati Bengals, and we appreciate what he did here. We hoped

Montoya missed just four non-strike games from 1980 to 1989.

he would have played out his career here, but he had a choice not to and decided he wouldn't. We wish him well."

Montoya, who left Cincinnati having appeared in a total of 157 games, 144 of which he started, ended up spending five seasons in Los Angeles, starting for the Raiders in four of those, before announcing his retirement after assuming a backup role in 1994.

Following his playing days, Montoya returned to Cincinnati, where he invested in Penn Station East Coast Subs and opened Montoya's Mexican Restaurant in Fort Mitchell, Kentucky. Montoya also spent five years helping coach the Beechwood High School football team. Now semi-retired,

Montoya lives with his wife, Patty, on a farm in Hebron, Kentucky, where he raises horses.

BENGALS CAREER HIGHLIGHTS

Best Season

Montoya had a tremendous year for the Bengals in 1988, when he helped them advance to the Super Bowl by allowing his opponent to hit the quarterback just once in 237 pass attempts at one point during the season, with his superior pass protection prompting *Pro Football Weekly* to name him the NFL's best pass-blocking guard. But Montoya performed even better the following year, earning his lone All-Pro nomination in 1989 by helping Bengals running backs average a robust 4.7 yards per carry.

Memorable Moments/Greatest Performances

Montoya helped the Bengals amass 571 yards of total offense during a 38–21 win over the Denver Broncos on November 22, 1981.

Montoya and his line-mates dominated the Dallas Cowboys at the point of attack on December 8, 1985, with the Bengals gaining a season-high total of 274 yards on the ground and amassing 570 yards of total offense during a convincing 50–24 victory.

Montoya and his cohorts manhandled the opposition again during a 31–7 win over the Patriots on December 7, 1986, with the Bengals rushing for 300 yards and gaining another 284 yards through the air.

Notable Achievements

- Started 105 consecutive games from 1980 to 1986.
- Three-time division champion (1981, 1982, and 1988).
- Two-time AFC champion (1981 and 1988).
- Three-time Pro Bowl selection (1986, 1988, and 1989).
- 1989 Second-Team All-Pro selection.
- Two-time First-Team All-AFC selection (1986 and 1988).
- 1989 Second-Team All-AFC selection.
- Pro Football Reference All-1980s First Team.
- Named to Bengals 40th Anniversary All-Time Team in 2007.
- Named to Bengals 50th Anniversary All-Time Team in 2017.

9

LEMAR PARRISH

One of the most dynamic players in franchise history, Lemar Parrish spent eight seasons in Cincinnati, teaming up with Ken Riley to form an exceptional cornerback tandem that ranks among the best in NFL history. The more colorful of the two, Parrish became known for his engaging personality, extravagant attire, and tremendous running ability, which made him a threat to score any time he got his hands on the football. The Bengals career leader for most touchdowns scored by a defender, Parrish crossed the opponent's goal line a total of 13 times, scoring seven times on defense and six times on special teams. Also ranking extremely high in team annals in interceptions, interception-return yards, punt-return yards, and fumble recoveries, Parrish proved to be a significant contributor to teams that won two division titles, with his outstanding play earning him six Pro Bowl selections, six All-AFC nominations, and a place on Pro Football Reference's All-1970s First Team. And even though Parrish ended up leaving Cincinnati on bad terms, the Bengals later named him to their 50th Anniversary All-Time Team.

Born in West Palm Beach, Florida, on December 13, 1947, Lemar R. Parrish attended John F. Kennedy High School in nearby Riviera Beach, where he starred as a running back on the gridiron. Offered a football scholarship to Lincoln University of Missouri, a small, historically Black college in Jefferson City, Parrish spent four years excelling at running back and punt-returner for the Blue Tigers, setting school records for the longest punt return (95 yards), most punt-return yards in a game (129), and highest career punt-return average (15.5 yards per return).

With Parrish having gained All-America recognition as a senior in 1969, the Bengals selected him in the seventh round of the 1970 NFL Draft, with the 163rd overall pick. Moved to defensive back following his arrival in Cincinnati, Parrish made an immediate impact after laying claim to the starting left cornerback job, earning Pro Bowl honors as a rookie by leading the team with five interceptions, while also amassing 676 yards and

Lemar Parrish combined with Ken Riley for eight seasons to form one of the finest cornerback tandems in NFL history.

scoring three times on special teams. Parrish followed that up with another strong season, earning his second straight Pro Bowl selection in 1971 by picking off seven passes and scoring two touchdowns on defense. Although Parrish failed to gain Pro Bowl recognition in either of the next two seasons, he earned consecutive All-AFC nominations by recording a total of seven interceptions, two of which he returned for touchdowns. Parrish also lit the scoreboard two other times, scoring once on a fumble return and once on a punt return.

Parrish subsequently failed to record a single interception in 1974. Nevertheless, his exceptional coverage skills and league-leading 18.8-yard punt-return average earned him Pro Bowl and Second-Team All-AFC honors for the first of four straight times. Also accorded unofficial All-Pro honors by the Newspaper Enterprise Association for the first of three times, Parrish became even better known throughout the league than his partner in crime, Ken Riley, whose quiet demeanor often caused him to be overshadowed by his more flamboyant teammate.

In discussing the differences between the two men, Bob Trumpy said, "As quiet and studious as Ken Riley was, Lemar Parrish was the exact opposite. He was a walking, lit-up, neon sign. When you heard cackling on the other side of the locker room—that's where the defense was—it was led by Lemar Parrish."

Also drawing attention to himself with the excitement he created every time he touched the football, Parrish thrilled even his own teammates with his exceptional running ability, with Trumpy saying, "When he was back returning punts, I went from the bench out to the sideline to watch him return punts. . . . A college running back converted to defensive back, and every time he touched the football—interception, fumble recovery, whatever—he was not looking to just possess it—he was looking to score. And every time he returned a punt, I was watching; he was that exciting."

Blessed with outstanding speed and exceptional moves, the 5-foot, 11-inch, 185-pound Parrish used the skills he developed in college to establish himself as one of the finest open-field runners in the game. An excellent one-on-one defender as well, Parrish did a superb job of sticking to his man and tracking the football, causing opposing quarterbacks to often avoid throwing to his side of the field.

Praising his former teammate for his superior athletic ability, Tommy Casanova said, "He was one of the most wonderful athletes I've ever seen. The guy would be running 100 miles per hour, stop on a dime, and go straight up. He was incredible. Lemar Parrish might be the best player I ever played with. He was really, really good."

Parrish also made a lasting impression on current Bengals owner and president Mike Brown, who stated, "Lemar was the most talented cornerback we ever had. He was the quickest. He could cover people with *ease*. Just stay right with 'em. He was also a great returner."

Unfortunately, Parrish's time in Cincinnati came to an end following the conclusion of the 1977 campaign. Unhappy over his treatment by Bengals head coach and general manager Paul Brown, who he claimed, "treated veterans like kids out of college," Parrish expressed a desire to go elsewhere,

Parrish scored more times on defense than any other player in team annals.

saying, "I just want out." Adding that Brown "never showed any affection for the guys. I don't care how good you are or how good you play, a guy likes to hear something from the coach," Parrish further exacerbated the situation by stating, "Paul wants to play his starters down; he doesn't want to pay anything."

With his contract set to expire, Parrish made it known that the Bengals needed to pay him much more if they wished to retain his services, saying, "No cornerback in the league is better than I am, but a lot are getting paid better than I am. If they can't meet my salary standards, I got to move. I can't spend glory."

Subsequently dealt to the Washington Redskins, along with star defensive end Coy Bacon, for Washington's first-round pick in the 1979 NFL Draft, Parrish left Cincinnati with career totals of 25 interceptions, 354 interception-return yards, 1,201 punt-return yards, 1,504 kickoff-return yards, 3,124 all-purpose yards, 10 fumble recoveries, and 13 touchdowns. The only player in franchise history ever to score two touchdowns on defense or special teams in the same game, Parrish accomplished the feat three times.

Continuing to perform at an elite level in Washington, Parrish earned two more trips to the Pro Bowl, two All-Pro nominations, and two First-Team All-NFC selections by recording a total of 21 interceptions over the course of the next four seasons, before ending his career as a backup with the Buffalo Bills in 1982. Retiring with 47 picks to his credit, Parrish registered the third most interceptions of any NFL player from 1970 to 1982, with only longtime teammate Ken Riley and Pittsburgh's Mel Blount picking off more passes during that time.

Following his playing days, Parrish struggled with drug addiction until turning his life around after he checked himself into a Tennessee rehab clinic in 1986. Eventually returning to his alma mater, Lincoln University of Missouri, Parrish earned a bachelor's degree in physical education and spent six seasons serving as head coach of the Blue Tigers football team, before retiring to private life in 2010.

BENGALS CAREER HIGHLIGHTS

Best Season

Although Parrish gained unofficial All-Pro recognition from the Newspaper Enterprise Association three straight times from 1974 to 1976, he had his finest all-around season for the Bengals in 1971, when, in addition to amassing 389 yards on special teams, he recorded seven interceptions, which he returned for a total of 105 yards, recovered two fumbles, and scored twice on defense.

Memorable Moments/Greatest Performances

Parrish earned NFL Defensive Player of the Week honors by picking off a pass, returning a kickoff 95 yards for a touchdown, and scoring again when he returned a blocked field goal attempt 83 yards for a TD during a 43–14 win over the Bills on November 8, 1970.

Parrish contributed to a 34–7 victory over the Steelers on November 22, 1970, by recording two interceptions in one game for the first time in his career.

Parrish scored his third touchdown on special teams when he returned a punt 79 yards for a TD during a 17–14 win over the Chargers on December 6, 1970.

Although the Bengals lost to the Steelers, 21–10, on September 26, 1971, Parrish lit the scoreboard again when he returned a fumble 14 yards for a touchdown.

Parrish scored again when he returned his interception of a Scott Hunter pass 65 yards for a touchdown during a 20–17 loss to the Packers on October 3, 1971.

Parrish contributed to a 31–7 win over the Patriots in the opening game of the 1972 regular season when he returned a punt 51 yards for a touchdown.

Parrish earned NFL Defensive Player of the Week honors by recording three interceptions, two of which he returned for touchdowns, during a 61–17 rout of the Houston Oilers in the 1972 regular-season finale.

Parrish scored again on defense when he returned a fumble 23 yards for a touchdown during a 27–0 shutout of the Vikings on December 2, 1973.

Parrish crossed the opponent's goal line again when he returned a punt 62 yards for a touchdown during a 33–7 win over the Browns in the 1974 regular-season opener.

Parrish proved to be a huge factor during a 28–17 win over Washington on October 6, 1974, returning a punt 90 yards for a touchdown, and scoring again when he ran 47 yards to paydirt after recovering a fumble.

Parrish scored his last points as a member of the Bengals on December 10, 1977, when he returned his interception of a Terry Bradshaw pass 47 yards for a touchdown during a 17–10 win over the Steelers.

Notable Achievements

- Scored seven defensive touchdowns.
- Scored six touchdowns on special teams.
- Recorded at least five interceptions three times.
- Amassed more than 100 interception-return yards once.
- Led NFL with an average of 18.8 yards per punt return in 1974.
- Led Bengals in interceptions four times.
- Holds Bengals career records for most touchdowns scored on defense (7) and most punt-return touchdowns (4).

- Ranks among Bengals career leaders with 25 interceptions (5th), 354 interception-return yards (3rd), four touchdown interceptions (2nd), 10 fumble recoveries (tied for 6th), and 1,201 punt-return yards (3rd).
- Two-time division champion (1970 and 1973).
- Two-time NFL Defensive Player of the Week.
- Six-time Pro Bowl selection (1970, 1971, 1974, 1975, 1976, and 1977).
- 1976 Newspaper Enterprise Association First-Team All-Pro selection.
- Two-time Newspaper Enterprise Association Second-Team All-Pro selection (1974 and 1975).
- 1972 First-Team All-AFC selection.
- Five-time Second-Team All-AFC selection (1973, 1974, 1975, 1976, and 1977).
- Pro Football Reference All-1970s First Team.
- Named to Bengals 40th Anniversary All-Time Team in 2007.
- Named to Bengals 50th Anniversary All-Time Team in 2017.

10

JOE BURROW

Although Joe Burrow has spent just four seasons in Cincinnati, he has already established himself as one of the finest players in team annals with his exceptional play behind center. Widely recognized as one of the two or three best quarterbacks in the game today, Burrow has received praise for his passing accuracy, outstanding pocket presence, high football IQ, and ability to remain calm under pressure, which has earned him the nicknames "Joe Cool" and "Joe Brrr." Despite missing significant playing time in two of his first four NFL seasons due to injury, Burrow has passed for more than 4,000 yards and thrown more than 30 touchdown passes twice each, earning in the process one Pro Bowl selection, two All-AFC nominations, and one top-five finish in the NFL MVP voting. Along the way, Burrow has helped restore the Bengals to prominence, leading them to two division titles and one AFC championship.

Born in Ames, Iowa, on December 10, 1996, Joseph Lee Burrow moved with his family to North Dakota in 2003, when his father, a former defensive back at the University of Nebraska and longtime college football coach, accepted the defensive coordinator position at North Dakota State University. Coming from a long line of outstanding athletes, Burrow, whose paternal grandmother once set a Mississippi state high school record by scoring 82 points in a basketball game, and whose paternal grandfather also starred on the hardwood at Mississippi State University, began playing football in youth leagues around North Dakota, before relocating again in 2005, when Ohio University in Athens offered his dad the same position he held at NDSU.

Eventually emerging as a star in multiple sports at Athens High School, Burrow excelled in basketball as well as football, earning First-Team All-State honors as a point guard his senior year. Even more proficient on the gridiron, Burrow led his school to three straight playoff appearances by passing for 11,416 yards and 157 touchdowns, while also rushing for 2,067 yards and 27 TDs, with his exceptional play in his final season

Joe Burrow has led the Bengals to two division titles and one AFC championship in his first four years in Cincinnati.
Courtesy of Keith Allison and All-Pro Reels Photography

gaining him recognition as Gatorade Player of the Year and the state of Ohio's "Mr. Football."

Offered an athletic scholarship to Ohio State University, Burrow redshirted as a freshman, before spending the next two years serving as a backup to starting quarterback J. T. Barrett. Realizing that the Buckeyes' coaching staff likely intended to anoint Dwayne Haskins as the starter in 2018, Burrow elected to transfer to Louisiana State University, telling reporters prior to making his decision, "I didn't come here [Ohio State] to sit on the bench for four years. I know I'm a pretty good quarterback. I want to play somewhere."

Following his arrival at LSU prior to the start of the 2018 campaign, Burrow laid claim to the starting quarterback job, after which he led the Tigers to a 10–3 record and a number six ranking in the final AP poll by throwing for 2,894 yards and 16 touchdowns, while also running for 399 yards and seven scores. Burrow followed that up with one of the greatest seasons in college football history, winning the Heisman Trophy and earning SEC Offensive Player of the Year, AP Player of the Year, and consensus All-America honors by passing for 5,671 yards and an FBS-record 60 touchdowns. Performing extraordinarily well during the College Football Playoffs, Burrow led LSU to a 63–28 win over fourth-ranked Oklahoma in the 2019 Peach Bowl by throwing for seven touchdowns and 493 yards, before amassing another 463 yards through the air and tossing five more TD passes during a 42–25 victory over Clemson in the National Championship Game.

Subsequently selected by the Bengals with the first overall pick of the 2020 NFL Draft, Burrow joined a team that had won just two games the previous year. Although the Bengals ended up posting just four victories in 2020, Burrow performed well before tearing the ACL and MCL in his left knee during the second half of a 20–9 loss to the Washington Football Team in Week 11, passing for 2,688 yards, throwing 13 TD passes and five interceptions, completing 65.3 percent of his passes, and compiling a passer rating of 89.8 in his 11 starts behind center.

Rejoining the Bengals in 2021 after undergoing successful knee surgery in December, Burrow stated upon his arrival in training camp that he wanted to get hit once or twice during the preseason, saying, "It doesn't really feel like football till you get hit a little bit. That's how it's been for me since the eighth grade."

Claiming that Burrow's proclamation revealed his inner toughness, Bengals offensive coordinator Brian Callahan commented, "I think he plays football like a defensive player sometimes. Contact has never been something he's been afraid of. It doesn't bother him. I think that's what makes him unique."

Bengals wide receiver Tyler Boyd added, "That's one thing I don't worry about is his toughness. He's as tough as it comes."

Proving himself fully healthy, Burrow led the Bengals to a regular-season record of 10–6 and the division title by completing a league-best 70.4 percent of his passes, placing near the top of the league rankings with 4,611 passing yards, 34 touchdown passes, and a passer rating of 108.3, and rushing for two TDs, with his outstanding play earning him First-Team All-AFC and NFL Comeback Player of the Year honors. Burrow then helped the Bengals advance to the Super Bowl for the first time in 33 years by leading them to playoff victories over the Las Vegas Raiders (26–19), Tennessee Titans (19–16), and Kansas City Chiefs (27–24 in OT), displaying his mettle against the Titans in the divisional round of the postseason tournament by completing 28 of 37 passes for 348 yards, despite being sacked nine times. Unfortunately, the Bengals came up just a bit short in their quest to capture their first NFL championship, suffering a heartbreaking 23–20 defeat at the hands of the Los Angeles Rams in Super Bowl LVI.

Cited by writers, coaches, and players throughout the league the following offseason as arguably the NFL's best young quarterback, Burrow drew praise for his ability to process opposing defenses quickly, with Charlie Goldsmith of the *Cincinnati Enquirer* writing that he possesses elite traits with regard to his "combination of picking up the blitz and his accuracy outside the pocket."

Brian Callahan also spoke of his quarterback's passing accuracy, saying that he has "an uncanny ability to place the ball accurately on the move anywhere on the field."

A master at managing the pocket, the 6'4", 220-pound Burrow avoids many would-be sacks by employing excellent footwork and moving well from side-to-side, with the *Athletic* commenting on his "ability to work a broken pocket," adding that he does an outstanding job of evading defenders and finding space to deliver a throw or run with the ball himself.

Extremely adept at protecting the football, Burrow avoids fumbles by always keeping both hands on the pigskin, prompting Bengals quarterbacks coach Dan Pitcher to say, "We see it every week across the league. A quarterback tries to spin out of something, he goes to avoid a guy, the ball is hanging out here, doesn't know someone is behind him, the ball is out. The way he is able to move in the pocket and be athletic and elusive without putting the ball in jeopardy is a big deal. . . . Joe is a guy who has incredible instincts and amazing spatial awareness. He doesn't have to see it; he can feel it. You'd be hard-pressed to find somebody better than he is in the pocket."

Meanwhile, Peter King of *Pro Football Talk* praised Burrow for his "cool" demeanor, both on and off the field, writing, "Burrow's steely mentality and his right arm are putting him on the path to greatness. I wouldn't bet against him."

An outstanding leader as well, Burrow, who possesses a strong work ethic and the ability to instill confidence in the other players around him,

Burrow holds single-season franchise records for most passing yards and touchdown passes.
Courtesy of Alexander Jonesi

quickly earned the respect of his veteran teammates, who voted him a team captain his first year in the league.

In discussing the leadership qualities of his close friend, Bengals star wide receiver Ja'Marr Chase, who has been a teammate of Burrow since their days together at LSU, said, "He's very different. He's very confident. He's someone you want to be around. He's growing as a person. I want to grow myself. . . . I just stay with him, ask him questions. I just lean on him like he's my older brother, basically."

Expressing his admiration for one of his fiercest rivals, Chiefs quarter-back Patrick Mahomes stated, "Not only is he a great football player; I think he's a great leader. He has that special knack where he can lead anybody."

Despite suffering a ruptured appendix just prior to the start of training camp in 2022 that required emergency surgery and hospitalization, Burrow had another great year, leading the Bengals to a record of 12–4 and their second straight division title by ranking among the league leaders with 4,475 passing yards, 35 touchdown passes, a pass-completion percentage of 68.3, and a passer rating of 100.8, while also throwing only 12 inter-ceptions and running for 257 yards and five TDs, with his fabulous perfor-mance earning him Pro Bowl honors and a fourth-place finish in the NFL MVP balloting. Burrow subsequently helped lead the Bengals to playoff victories over Baltimore (24–17) and Buffalo (27–10), before throwing one TD pass and two picks during a 23–20 loss to Kansas City in the AFC Championship Game.

The 2023 campaign began ominously for Burrow and the Bengals, with the quarterback missing the entire preseason with a strained calf muscle that ended up limiting his mobility the first few weeks of the regular season. And with Burrow at less than 100 percent, the Bengals lost three of their first four contests, before a return to full health by their signal-caller enabled them to reel off four straight victories. But after the Bengals suffered a 30–27 defeat at the hands of the Houston Texans on November 12, Burrow tore a ligament in his throwing hand during a 34–20 loss to the Baltimore Ravens four days later that forced him to undergo season-ending surgery.

Burrow, who is expected to be fully recovered by the start of the 2024 season, will enter the campaign with career totals of 14,083 passing yards, 97 touchdown passes, and 37 interceptions, a pass-completion per-centage of 68.0, and a passer rating of 98.6. He has also run for 605 yards and 10 touchdowns. With most of Burrow's career still ahead of him, he figures to earn an even more prominent place in these rankings before his time in Cincinnati comes to an end.

CAREER HIGHLIGHTS

Best Season

Burrow performed magnificently in both 2021 and 2022, posting extremely similar numbers those two years. But while Burrow failed to finish in the league's top five in either passer rating or yards per pass attempt in 2022, he ranked second among all NFL quarterbacks with a passer rating of 108.3 the previous year even though he also led the league with an average of 8.9 yards per pass attempt. More importantly, the Bengals advanced to the Super Bowl in 2021, while they came up just a bit short in the AFC Championship Game the following year. That being the case, we'll identify the 2021 campaign as Burrow's finest to this point in his career.

Memorable Moments/Greatest Performances

Burrow led the Bengals to a 33–25 victory over Jacksonville on October 4, 2020, by throwing for 300 yards and one touchdown, earning in the process his first win as an NFL quarterback.

Burrow starred in defeat on October 25, 2020, running for one score and passing for 406 yards and three touchdowns during a 37–34 loss to the Browns.

Burrow earned AFC Offensive Player of the Week honors for the first time by throwing for 348 yards and two touchdowns during a 24–21 win over Jacksonville on September 30, 2021.

Burrow led the Bengals to a lopsided 41–17 victory over the Baltimore Ravens on October 24, 2021, by throwing for 416 yards and three touchdowns, the longest of which came on an 82-yard connection with Ja'Marr Chase.

Burrow had another huge game against Baltimore on December 26, 2021, earning AFC Offensive Player of the Week honors by throwing for 525 yards and four touchdowns during a 41–21 Bengals win.

Burrow helped the Bengals overcome a 14-point, second-quarter deficit to the Chiefs on January 2, 2022, by throwing for 446 yards and four touchdowns during a 34–31 win, with three of his TD passes going to Ja'Marr Chase.

Burrow earned AFC Offensive Player of the Week honors by running for one score and completing 34 of 42 passes for 481 yards and three touchdowns during a 35–17 win over Atlanta on October 23, 2022.

Burrow earned that distinction again by passing for 286 yards and two touchdowns, while also running for 46 yards and a third score, during a 27–24 win over the Chiefs on December 4, 2022.

Burrow again gained recognition as AFC Offensive Player of the Week by completing 40 of 52 passes for 375 yards and three TDs during a 22–18 win over the Patriots on December 24, 2022.

Burrow led the Bengals to a 34–20 victory over the Arizona Cardinals on October 8, 2023, by completing 36 of his 46 pass attempts for 317 yards and three touchdowns, all of which went to Ja'Marr Chase.

Notable Achievements

- Has passed for more than 4,000 yards twice.
- Has thrown more than 30 touchdown passes twice.
- Has completed more than 70 percent of his passes once.
- Has posted touchdown-to-interception ratio of better than 2–1 four times.
- Has posted passer rating above 100.0 twice.
- Has led NFL in pass-completion percentage once.
- Has finished second in NFL in touchdown passes once, pass-completion percentage once, and passer rating once.
- Holds Bengals single-season records for most passing yards (4,611 in 2021), most touchdown passes (35 in 2022), highest pass-completion percentage (70.4 in 2021), and highest passer rating (108.3 in 2021).
- Holds Bengals career records for highest pass-completion percentage (68.0) and highest passer rating (98.6).
- Ranks among Bengals career leaders with 1,895 pass attempts (6th), 1,288 pass completions (5th), 14,083 passing yards (6th), and 97 touchdown passes (5th).
- Two-time division champion (2021 and 2022).
- 2021 AFC champion.
- Six-time AFC Offensive Player of the Week.
- 2021 NFL Comeback Player of the Year.
- Finished second in 2022 NFL Offensive Player of the Year voting.
- Finished fourth in 2022 NFL MVP voting.
- 2022 Pro Bowl selection.
- 2021 First-Team All-AFC selection.
- 2022 Second-Team All-AFC selection.

11

ISAAC CURTIS

The first in a long line of outstanding wide receivers to don a Bengals uniform, Isaac Curtis spent his entire 12-year career in Cincinnati, establishing himself as one of the game's top deep threats. A world-class sprinter who possessed so much speed and game-breaking ability that the NFL had to install new rules to prevent opposing defensive backs from manhandling him as he headed downfield, Curtis averaged more than 20 yards per reception twice, leading the league once with an average of 21.2 yards per catch. Ranking extremely high in team annals in every major pass-receiving category, Curtis led the Bengals in receptions four times and receiving yards five times, earning in the process four trips to the Pro Bowl, three All-Pro nominations, and four All-AFC selections. A major contributor to teams that won three division titles and one AFC championship, Curtis later received the additional honors of being named to the Bengals 50th Anniversary All-Time Team and gaining induction into the team's Ring of Honor.

Born in Santa Ana, California, on October 20, 1950, Isaac Fischer Curtis starred in multiple sports at Santa Ana High School, excelling as a running back in football and a sprinter and hurdler in track. With former Santa Ana head football coach Tom Baldwin later calling him "the best running back to ever play in Orange County," Curtis received a football scholarship to the University of California–Berkeley, where he continued to compete in both sports the next three years, serving as a member of the school's track team, while also excelling as a running back and kick returner on the gridiron.

Choosing to transfer to San Diego State University prior to the start of his senior year after the NCAA placed Cal-Berkeley's football team on probation for 21 rules infractions, Curtis, who posted a personal-best time of 9.3 seconds in the 100-yard dash while at Cal, passed up an opportunity to compete in the 1972 Olympics, remembering, "I was running well. I don't think there's any doubt I would have made the Olympic team. But the problem was, I was a football player first. I was not a track guy. I was transferring and moving positions. It was my senior year. If I made the Olympic team, I would have missed the first part of the football season. I couldn't afford to do that. I was a football player first. I wasn't going to go to the trials, bump somebody off the team, and then turn around and not go to the Olympics."

Isaac Curtis's exceptional running speed forced the NFL to install new rules to protect wide receivers.

Switched from running back to wide receiver by San Diego State head coach Don Coryell, Curtis transitioned seamlessly to his new post, making 44 receptions for 832 yards and seven touchdowns. Commenting on his move to wideout years later, Curtis said, "I always felt it was a natural position for me. I could always catch. I always considered myself a football player first. Some of these sprinters come into the pros, they're afraid of contact. They only know how to run straight ahead."

Although Curtis had spent just one season at wideout, the Bengals selected him in the first round of the 1973 NFL Draft, with the 15th overall pick, with Paul Brown later revealing that the receiver's quiet demeanor impressed him more than anything else, saying, "He's a very gentle person . . . no jumping up and down, spiking it, or trash talking."

Meanwhile, Bengals quarterback Ken Anderson, then just beginning his second season as the team's full-time starter at that post, recalled the first time he saw the 6'1", 192-pound Curtis, telling Bengals.com, "He had size. He had world-class speed. He was not a sprinter that played football. He was a football player that was also a sprinter. There's a big difference. . . . When you look at his rookie year and what he did, he had the same kind of impact on the NFL that Jerry Rice did."

After earning a starting job during training camp, Curtis helped lead the Bengals to their second division title by making 45 receptions and ranking among the league leaders with 843 receiving yards and nine touchdown catches, with his exceptional play earning him a trip to the Pro Bowl, Second-Team All-AFC honors, and a third-place finish in the NFL Offensive Rookie of the Year voting. However, with the Miami Dolphins defense taking full advantage of the rules in effect at the time, Curtis proved to be a non-factor in the divisional round of the playoffs. Mauled throughout the contest by Miami's defensive secondary, Curtis made just one catch for 9 yards during a 34–16 loss to the defending Super Bowl champions.

Still fuming over the mistreatment of his star wide receiver, Paul Brown insisted at the next owners' meetings that the league take steps to liberalize the passing game. Subsequently putting into effect the "Isaac Curtis Rule," the NFL made it illegal for defensive backs to touch receivers more than 5 yards from the line of scrimmage. Known to others as the "Mel Blount Rule" (in deference to the Pittsburgh cornerback who regularly manhandled every receiver he covered), the new rule stipulated, "A defender is allowed to block a receiver within five yards of the line of scrimmage. After the initial yards, any contact will be considered holding, which is a five-yard penalty and an automatic first down."

Recalling the challenges that he faced during the early stages of his career, Curtis said, "They could hit you anywhere on the field. They would run you out of bounds downfield. You'd be 15 yards downfield, and the cornerback would roll up on you. Or the corner would hold you up, and here would come an outside linebacker cutting you. I didn't complain because that's the way the game was played. I was happy when it was changed. It made the game better and opened it up, but it took a while to take hold, too."

Curtis added, "They certainly found a way to try and keep me down. I'm sure that was going to happen to a lot of players around the league as well, it wasn't just going to happen to me, but they definitely took a lot of it out on me. . . . I think that really opened up the game and has made the passing game what it is today."

Former Bengals receiver Cris Collinsworth, who spent his first four years in the league playing with Curtis, said of his one-time teammate, "He changed the game. There's no question because no one could keep up with him. They put in the five-yard bump rules, and all that crazy stuff that it all eventually became."

Although the Bengals failed to capture the division title in any of the next three seasons, Curtis earned Pro Bowl, First-Team All-AFC, and Second-Team All-Pro honors each year, totaling 115 receptions, 2,333 receiving yards, and 23 touchdowns from 1974 to 1976. Particularly outstanding in 1975, Curtis caught 44 passes, finished second in the league with 934 receiving yards, made seven touchdown catches, and led the NFL with an average of 21.2 yards per reception.

After missing half of the 1977 season due to injury, Curtis had four more extremely productive years for the Bengals, averaging 40 receptions, 640 receiving yards, and four touchdowns from 1978 to 1981. Most effective in 1978 and 1979, Curtis made a career-high 47 receptions for 737 yards and three touchdowns in the first of those campaigns, before amassing 605 receiving yards and making eight TD catches in the second.

Having lost some of his great speed by 1982, Curtis developed into more of a possession receiver, making just 23 receptions for 320 yards and one touchdown during the strike-shortened campaign, before increasing his offensive output the following season, when he caught 42 passes, amassed 571 receiving yards, and scored two TDs. Reduced to a part-time role in 1984, Curtis made only 12 receptions for 135 yards and no touchdowns, prompting him to announce his retirement at the end of the year.

In his 12 seasons with the Bengals, Curtis made 416 receptions, amassed 7,101 receiving yards, caught 53 touchdown passes, and averaged

Curtis led the NFL with an average of 21.2 yards per reception in 1975.
Courtesy of RMYAuctions.com

17.1 yards per reception. While those numbers might seem modest by today's standards, they compare quite favorably to those compiled by Hall of Fame receivers Lynn Swann and John Stallworth, particularly Swann, who caught 90 fewer passes and accumulated almost 1,600 fewer receiving yards. Yet, Curtis has never come close to gaining admittance to the Pro Football Hall of Fame, a fact that former Bengals cornerback Louis Breeden addressed when he said, "I think both Swann and Stallworth were great players, but I played against Isaac Curtis every single day, and those guys were not better football players than Isaac Curtis. Isaac Curtis had similar numbers, but they have more Super Bowls, and that's the difference."

Breeden continued, "I don't think people realized how unique he [Curtis] was. He was a world-class sprinter. A lot of guys can't make that transition from sprinting to the football field. But he did play football (in college). But not only did he play football, not only was he fast, but he had that kind of physical dexterity where he could run patterns; he could catch the football; he was athletic. He was this quiet, unassuming guy that, when he got on the football field, he was a killer."

Following his playing days, Curtis, who spent his last few offseasons working for the Cincinnati-based hotel management and development company Winegardner and Hammons, became the company's longtime director of sports marketing. Eventually retiring to his home state of California, Curtis now looks back fondly on his years in Cincinnati, saying, "I had such a great relationship with the fans, and they've always showed me their appreciation, and it made me feel so good. I was very fortunate to be in Cincinnati because there was another place I almost ended up. I'm glad that didn't happen. I'm so appreciative of being in Cincinnati."

CAREER HIGHLIGHTS

Best Season

Although Curtis made a career-high 10 touchdown receptions the previous year, he had his finest all-around season in 1975, when he gained consensus All-Pro recognition by catching 44 passes, amassing 934 receiving yards, and scoring seven TDs, with both the Newspaper Enterprise Association and *Pro Football Weekly* according him First-Team honors.

Memorable Moments/Greatest Performances

Although the Bengals lost to the Browns, 17–10, on October 7, 1973, Curtis scored the first touchdown of his career when he gathered in a 60-yard pass from Ken Anderson.

Curtis helped lead the Bengals to a 34–17 win over the Browns in the second meeting between the two teams on December 9, 1973, by making five receptions for 117 yards and three touchdowns, the longest of which covered 70 yards.

Curtis contributed to a 24–14 victory over the Baltimore Colts on November 3, 1974, by making five receptions for 166 yards and two touchdowns, which came on connections of 77 and 45 yards with Ken Anderson.

Curtis torched the Cleveland defensive secondary for six catches, 127 receiving yards, and one touchdown during a 24–17 Bengals win in the opening game of the 1975 regular season.

Curtis continued to be a thorn in the side of the Browns on October 31, 1976, making six receptions for 116 yards and one touchdown during a 21–6 Bengals win, with his TD coming on a 69-yard hookup with Ken Anderson.

Curtis helped lead the Bengals to a 31–27 win over the Houston Oilers on November 14, 1976, by making four receptions for 116 yards and one touchdown, which came on a 47-yard connection with Ken Anderson late in the fourth quarter that provided the margin of victory.

Although Curtis made just one reception during a 42–3 pasting of the Jets in the final game of the 2016 regular season, it went for a career-long 85-yard touchdown.

Curtis starred in defeat on November 4, 1979, making five receptions for 144 yards and three touchdowns during a 38–28 loss to the Colts, with the longest of his TDs covering 67 yards.

Curtis helped the Bengals gain a measure of revenge against the Colts on December 7, 1980, by making seven receptions for 176 yards and one touchdown during a 34–33 win, scoring his TD on a 67-yard connection with Ken Anderson.

Curtis had another big game on November 8, 1981, making eight receptions for 147 yards and one touchdown during a lopsided 40–17 victory over the Chargers.

Notable Achievements

- Finished second in NFL with 934 receiving yards in 1975.
- Finished second in NFL with 10 touchdown receptions in 1974.
- Averaged more than 20 yards per reception twice, leading NFL with 21.2-yard average in 1975.
- Led Bengals in receptions four times and receiving yards five times.
- Ranks among Bengals career leaders with 416 receptions (7th), 7,101 receiving yards (3rd), 7,177 yards from scrimmage (6th), 7,177 all-purpose yards (7th), 318 points (14th), 53 touchdowns (7th), and 53 touchdown receptions (4th).
- Three-time division champion (1973, 1981, and 1982).

- 1981 AFC champion.
- Finished third in 1973 NFL Offensive Rookie of the Year voting.
- Four-time Pro Bowl selection (1973, 1974, 1975, and 1976).
- Three-time Second-Team All-Pro selection (1974, 1975, and 1976).
- Three-time First-Team All-AFC selection (1974, 1975, and 1976).
- 1973 Second-Team All-AFC selection.
- Named to Bengals 50th Anniversary All-Time Team in 2017.
- Inducted into Bengals Ring of Honor in 2022.

12

COREY DILLON

One of the most controversial figures in franchise history, Corey Dillon spent seven tumultuous years in Cincinnati, during which time he became known to many as a selfish malcontent who cared little about his team or his teammates. However undeserving that reputation may have been, Dillon also established himself as one of the finest running backs in the game, gaining more than 1,000 yards on the ground six straight times, while also amassing more than 1,500 yards from scrimmage on three separate occasions. The Bengals' all-time leading rusher, Dillon also ranks extremely high in team annals in yards from scrimmage, all-purpose yards, rushing touchdowns, and total touchdowns, with his superior play earning him three Pro Bowl selections and a spot on the Bengals 50th Anniversary All-Time Team. And after leaving Cincinnati, Dillon silenced his critics by helping the Patriots win the NFL championship his first year in New England.

Born in Seattle, Washington, on October 24, 1974, Corey James Dillon grew up in a single-parent household in the city's depressed Capitol Hill district. Introduced to football by his two older brothers at the age of seven, Dillon actively participated in sports as a youth, often using the playing field to escape the harsh realities of life in the ghetto. But, with Dillon lacking a strong father figure in his life, he gradually began to experience problems with the law as a teenager, being charged with seven different offenses in juvenile court, the most serious of which came after he turned 15, when he was arrested and convicted for conspiracy to sell cocaine to an undercover cop.

Hoping to change his ways, Dillon began focusing more on further developing his athletic skills after he enrolled at Franklin High School. Starring in multiple sports, Dillon excelled as a power-hitting outfielder in baseball and a running back in football, performing so well on the gridiron as a senior that he earned First-Team All-State and All-Metro Player of the Year honors. Meanwhile, the speed and power that Dillon exhibited on the

Corey Dillon gained more yards on the ground than anyone else in franchise history.
Courtesy of RMYAuctions.com

diamond prompted the San Diego Padres to select him in the 1993 MLB Draft.

Rejecting the Padres because he believed that his future in professional sports lay in football, Dillon decided to attend college instead. But, with Dillon failing to meet the NCAA's minimum academic requirements, and his earlier run-ins with the law scaring off most of the nation's top programs, he ended up spending two years trying to improve his grades and reputation at various community colleges. Experiencing numerous setbacks along the way, Dillon quit one school and found himself being kicked out of another for skipping classes and fighting. However, after landing at Dixie College in St. George, Utah, Dillon finally demonstrated the initiative to make something of himself. And with Dillon earning Junior College Offensive Back of the Year honors from *College Sports* magazine in 1995 by rushing for 1,899 yards and 20 touchdowns, the University of Washington offered him a football scholarship.

Making the most of his opportunity in his hometown of Seattle, Dillon helped lead the Huskies to a 9–3 record in 1996 by rushing for 1,695 yards and 24 touchdowns. Subsequently choosing to forgo his senior year, Dillon declared himself eligible for the 1997 NFL Draft, where the Bengals selected him in the second round, with the 43rd overall pick.

Upon his arrival in Cincinnati, Dillon made an immediate impression on veteran Bengals quarterback Boomer Esiason, who recalled, "I saw a kid who was going to be a superstar. He had the instincts, the ability, and the raw talent to play what is physically the toughest position in football. But I also saw someone who was impatient, who wanted everything right now."

With Esiason taking Dillon under his wing, the rookie running back soon emerged as the Bengals' top offensive weapon. After spending the first half of the 1997 campaign backing up Ki-Jana Carter, Dillon supplanted the former Nittany Lion as the starter in Week 11. Despite starting just six games, Dillon ended up earning a spot on the NFL All-Rookie Team and a runner-up finish in the NFL Offensive Rookie of the Year voting by gaining 1,129 yards on the ground, amassing 1,388 yards from scrimmage, accumulating 1,574 all-purpose yards, and scoring 10 touchdowns. Dillon followed that up with five more extremely productive seasons, posting the following numbers from 1998 to 2002:

YEAR	YDS RUSHING	RECS	REC YDS	YDS FROM SCRIMMAGE	TDS
1998	1,130	28	178	1,308	5
1999	1,200	31	290	1,490	6
2000	1,435	18	158	1,593	7
2001	1,315	34	228	1,543	13
2002	1,311	43	298	1,609	7

A Pro Bowler in three of those five seasons, Dillon annually ranked among the league leaders in rushing yards, placing as high as fifth in 2000. A true workhorse, Dillon also typically placed near the top of the league rankings in rushing attempts, finishing second in the circuit with 340 carries in 2001.

A punishing runner whom opposing defenders had a difficult time bringing down one-on-one, Dillon also proved to be extremely shifty, frequently outmaneuvering would-be tacklers at the point of first contact. Blessed with good speed and excellent acceleration, Dillon also had the ability to run away from defenders once he broke into the open field, although he often preferred to use his powerful 6'1", 225-pound frame to run over people, rather than avoid them. Meanwhile, Dillon's soft hands and feel for the soft spots in the opposing defense made him an excellent safety valve for Bengals quarterbacks.

Despite his outstanding play, Dillon shared a somewhat contentious relationship with the local media, his coaches, and even some of his teammates. Upset over playing for a team that consistently finished with one of the league's worst records, Dillon often expressed his dissatisfaction to the press, once telling a Cincinnati radio station that he would rather flip burgers for a living than continue to play for a losing team. Dillon's occasional off-field transgressions provided additional fodder for the local media, which lambasted him when he had to spend a day in jail and attend an alcohol information program after pleading guilty to negligent driving and driving with a suspended license in March 1998. Some 17 months later, just weeks before the start of the 2000 NFL season, police arrested Dillon on a charge of fourth-degree assault against his wife, Desiree, whom he had married six months earlier.

Dillon's situation in Cincinnati grew increasingly worse in 2003, when, after being slowed by an injury during the early stages of the campaign, he found himself relegated to backup duty by new head coach Marvin Lewis, who replaced him in the starting backfield with Rudi Johnson. Although the Bengals finished the season with a record of 8–8 that represented their best mark since 1996, an unhappy Dillon spent most of the year campaigning to be traded, alienating in the process his teammates and coaching staff. After Dillon further angered team management the following offseason by appearing on national TV in an Oakland Raiders jersey, the Bengals granted his wish, trading him to the Patriots in April 2004 for a second-round draft pick.

Dillon, who left Cincinnati with career totals of 8,061 rushing yards, 192 receptions, 1,482 receiving yards, 9,543 yards from scrimmage, 9,724 all-purpose yards, 45 rushing touchdowns, and 50 touchdowns, ended up spending three years in New England, during which time he changed the overall perception that others held toward him by proving

Dillon rushed for more than 1,000 yards six times as a member of the Bengals.

to be an exceptional leader and an outstanding teammate. Fueled by an intense desire to win, the enigmatic running back thrived in an environment in which he found himself surrounded by like-minded people, supporting the contention he made when he said, "My thing has always been, sit down with me for an hour and base your judgments off that. That's all I ask. Don't go by what you read in the paper or hear in the streets."

Gradually earning the admiration and respect of his teammates, Dillon drew praise from Patriots linebacker Mike Vrabel, who said, "He [Dillon] brings a toughness and an attitude here. I think he's very happy to be part of our team."

Offensive lineman Matt Light noted, "The guy's a workhorse. You need people like that on your team."

Tight end Christian Fauria suggested, "Having him is just a plus, because he plays with so much heart and effort, and it's just contagious."

Addressing the somewhat questionable reputation that Dillon brought with him to the team, Tom Brady commented, "He's really been a great leader. I don't care what someone's reputation is. Corey had a great attitude coming in, and it's only gotten better."

Meanwhile, in discussing Dillon's running style, Patriots head coach Bill Belichick noted, "He's a powerful guy who can break tackles. And, when he gets in the open field, you don't see him get run down a lot."

Excelling in his first year in New England, Dillon helped lead the Patriots to the NFL championship by rushing for 1,635 yards, amassing 1,738 yards from scrimmage, and scoring 13 touchdowns, earning in the process the last of his four Pro Bowl nominations. Although Dillon proved to be somewhat less productive the next two seasons, he led the Patriots in rushing both years, gaining a total of 1,545 yards on the ground, while also scoring 26 touchdowns.

With Dillon approaching his 33rd birthday, the Patriots released him prior to the start of the 2007 campaign. After briefly considering playing for another team, Dillon elected to announce his retirement, ending his career with 11,241 rushing yards, 244 pass receptions, 1,913 receiving yards, 13,154 yards from scrimmage, 13,335 all-purpose yards, 89 touchdowns, and a rushing average of 4.3 yards per carry.

Although Dillon has led a mostly quiet, anonymous life since retiring from the NFL, his name appeared in the tabloids in early May 2010, less than one month after his wife filed for divorce, when police arrested him on suspicion of assaulting her at their home in Calabasas, California.

Meanwhile, Dillon continued to distance himself from the Bengals until the summer of 2017, when he reached out to them for the first time in well over a decade by saying that he had no ill will toward the organization and admitted that he made some mistakes during his time in Cincinnati, stating, "I am a grown man. I can admit when I'm wrong. I did some stuff that was not cool, okay? Not cool at all. . . . But hey, at the end of the day, I got the end result that I wanted. That was to play on a stage and actually win a Super Bowl. Do I wish it would have been with them? Absolutely. It didn't work out that way. I don't have no ill will toward nobody there."

Dillon added, "People want to say I was the bad guy in that situation? No, that's not the case. It comes down to we play this football game to win football games. That's what you play for. I don't know what was on everybody else's agenda."

BENGALS CAREER HIGHLIGHTS

Best Season

Although Dillon rushed for more yards (1,435) in 2000 and amassed more yards from scrimmage (1,609) in 2002, he had his finest all-around season for the Bengals in 2001, when, in addition to gaining 1,315 yards on the ground and accumulating 1,543 yards from scrimmage, he scored 13 touchdowns.

Memorable Moments/Greatest Performances

Dillon went over 100 yards rushing for the first time in his career when he carried the ball 19 times for 123 yards and one touchdown during a 38–31 win over the Chargers on November 2, 1997, scoring his TD on a 71-yard run.

Dillon earned AFC and NFL Offensive Player of the Week honors by rushing for 246 yards and four touchdowns during a 41–14 victory over the Tennessee Oilers on December 4, 1997, with his 246 yards rushing establishing a new single-game league record for rookies.

Dillon helped lead the Bengals to an 18–17 win over the Browns on October 10, 1999, by carrying the ball 28 times for 168 yards.

Dillon again proved to be too much for the Cleveland defense to handle in the second meeting between the two teams on December 12, 1999, rushing for 192 yards and three touchdowns during a 44–28 Bengals win.

Dillon earned AFC and NFL Offensive Player of the Week honors for the second time by carrying the ball 22 times for a then-NFL record 278 yards and two touchdowns during a 31–21 win over the Denver Broncos on October 22, 2000, scoring his TDs on runs of 65 and 41 yards.

Dillon led the Bengals to a 24–13 victory over the Arizona Cardinals on December 3, 2000, by rushing for 216 yards and one touchdown.

Dillon earned AFC Offensive Player of the Week honors for the third and final time as a member of the Bengals by rushing for 184 yards, amassing 202 yards from scrimmage, and scoring three touchdowns during a 31–27 win over the Lions on October 28, 2001, with one of his TDs coming on a 96-yard run that represents the longest run from scrimmage in franchise history.

NOTABLE ACHIEVEMENTS

- Rushed for more than 1,000 yards six times.
- Amassed more than 1,500 yards from scrimmage three times.
- Amassed more than 1,500 all-purpose yards four times.
- Scored at least 10 touchdowns twice.
- Led Bengals in rushing six times.
- Holds Bengals record for longest rushing touchdown in franchise history (96 yards).
- Holds Bengals single-game records for most rushing yards (278) and rushing touchdowns (4).
- Holds Bengals career records for most rushing attempts (1,865) and rushing yards (8,061).
- Ranks among Bengals career leaders with 9,543 yards from scrimmage (2nd), 9,724 all-purpose yards (3rd), 45 rushing touchdowns (4th), and 50 touchdowns (8th).
- Member of 1997 NFL All-Rookie Team.
- Finished second in 1997 NFL Offensive Rookie of the Year voting.
- Three-time AFC Offensive Player of the Week.
- Two-time NFL Offensive Player of the Week.
- Three-time Pro Bowl selection (1999, 2000, and 2001).
- Named to Bengals 50th Anniversary All-Time Team in 2017.

13

BOB JOHNSON

Often referred to as "the Original Bengal," Bob Johnson holds the distinction of being the first player ever drafted by the organization. The Bengals' starting center in each of their first 10 seasons, Johnson spent his entire 12-year professional career in Cincinnati, establishing himself as one of the game's finest players at his position. A team captain for 11 years, Johnson contributed significantly to squads that made three playoff appearances and won two division titles, with his consistently excellent play earning him one All-AFL nomination and four All-AFC selections. And following the conclusion of his playing career, Johnson received the additional honors of being named to the Bengals 50th Anniversary All-Time Team and having his jersey number retired by the organization, making him the only player to be so honored.

Born in Gary, Indiana, on August 19, 1946, Robert Douglas Johnson grew up in Cleveland, Tennessee, where he excelled both on the football field and in the classroom at Bradley High School. An honor student, Johnson also performed so well on the gridiron that the University of Tennessee offered him an athletic scholarship.

Continuing his exceptional play at Tennessee, Johnson started at center for three years, leading the Vols to an overall record of 25-6-2 and the SEC title in 1967, when he earned his second consecutive All-America nomination and a sixth-place finish in the Heisman Trophy balloting. Also named the SEC's Most Outstanding Lineman by the Birmingham Touchdown Club and the winner of the Jacobs Trophy, presented annually to the conference's best blocker, Johnson received high praise from Vols head coach Doug Dickey, who said, "It's impossible for a boy to contribute more to a team than Johnson does. As captain, he provides leadership, both on and off the field."

A National Football Foundation Scholar Athlete, Johnson, who earned his degree in industrial engineering, received an offer to attend the Harvard Business School. However, he chose to pursue a career in professional

Bob Johnson started for the Bengals at center in each of their first 10 seasons.

football instead after the expansion Bengals selected him with the second overall pick of the 1968 NFL/AFL Common Draft.

Pleased with his selection of Johnson, Bengals general manager and head coach Paul Brown told the press, "This is the fellow we planned to take all the way. Johnson seals up our snap problem. To me, a center is like a catcher in baseball. It's the heart of your ball club. Pitching and catching. We now have both."

Brown then added, "Johnson has tremendous speed and quickness. He's a class person. The kind you build with."

Revealing that he knew very little about the Bengals prior to the draft, Johnson recalled, "I knew it was an expansion team. I knew it was in Cincinnati. I knew Coach Brown was head of it. That's about all I knew. . . . I grew up in Cleveland, Tennessee, and the closest teams were Washington and Cleveland, so the Browns were on TV quite a bit, and I knew who Coach Brown was. So did the people in Cincinnati. You walked in with a built-in respect, and the fans had it. We had a terrific original fan base."

Johnson continued, "I never dreamed I'd be the second pick in the draft. The only team that contacted me before the draft was Chicago, and they were picking 16, and they were going to switch me to defense. I wasn't going to talk them out of taking me in the first round, but I hardly ever played defense at Tennessee."

Immediately establishing himself as one of the team's foremost members upon his arrival in Cincinnati, Johnson laid claim to the starting center job, after which he went on to start every game the Bengals played for the first of six straight seasons, earning in the process AFL All-Star (Pro Bowl) and Second-Team All-AFL (All-Pro) honors. After performing well once again in 1969, Johnson continued to excel following the NFL/AFL merger one year later, gaining All-AFC recognition four times between 1970 and 1976, a period during which the Bengals made three playoff appearances and won two division titles.

The unquestioned leader of the Bengals during their formative years, Johnson became the player everyone else turned to for advice and guidance, with current team owner and president Mike Brown (then the team's assistant GM) telling Bengals.com during a 2016 interview, "Bob was a very solid player. During his time here, he was always one of the leaders of the team. The other players listened to him because they respected his intelligence, the way he lived his life, the way he practiced and comported himself around the team."

In expressing his admiration for his former line-mate, Dave Lapham said, "His intangibles are as high as anybody I've ever been around. Supremely intelligent. Leadership skills off the charts. I tried to get under his wing. I respected Bob's football acumen and IQ. I liked to hang with him. Smart guy."

An outstanding player as well, the 6'5", 262-pound Johnson proved to be equally effective in pass protection and run-blocking. Big and strong, Johnson did an excellent job of protecting his quarterback from interior pass-rushers and creating holes for Bengals runners. Meanwhile, he used his speed, quickness, and superior technique to outmaneuver his man at the line of scrimmage and provide blocks downfield.

Johnson holds the distinction of being the only Bengals player to have his number officially retired by the team.

After sitting out four contests in 1974 due to injury, Johnson began a new string of consecutive starts the following year, manning his familiar position of center in all 14 games the Bengals played in each of the next three seasons. Seeming somewhat surprised at how fast the time had passed, Johnson stated at one point during the 1976 campaign, "You know, it doesn't seem like nine years since I joined the Bengals, but, if you go back year-by-year, we have played so many games that it seems like more than nine years."

Johnson added, "Personally, I am glad to be here. People kid me about being the original Bengal, but I've seen everything that's ever happened to this franchise. It gets exciting sometimes to think back to the first training camp we ever had and see the type of team we have now."

Johnson continued to anchor the Bengals offensive line from his center position until 1978, when he lost his starting job to Blair Bush. With Johnson making it known that he intended to retire at the end of the year, the Bengals honored him during a special ceremony held on the final day of the regular season by retiring his #54. However, after Bush suffered a knee injury the following year, the Bengals convinced Johnson to temporarily come out of retirement and serve as a long snapper on punts, field goals, and extra points. Hanging up his cleats for good after appearing in five games in 1979, Johnson retired as the last original member of the Bengals.

Following his playing days, Johnson settled with his family in the Cincinnati suburb of Glendale, Ohio, where, after spending five years working as a color analyst on Bengals radio, he became president of Imperial Adhesives Corporation. Selling the company after overseeing its operations for several years, Johnson became director of the industrial adhesives group for Henkel Technologies, a Germany-based corporation, where he remained for more than a decade before retiring to private life.

CAREER HIGHLIGHTS

Best Season

Although Johnson gained AFL All-Star and Second-Team All-AFL recognition as a rookie in 1968, he perhaps played his best ball for the Bengals in 1973, when he helped lead them to a regular-season record of 10–4 and their second division title, prompting the Newspaper Enterprise Association (NEA) to accord him unofficial First-Team All-Pro honors.

Memorable Moments/Greatest Performances

Johnson helped the Bengals gain 180 yards on the ground and amass 472 yards of total offense during a 34–20 win over the San Diego Chargers on September 21, 1969.

Johnson's superior blocking up front helped the Bengals rush for 236 yards and amass 532 yards of total offense during a 37–14 victory over the Philadelphia Eagles in the 1971 regular-season opener.

Johnson again did yeoman's work during a 30–7 win over the Houston Oilers on October 29, 1972, with the Bengals gaining 244 yards on the ground and another 252 yards through the air.

Notable Achievements

- Started 84 consecutive games from 1968 to 1973.
- Two-time division champion (1970 and 1973).
- 1968 AFL All-Star selection.
- 1968 Second-Team All-AFL selection.
- 1972 First-Team All-AFC selection.
- Three-time Second-Team All-AFC selection (1970, 1974, and 1976).
- Named to Bengals 50th Anniversary All-Time Team in 2017.
- #54 retired by Bengals.

14

REGGIE WILLIAMS

One of the most beloved players in franchise history, Reggie Williams spent his entire 14-year NFL career in Cincinnati, serving as a key member of teams that won three division titles and two AFC championships. An outstanding all-around defender, Williams excelled in every aspect of linebacker play, recovering more fumbles than anyone else in team annals, while also ranking among the franchise's all-time leaders in tackles, sacks, interceptions, and forced fumbles. Extremely durable, Williams missed just six games his entire career, at one point starting 136 consecutive contests from his post at right-outside linebacker, with his many contributions to the organization landing him a spot on the Bengals 50th Anniversary All-Time Team.

Born in Flint, Michigan, on September 19, 1954, Reginald Williams moved with his family at a young age from a low-income section of the city to a more affluent, fully integrated area, where he struggled in school. Although intelligent and well-read, Williams, who lisped badly, found it difficult to communicate with others and had a hard time coming up with the correct answers in class, causing him to become painfully shy. Discovered to have a 40 percent hearing loss in both ears after undergoing a battery of tests, Williams recalled how his impediment affected him, saying, "Unless you've been there yourself, you can't begin to imagine how even a small handicap can make such a tremendous difference. It's like walking in quicksand."

Subsequently enrolled in the Michigan School for the Deaf and Dumb, Williams felt lost, refusing to speak to anyone at first, until an innocuous cookies-and-milk session finally helped him come out of his shell, with Williams later saying, "I've always been a cookie monster."

Gradually improving his communication skills and ability to interact with others, Williams eventually returned to the public school system, developing into an exceptional student and athlete at Flint Southwestern High School, where he wrestled and played football. Performing so well

Reggie Williams ranks among the franchise's career leaders in most defensive categories.

on the gridiron at linebacker and fullback that the University of Michigan offered him a full scholarship, Williams, who grew up dreaming of one day playing linebacker for the Wolverines, remembered, "I was offered a full scholarship at Michigan, a full ride, even though (head coach) Bo

Schembechler didn't seem much interested in me. Then I visited Hanover through the Sponsorship Program and went to the banquet celebrating Dartmouth's third straight Ivy championship. That did it. If Dartmouth was going to let me in, I was going to come."

Able to attend Dartmouth with the help of his father, who took a second job driving a cab and a third job selling real estate to finance his education, Williams ended up excelling in both the classroom and on the football field, graduating in less than four years, while also earning All–Ivy League honors three times at linebacker. An outstanding wrestler as well, Williams won the Ivy League heavyweight wrestling championship as a senior in 1975, once pinning an opponent in just 16 seconds.

Making an extremely favorable impression on other Ivy League coaches with his exceptional play on the gridiron, Williams drew praise from Harvard head coach, Joe Restic, who proclaimed, "Reggie Williams is the best linebacker I've seen this year—live or on film."

Yale head coach Carmen Cozza, who had been at the school since 1963, took it one step further, saying of Williams, "He's by far the best linebacker we've ever faced since I've been at Yale."

Selected by the Bengals in the third round of the 1976 NFL Draft, with the 82nd overall pick, Williams laid claim to the starting right-outside linebacker job during the early stages of his first NFL season, earning a spot on the NFL All-Rookie Team by recording 109 tackles (83 solo), two sacks, and one interception. Continuing to perform well the next four seasons, Williams picked off eight passes, registered 9 1/2 sacks, and averaged 94 tackles from 1977 to 1980, with his team-leading 120 stops (104 solo) in the first of those campaigns representing the highest single-season mark of his career.

Employed more as a pass-rusher in the team's new 3–4 defensive scheme in 1981, Williams helped lead the Bengals to the division title and AFC championship by recording a career-high 11 sacks, while also making 109 tackles, intercepting four passes, forcing three fumbles, and recovering three others.

A complete linebacker who performed equally well in a 4–3 or 3–4 defense, the 6'1", 228-pound Williams possessed the speed and quickness to cover running backs and tight ends downfield, the moves and agility to apply pressure to opposing quarterbacks off the edge, and the strength and tackling ability to bring down runners at or beyond the line of scrimmage. An effective blitzer, Williams recorded at least seven sacks in a season on three separate occasions. An extremely instinctual player who displayed a nose for the football throughout his career, Williams led the NFL in fumble recoveries once and registered a total of 16 interceptions, which places him first all-time among Bengals linebackers.

Perhaps Williams's greatest strengths, though, lay in his superior leadership ability and tremendous determination, which allowed him to appear in all but six games from 1976 to 1989, even though he spent most of that time playing on an injured knee that eventually required more than two dozen surgeries. A pillar within the community as well, Williams won the NFL Alan Page Community Award in 1984 and the NFL Man of the Year award two years later for his work off the playing field.

Following his outstanding 1981 season, Williams remained a fixture at right-outside linebacker for eight more years, starting every game the Bengals played from 1982 to 1989, with his consistently excellent play helping them win another two division titles and their second AFC championship. Performing especially well in 1983 and 1984, Williams recorded 90 tackles, registered 7 1/2 sacks, forced three fumbles, recovered four others, and scored a touchdown in the first of those campaigns, before making 92 tackles, recording nine sacks, and intercepting two passes in the second. But, after registering 3 1/2 sacks and just 48 tackles in 1989, Williams chose to announce his retirement, ending his career with 1,161 tackles (865 solo), 63 1/2 sacks, 16 interceptions, 194 interception-return yards, 16 forced fumbles, 23 fumble recoveries, three touchdowns, and two safeties.

Following his playing days, Williams, who, during his last two seasons with the Bengals, served as a member of the Cincinnati City Council, moved to Florida, where he became Walt Disney World's first Black vice president and helped create the ESPN Wide World of Sports Complex. Williams also later served as vice president and general manager of the New Jersey Knights of the World League of American Football, before returning to the NFL in a front office capacity.

Plagued by health problems in retirement, Williams, who went under the knife for the first time in 1979, has had a total of 25 knee operations, including four right knee replacements and one left knee replacement. Diagnosed with the bone infection osteomyelitis in 2008, Williams underwent surgery eight times in that year alone. His right leg now 2 5/8 inches shorter than his left leg, Williams has struggled to avoid having it amputated. Williams uses cannabis to treat the pain and inflammation in his knee, claiming that doing so has allowed him to walk without crutches again.

Williams, who is 69 years old as of this writing, has also suffered a stroke, broken his hip, and experienced symptoms of chronic traumatic encephalopathy (CTE). Known to have suffered at least four concussions during his playing career, Williams has pledged to donate his brain to the Concussion Legacy Foundation to advance research on CTE, saying in 2020, "I'm now at a point where I'll break into tears because of the slightest trigger, and I often get hot flashes of anger; it's a constant struggle to control my mood and emotions. I have a very strong feeling that I have CTE, so it was a simple decision for me to pledge to donate my brain. I want to do anything I can to make football safer and help the next generation of athletes."

CAREER HIGHLIGHTS

Best Season

Williams performed exceptionally well in 1977, registering a career-high 120 tackles, recovering two fumbles, and recording three interceptions, one of which he returned for a touchdown. However, Williams made his greatest overall impact during the AFC championship campaign of 1981, when, in addition to making 109 tackles, he collected a career-high 11 sacks, picked off four passes, forced three fumbles, and recovered three others.

Memorable Moments/Greatest Performances

Williams recorded the first interception of his career during a 31–27 win over the Houston Oilers on November 14, 1976, subsequently returning the ball 17 yards.

Williams scored his first career touchdown when he ran 54 yards to pay dirt after intercepting a Jim Zorn pass during a 42–20 win over the Seattle Seahawks on September 25, 1977.

Williams lit the scoreboard again when he recovered a fumble in the end zone on special teams during a 20–14 loss to the Steelers on October 17, 1977.

Williams contributed to a 34–10 win over the Steelers on October 14, 1979, by intercepting Terry Bradshaw twice.

Williams registered two sacks during a 27–6 win over Houston in the 1982 regular-season opener.

Williams recorded a safety when he sacked Ron Jaworski in the end zone during an 18–14 win over the Eagles on November 21, 1982.

Williams helped lead the Bengals to a 55–14 rout of the Oilers on November 6, 1983, by recording two sacks and recovering a fumble, which he returned 59 yards for a touchdown.

Williams continued to torment Houston on October 28, 1984, registering a sack and an interception during a 31–13 Bengals win.

Although the Bengals suffered a 20–16 defeat at the hands of the San Francisco 49ers in Super Bowl XXIII, Williams performed extremely well, recording a sack and leading both teams with 10 tackles, including seven of the solo variety.

Notable Achievements

- Started 136 consecutive games from 1981 to 1989.
- Scored three touchdowns.
- Recorded more than 100 tackles three times.
- Recorded 11 sacks in 1981.
- Led NFL with four fumble recoveries in 1982.
- Led Bengals in tackles and sacks three times each.
- Holds Bengals career record for most fumble recoveries (23).
- Ranks among Bengals career leaders with 1,161 tackles (2nd), 63 1/2 sacks (4th), 16 forced fumbles (2nd), 16 interceptions (tied for 9th), 14 seasons played (tied for 3rd), and 206 games played (3rd).
- Three-time division champion (1981, 1982, and 1988).
- Two-time AFC champion (1981 and 1988).
- Member of 1976 NFL All-Rookie Team.
- 1984 NFL Alan Page Community Award winner.
- 1986 NFL Walter Payton Man of the Year.
- Named to Bengals 40th Anniversary All-Time Team in 2007.
- Named to Bengals 50th Anniversary All-Time Team in 2017.

15

TIM KRUMRIE

The heart and soul of the Bengals defense for more than a decade, Tim Krumrie spent his entire 12-year NFL career in Cincinnati, inspiring his teammates with his tremendous determination and relentless style of play. An extremely aggressive and hard-nosed player who tried to instill in others the same intensity he brought with him to the playing field, Krumrie served as the Bengals' starting nose tackle from 1984 to 1993, a period during which he started every non-strike game. An exceptional run-stuffer and solid interior pass-rusher, Krumrie ranks among the franchise's all-time leaders in both tackles and sacks, with his 1,017 career stops representing the third-highest total in team annals. One of the central figures on teams that won two division titles and one AFC championship, Krumrie earned two Pro Bowl selections and two All-Pro nominations, before being further honored in retirement by being named to the Bengals 50th Anniversary All-Time Team.

Born in Eau Claire, Wisconsin, on May 20, 1960, Timothy Alan Krumrie grew up on a dairy farm located some 20 miles south, just outside the town of Mondovi. A star athlete at Mondovi High School, Krumrie excelled for the Buffaloes in football and wrestling, winning the heavyweight state championship as a senior in 1979.

Choosing to remain close to home, Krumrie accepted an athletic scholarship to the University of Wisconsin–Madison, where he continued to compete in both sports. Although originally recruited as an inside linebacker, Krumrie spent his entire college career starting at nose tackle, leading the Badgers in tackles four straight times, en route to establishing a school record that still stands for most solo tackles in a career (276). A three-time All–Big Ten selection and a consensus All-American in 1981, Krumrie assumed the role of team captain as a senior in 1982, after spending his first two seasons at Wisconsin also serving as a member of the school's wrestling team.

Tim Krumrie started at nose tackle for the Bengals from 1984 to 1993.

Despite his accomplishments at the collegiate level, Krumrie had to wait until the 10th round of the 1983 NFL Draft to hear his name called, with the Bengals finally selecting him with the 276th overall pick. Seeking to prove himself worthy of a much higher selection at his first pro training camp, the 6'2", 270-pound Krumrie did so at the expense of rookie Dave Rimington, a 315-pound All-America center whom the Bengals had claimed in the first round of that year's draft. Making a statement during the team's daily one-on-one "nutcracker" drill, Krumrie totally dominated Rimington, with former Bengals offensive line coach Jim McNally remembering, "You wouldn't believe what Krumrie did to Rimington that first week. They went at it 10 times, and Tim buried him into the ground all 10 times. Even after he had Rimington down, Tim kept at him like he wanted to push him under the dirt. Tim didn't know when to quit. The coaches had to pull him off Rimington 10 times. . . . Every now and then, the coaches pull that film out and play it back. It's an awesome display of blood and guts."

Recalling his motivation at the time, Krumrie said, "Tenth-round draft choices aren't supposed to make the team, but the No. 1 is a shoo-in. If I beat the No. 1 guy, I figured they had to look at me."

Meanwhile, Anthony Muñoz stated, "I remember saying, 'Thank God he's a nose tackle and not a defensive end.' From that day on, he had everybody's respect."

After earning a spot on the Bengals roster, Krumrie spent most of the 1983 campaign assuming a part-time role in the team's 3–4 defense, recording 53 tackles and 1 1/2 sacks, before registering 84 tackles and five sacks the following year after displacing Jerry Boyarsky as the full-time starter at nose tackle. Continuing to improve upon his performance in each of the next two seasons, Krumrie recorded 96 tackles and 3 1/2 sacks in 1985, before making 113 stops, registering one sack, and recovering two fumbles the following year.

After starting 48 consecutive games over the course of the previous three seasons, Krumrie missed three contests in 1987 due to the players' strike. Nevertheless, he earned Pro Bowl, All-Pro, and All-AFC honors for the first of two straight times by recording 88 tackles and 3 1/2 sacks in only 12 games. Krumrie subsequently helped lead the Bengals to the division title and AFC championship in 1988 by registering three sacks, recovering three fumbles, and making a career-high 152 tackles, prompting three writers to place his name on their ballots in the voting for NFL Defensive Player of the Year.

Still fueled by his unexpectedly late selection in the 1983 NFL Draft, Krumrie became almost fanatical in his desire to prove his doubters wrong, saying after his sixth year in the league, "That's what drives me, going so low in the draft. A lot of guys work hard, make All-Pro, and then they let up a little because they have reached the top. I'll never let up. I've made All-Pro the last two years but being picked in the 10th round will always be with me and motivate me."

Krumrie added, "What the computers failed to measure was the size of my heart. I'm a little bit short, but I play tall. I'm not that fast, but I can get to the runner and make tackles. I'm not an athlete, but I can play a hell of a game of football."

A raving lunatic on game day, Krumrie frightened even his own teammates, with Bengals cornerback Eric Thomas saying, "I try to stay as far away from him as I can before a game. Whenever I see him in the dressing room, I head the other way. . . . Before one game, he grabbed me by the shoulder pads, shook me around, started screaming in my ear, and then shoved me to the floor. His nose was already bleeding from slapping himself on the helmet so many times. During the National Anthem, he just stood there trembling. . . . He was ready to play, and he was trying to get me ready. He almost killed me."

Bengals head coach Sam Wyche added, "The only danger with Tim Krumrie is you've got to stay a little away from him before game time, or he'll beat the crap out of you trying to get you up."

One of the NFL's best interior defensive linemen, Krumrie proved to be extremely difficult to block despite his relatively short stature and somewhat limited athletic ability. Particularly effective against the run, Krumrie did an outstanding job of clogging up the middle by imposing his will against opposing centers and guards. Always in excellent condition, Krumrie, who spent his offseasons running, lifting weights, riding mountain bikes, and skiing cross country, pursued ball-carriers from sideline to sideline, enabling him to lead the Bengals in tackles on five separate occasions.

In discussing Krumrie, former Buffalo Bills center Ken Hull stated, "He makes tackles all over the place. There's a lot of people who move well inside, but they don't make tackles from sideline to sideline like he does. He's almost like a linebacker in a three- or four-point stance. That's how mobile he is. He's the type of person that if you ever get him on the ground, you better hold him down. Because if he gets up, he's going to make the tackle."

Blessed with superior instincts, Krumrie said, "Most of the time, I can tell you where my opponent is going before he goes there. You have to have a sense of pressure, of how the guy is leanin' on you, of how to find the ball. There's a whole system. I used to be a two-man reader. Now, I read the whole line. Now, I'm thinkin,' 'What's this guy doin'? Is that guy's stance funny? Is he set? Does he have his foot back?'"

Identified by Bengals linebacker Kevin Walker as "one of the most ferocious, intense guys I've ever had the opportunity to play with," Krumrie exhibited his intensity in Super Bowl XXIII, when, after suffering a broken tibia and fibula during the contest, he remained on the sideline with an inflatable splint stabilizing his leg, refusing to go to the hospital until paramedics told him he might go into shock.

Ready to return to action by the start of the 1989 regular season after having a 15-inch steel rod surgically implanted in his leg, Krumrie continued to start for the Bengals at nose tackle for five more years, recording a team-high 97 tackles in 1992, before assuming a part-time role when

Krumrie's 1,017 career tackles rank as the third-highest total in team annals.

the team switched to a 4–3 defense in 1994. Choosing to announce his retirement at the end of the year, Krumrie ended his playing career with 1,017 tackles (700 solo), 34 1/2 sacks, 13 fumble recoveries, and 11 forced fumbles. In addition to ranking among the franchise's all-time leaders in each of those categories, Krumrie appeared in the sixth-most games (188) of any player in team annals.

Paying homage to Krumrie during the latter stages of his career, long-time Bengals strength and conditioning coach Kim Wood stated, "I look at Tim as a success story, a person who's gotten everything through hard work. He's the same guy he was when he showed up here eleven years ago. He made the team because he worked hard. He's just that way. As a football player, he's everything you want. He plays hurt. He breaks his leg in the Super Bowl, it's dangling there, and he tries to get up. What I'm saying is, he's just an impressive man, a man's man. The Reggie Williamses and Anthony Muñozes, and James Brookses, guys who were leaders of men and leaders by example, all seem to be gone. Timmy is the last one."

After retiring as an active player, Krumrie spent 15 seasons serving as defensive line coach for three different teams, fulfilling that role for the Bengals from 1995 to 2002, before moving on to Buffalo (2003–2005) and Kansas City (2006–2009). Although Krumrie discovered in 2010 that he had symptoms of brain trauma, he has since received treatment that he says has improved his health.

Now living in Cincinnati, the 64-year-old Krumrie proudly accepts the costs of his life's work. Asked if he would pursue the same career path if he had a chance to do it again, Krumrie says, "In a second. In a second. You put me in the Super Bowl, you can break my leg—two of 'em! It's that important."

CAREER HIGHLIGHTS

Best Season

Krumrie had the finest season of his career in 1988, when he earned his lone First-Team All-Pro nomination by finishing fourth in the NFL with 152 combined tackles—an extraordinary number for an interior defensive lineman.

Memorable Moments/Greatest Performances

Krumrie recorded his first sack as a pro when he brought down Cliff Stoudt behind the line of scrimmage during a 23–10 win over the Steelers on December 4, 1983.

Krumrie earned AFC Defensive Player of the Week honors by registering two sacks during a 45–27 victory over the Houston Oilers on December 1, 1985.

Krumrie gained recognition from the Pro Football Writers as NFL Defensive Player of the Week by helping to limit the Steelers to 198 yards of total offense during a 42–7 Bengals win on November 6, 1988.

Krumrie starred in defeat the following week, recording an unofficial total of 21 tackles during a 31–28 loss to the Kansas City Chiefs on November 13, 1988.

Krumrie's superb play at the point of attack helped limit the Seahawks to just 18 yards rushing during a 21–13 Bengals win in the divisional round of the 1988 playoffs.

Krumrie contributed to a 24–21 overtime victory over the Los Angeles Raiders on September 13, 1992, by sacking Jay Schroeder twice.

Notable Achievements

- Never missed a game entire career, appearing in 188 consecutive non-strike contests.
- Recorded more than 100 tackles twice.
- Finished fourth in NFL with 152 combined tackles in 1988.
- Led Bengals in tackles five times.
- Ranks among Bengals career leaders with 1,017 tackles (3rd), 11 forced fumbles (tied for 4th), 13 fumble recoveries (4th), 34 1/2 sacks (12th), and 188 games played (6th).
- Two-time division champion (1988 and 1990).
- 1988 AFC champion.
- 1985 Week 14 AFC Defensive Player of the Week.
- 1988 Week 11 NFL Defensive Player of the Week.
- November 1988 AFC Defensive Player of the Month.
- Two-time Pro Bowl selection (1987 and 1988).
- 1988 First-Team All-Pro selection.
- 1987 Second-Team All-Pro selection.
- 1988 First-Team All-AFC selection.
- 1987 Second-Team All-AFC selection.
- Named to Bengals 40th Anniversary All-Time Team in 2007.
- Named to Bengals 50th Anniversary All-Time Team in 2017.

16

BOOMER ESIASON

The man who succeeded Ken Anderson as the starter at quarterback in Cincinnati, Boomer Esiason performed nearly as well as his predecessor from 1984 to 1992, throwing for more than 3,500 yards and 25 touchdowns three times each, in leading the Bengals to two division titles and one AFC championship. A master at reading defenses and employing the play-action pass, Esiason did an excellent job of running the no huddle offense devised by head coach Sam Wyche, with his strong play earning him three Pro Bowl selections, one All-Pro nomination, one NFL MVP trophy, and a place on the Bengals 50th Anniversary All-Time Team. Returning to the Bengals for a second tour of duty with the club in 1997, Esiason spent one final season in the city where his career began, before retiring as one of the franchise's all-time leaders in virtually every major passing category.

Born in East Islip, New York, on April 17, 1961, Norman Julius Esiason grew up on the South Shore of Long Island, where his father raised him and his two sisters by himself after his wife died of ovarian cancer seven years after giving birth to her only son. Nicknamed "Boomer" by his mother for his constant kicking prior to his birth, Esiason went on to star in multiple sports at East Islip High School, excelling in football, baseball, and basketball.

Offered an athletic scholarship to the University of Maryland, Esiason spent his college career playing for head coaches Jerry Claiborne and Bobby Ross, throwing for 6,169 yards and 42 touchdowns, en route to setting 17 school records. After gaining honorable mention All-America recognition for the second straight time as a senior in 1983, Esiason entered the 1984 NFL Draft, where the Bengals selected him in the second round, with the 38th overall pick, making him the first quarterback to come off the board in a lean year for signal-callers.

Esiason subsequently spent most of his first year in Cincinnati serving as a backup to Ken Anderson, before replacing him behind center during the latter stages of the campaign. After leading the Bengals to victories in

Boomer Esiason earned NFL MVP honors in 1988, when he led the Bengals to their second Super Bowl appearance.
Courtesy of RMYAuctions.com

three of his four starts, Esiason became the full-time starter in 1985, when he established himself as one of the NFL's better quarterbacks by throwing for 3,443 yards, completing 58.2 percent of his passes, and finishing second in the league with 27 touchdown passes and a QBR of 93.2, while tossing only 12 interceptions. Esiason followed that up with another outstanding season, earning Pro Bowl honors in 1986 by again completing 58.2 percent of his passes and ranking among the league leaders with 3,959 passing yards, 24 TD passes, and a QBR of 87.7 for a Bengals team that compiled a record of 10–6 that nearly earned them a spot in the playoffs.

But with the well-paid Esiason joining his teammates in a month-long players' strike in 1987 and struggling upon his return to action, he incurred the wrath of the hometown fans, who booed him constantly, causing him to express an interest in perhaps going elsewhere. However, the boos turned to cheers the following year, when Esiason led the Bengals to the AFC championship by passing for 3,572 yards, throwing 28 touchdown passes and only 14 interceptions, and leading the league with a QBR of 97.4, earning in the process Pro Bowl, First-Team All-Pro, and NFL MVP honors. Performing extremely well again in 1989, Esiason gained Pro Bowl recognition for the second straight time by ranking among the league leaders with 3,525 passing yards, 28 TD passes, and a QBR of 92.1.

Big and strong at 6'5" and 225 pounds, the left-handed-throwing Esiason saw the field well, moved well in the pocket, and possessed a powerful throwing arm that enabled him to deliver the ball deep downfield to his receivers. A deft handler of the football, Esiason excelled at deceiving the opposition with fake handoffs, making the play-action pass a staple of the Bengals offense. Meanwhile, Esiason's ability to read opposing defenses and make quick decisions made him the perfect quarterback to run head coach Sam Wyche's high tempo no-huddle offense that served as a precursor to the one the Buffalo Bills employed during their Super Bowl run a few years later. A tremendous leader of men as well, Esiason is regarded as the greatest locker-room leader the Bengals have ever had.

Although Esiason never again reached such heights during his three remaining years in Cincinnati, he managed to lead the Bengals to a 9–7 record and the division title in 1990 by throwing for 3,031 yards and 24 touchdowns, despite leading the league with 22 interceptions. But after posting an overall record of just 8–24 over the course of the next two seasons, the Bengals decided to clean house, parting ways with several veterans, including Anthony Muñoz, wide receiver Tim McGee, tight end Rodney Holman, and Esiason, whom they traded to the New York Jets on March 17, 1993, for a third-round pick in that year's NFL Draft.

Esiason ended up spending three years in New York, playing his best ball for the Jets in 1993, when he earned his final trip to the Pro Bowl by completing close to 61 percent of his passes and ranking among the league leaders with 3,421 passing yards. Released by the Jets following the conclusion of the 1995 campaign, Esiason subsequently signed with the Arizona Cardinals, for whom he started eight games in 1996. Esiason then spent most of the following offseason contemplating retirement, before deciding to return to Cincinnati when the Bengals talked him into playing one more year.

After backing up Jeff Blake for most of 1997, Esiason replaced him behind center for the season's final five games, leading the struggling Bengals to a record of 4–1 in his five starts by passing for 1,478 yards, throwing 13 touchdown passes and only two interceptions, completing 63.4 percent of his passes, and posting a QBR of 106.9.

Despite his strong performance, the 36-year-old Esiason chose to announce his retirement at season's end, telling Paul Dehner Jr. of the *Cincinnati Enquirer* some 20 years later, "I really was close to coming back. I loved my time that last year. Bruce Coslet was now my head coach, and Kenny Anderson was my quarterback coach. It was the perfect situation for me: a veteran quarterback who knew the offense as much as the coaches did."

Esiason continued, "Unfortunately for Jeff Blake, he was struggling that year. As soon as the season was over, believe you me, I was so hyped and jacked and so proud of what we were able to accomplish, it really did take a lot to take me off the football field. I think I was a realist at that time. I remember telling Mike Brown, 'Look, if you want to give me some contract that I can't say no to, then I will come back and do that.'"

But, with ABC seeking to add him to its *Monday Night Football* broadcast team, Esiason, who had previously done color commentary for the USA Network on its telecasts of the World League of American Football, found it impossible to turn down such a prestigious offer, later saying, "If I didn't get it then, I don't know that I would have ever gotten it after that. It was a great run for me at the end of that season; my young teammates all bought into what I was selling. To watch guys like Corey Dillon and Ki-Jana Carter and James Hundon and Marco Battaglia and a host of guys get to another level that I don't think they thought was possible was probably one of the most satisfying aspects of finishing up as a Cincinnati Bengal."

Esiason ended his playing career with 37,920 passing yards, 247 touchdown passes, 184 interceptions, a pass-completion percentage of 57, a QBR of 81.1, 1,598 rushing yards, and seven rushing touchdowns. During his time in Cincinnati, he passed for 27,149 yards and 187 touchdowns, threw 131 interceptions, completed 56.5 percent of his passes, compiled a QBR of 83.1, gained 1,355 yards on the ground, and ran for five touchdowns.

After working alongside play-by-play announcer Al Michaels and fellow analyst Dan Dierdorf on ABC's *Monday Night Football* telecasts for two years, Esiason was relieved of his duties due to differences with Michaels. Following his dismissal by ABC, Esiason joined the Westwood

One radio network, where he spent the next 19 years serving as the lead analyst for radio broadcasts of *Monday Night Football* and Super Bowl games. While fulfilling that role, Esiason also began working at the CBS television network, where he has spent more than two decades serving as an in-studio analyst for *The NFL Today*. Esiason also co-hosts *Boomer and Gio*, a syndicated sports talk radio program that airs on WFAN in New York. In his spare time, Esiason remains involved in the Gunnar H. Esiason Cystic Fibrosis Center in the Pulmonary Division of Cincinnati Children's Hospital that he established during his playing days to honor his son, who has battled the disease since the age of two.

Continuing to hold the Bengals, their fans, and the city of Cincinnati close to his heart, Esiason says, "Even the minutes where we lost, even the strike season to the Super Bowl year to the playoff year where Bo Jackson gets hurt in our game. There are so many memories there and really great memories. I have nothing but positive feelings towards the Brown family, towards the Cincinnati Bengals and their fan base, the city. Everything that goes into analyzing a career and looking back on it is—I don't have any regrets. It's regretful we didn't win the Super Bowl, of course, but for 10 years it was great."

BENGALS CAREER HIGHLIGHTS

Best Season

Although Esiason threw for more yards (3,959) and completed a slightly higher percentage of his passes (58.2) two years earlier, he had the finest season of his career in 1988, when he earned his lone All-Pro selection and NFL MVP, *Sporting News* NFL Player of the Year, and UPI NFL Offensive Player of the Year honors by passing for 3,572 yards, completing 57.5 percent of his passes, finishing second in the league with 28 touchdown passes, and leading all NFL quarterbacks with a passer rating of 97.4.

Memorable Moments/Greatest Performances

Esiason earned AFC Offensive Player of the Week honors for the first time by throwing for 320 yards and three touchdowns during a 45–27 win over the Houston Oilers on December 1, 1985.

Esiason earned that distinction again by running for one touchdown and passing for two others during a 36–33 OT win over the Bills on

September 14, 1986, with his 2-yard TD run in the closing moments of regulation sending the game into overtime.

Esiason led the Bengals to a 52–21 blowout of the Jets in the final game of the 1986 regular season by throwing for 425 yards and five touchdowns, earning in the process his third AFC Offensive Player of the Week nomination.

Esiason again earned AFC Offensive Player of the Week honors by passing for 368 yards and two touchdowns during a 30–27 win over the Jets on December 6, 1987.

Esiason helped the Bengals begin the 1988 campaign on a positive note by throwing for 271 yards and three TDs during a 21–14 win over the Phoenix Cardinals in the regular-season opener.

Esiason followed that up by passing for 363 yards and four touchdowns during a 28–24 win over the Eagles in Week 2, earning in the process NFL Offensive Player of the Week honors.

Esiason again gained recognition as NFL Offensive Player of the Week by throwing five touchdown passes during a 56–23 win over Tampa Bay on October 29, 1989, connecting once with Tim McGee and twice each with Rodney Holman and Eddie Brown.

Esiason led the Bengals to a 42–7 rout of the Detroit Lions on November 19, 1989, by completing 30 of 39 passes for 399 yards and three touchdowns.

Esiason earned NFL Offensive Player of the Week honors for the third time in 1989 by throwing for 326 yards and four touchdowns during a 61–7 mauling of the Houston Oilers on December 17, with the longest of his TD passes going 74 yards to Tim McGee.

Esiason had a huge game against the Los Angeles Rams on October 7, 1990, earning AFC Offensive Player of the Week honors by throwing for 490 yards and three touchdowns during a 34–31 Bengals overtime win.

Esiason made the last pass of his career a memorable one, providing the winning margin in a 16–14 victory over the Baltimore Ravens in the final game of the 1997 regular season when he connected with Darnay Scott on a 77-yard scoring play with just under four minutes left in regulation.

Notable Achievements

- Passed for more than 3,000 yards six times, topping 3,500 yards three times.
- Threw more than 25 touchdown passes three times.
- Posted touchdown-to-interception ratio of better than 2–1 four times.

- Posted passer rating above 90.0 four times, finishing with mark above 100.0 once.
- Led NFL with passer rating of 97.4 in 1988.
- Finished second in NFL in passing yards once, touchdown passes three times, and passer rating twice.
- Ranks among Bengals career leaders with 3,564 pass attempts (3rd), 2,015 pass completions (4th), 27,149 passing yards (3rd), and 187 touchdown passes (3rd).
- Two-time division champion (1988 and 1990).
- 1988 AFC champion.
- Nine-time AFC Offensive Player of the Week.
- Six-time NFL Offensive Player of the Week.
- September 1988 AFC Offensive Player of the Month.
- 1988 NFL MVP.
- 1988 *Sporting News* NFL Player of the Year.
- 1988 United Press International NFL Offensive Player of the Year.
- Three-time Pro Bowl selection (1986, 1988, and 1989).
- 1988 First-Team All-Pro selection.
- Two-time First-Team All-AFC selection (1988 and 1989).
- Named to Bengals 50th Anniversary All-Time Team in 2017.
- Inducted into Bengals Ring of Honor in 2023.

17

JIM LECLAIR

A powerful run-stuffing inside linebacker who inspired his teammates with the intensity he brought with him to the playing field, Jim LeClair spent his entire 12-year NFL career in Cincinnati, proving to be one of the league's better players at his position most of that time. The centerpiece of the Bengals defense for nearly a decade, LeClair recorded more tackles than anyone else in franchise history, leading the team in that category on five separate occasions. A member of Bengals teams that won three division titles and one AFC championship, LeClair earned one Pro Bowl selection and one All-AFC nomination, before being further honored by being named to the Bengals 50th Anniversary All-Time Team.

Born in St. Paul, Minnesota, on October 30, 1950, James Michael LeClair attended South St. Paul High School, where he made a name for himself as a star football player and wrestler. Continuing to compete in both sports after he enrolled at the University of Minnesota Crookston, LeClair earned Minnesota College Athletic Conference (MCAC) All-Conference and NCJAA All-Region honors in football and ranked first in Minnesota and fourth in the nation in wrestling during the 1969–1970 season, before transferring to the University of North Dakota prior to the start of his junior year. Named to both the Little All-America and the College Division All-America teams as a senior in 1971 after he led North Dakota to its 12th North Central Conference championship by recording 187 tackles, three interceptions, four fumble recoveries, 11 forced fumbles, and 20 tackles for loss, LeClair received the additional honor of being named the conference's most valuable defensive lineman.

Selected by the Bengals in the third round of the 1972 NFL Draft, with the 54th overall pick, LeClair spent his first three seasons in Cincinnati playing mostly on special teams and serving as a backup linebacker, before joining the starting unit in 1975. Beginning a string of six straight seasons in which he started every game at middle linebacker, LeClair helped the Bengals compile a record of 11–3 that earned them a trip to the playoffs by

Jim LeClair recorded more tackles than anyone else in franchise history.

picking off three passes and recovering three fumbles. LeClair subsequently gained Pro Bowl recognition for the only time in his career in 1976, when he led the Bengals in tackles for the first of five times over the course of the next six seasons.

Although LeClair also did a good job in pass coverage, he became best known for his ability to defend against the run, where he used his aggressiveness and great strength to impose his will against the opposition. After entering the league at a svelte 6'3" and 210 pounds, LeClair gradually evolved into the team's strongest player by adding some 25 pounds of muscle onto his frame, with former Bengals strength and conditioning coach

Kim Wood later saying, "He was one of the strongest men I've ever seen. A real man's man."

Meanwhile, longtime teammate Dave Lapham recalled the advice he received from veteran offensive tackle Stan Walters while working against LeClair during blocking drills at his first pro training camp, remembering that Walters told him, "There's one thing you better not do. When you come off the double team, don't peek. LeClair will take your head off."

Lapham then added, "And he would. He had forearms that would rip you. He'd bring it, now. Big, broad shoulders. He was hard core."

An exceptional team leader, LeClair served as defensive captain most of his time in Cincinnati, fulfilling that role in 1981, when the Bengals won the AFC championship, and in 1983, when they boasted the NFL's top-ranked defense.

In discussing the lessons that he learned from LeClair, fellow Bengals linebacker Reggie Williams said, "Jimmy taught me the intensity level necessary for a linebacker to make the leap from the Ivy League to the NFL. Jimmy had an amazing intensity, but I never saw it in anger. We never had an argument in all the years (eight) we played together."

Recalling how he reacted when, as a rookie in 1976, he heard LeClair emit an ear-piercing scream while taking on two offensive linemen at the same time during a preseason goal-line stand, Williams stated, "He didn't give an inch. I had the best seat in the house for the Jimmy LeClair House of Horrors. . . . I knew then that I needed to step up my intensity to play beside this competitor."

LeClair's tremendous competitive spirit and incredible strength both came in handy on January 31, 1974, when he squared off against a previously undefeated 457-pound bear named Victor in a promotional wrestling match held at a downtown Cincinnati sports and travel show. Describing the events that transpired, Dave Lapham remembered, "The bear was huge. He's batting guys into a pool with his arm. Jimmy was out there shooting the bear's legs, putting wrestling moves on him. He got the bear off his feet. I guess that almost never happened. The bear's handler wanted to stop it because he knew Jimmy knew what he was doing."

Also in attendance was Kim Wood, who recalled, "It was a takedown. He took his heel to get behind the bear's heel and tripped him. That got the bear on his back and (LeClair) went up and covered him for the pin. I'm telling you; he pinned him. . . . They said that Victor was undefeated. But I'm telling you, Jim beat him. That bear was 35,000-and-1."

LeClair continued to excel on the football field after he moved to left-inside linebacker when the Bengals switched to a 3–4 defense in

1980, leading the team in tackles for the third of four straight times. But after three more years in Cincinnati, LeClair signed with the New Jersey Generals of the USFL. During his 12 seasons with the Bengals, LeClair amassed a franchise-record 1,212 tackles and registered 10 interceptions, 7 1/2 sacks, and 10 fumble recoveries, one of which he returned for a touchdown. Although LeClair never earned First- or Second-Team All-Pro honors because he had to compete against the likes of Hall of Fame middle linebackers Willie Lanier and Jack Lambert for recognition, he collected five All-Pro first-alternate selections.

After leaving Cincinnati, LeClair spent two years playing for the Generals, before announcing his retirement following the conclusion of the 1985 campaign. He subsequently became head football coach at Mayville State University, in Mayville, North Dakota, remaining in that post from 1986 to 1988, until retiring from football. LeClair then opened an insurance agency and later became mayor of Mayville. Eventually diagnosed with early-onset Alzheimer's disease, LeClair lived until November 4, 2019, when he passed away just five days after turning 69 years of age.

Upon learning of LeClair's passing, longtime Bengals defensive lineman Tim Krumrie said on Twitter: "I lost a teammate and friend today. Not only did No. 55, Jim LeClair, take me under his wing as a rookie, but he trained me in my comeback from my broken leg in 1989. What a great guy. RIP my friend."

Meanwhile, LeClair's wife of 49 years, Betty McGinn LeClair, said, "He was a tough one. He meant business. He loved playing the game. If he had to live life all over again, he would have done it again. He said God made him to be a football player."

CAREER HIGHLIGHTS

Best Season

LeClair performed extremely well in both 1975 and 1981, recording a career-high three interceptions and recovering three fumbles in the first of those campaigns, before helping to lead the Bengals to a regular-season record of 12–4 and the AFC championship in the second. But LeClair received his only Pro Bowl nomination in 1976, when he served as one of the key figures on a Bengals team that finished 10–4, with Pro Football Reference later assigning him an "Approximate Value" of 9 that represented the highest mark of his career.

Memorable Moments/Greatest Performances

LeClair contributed to a 21–0 shutout of the Saints on September 28, 1975, by recording his first career interception, which he subsequently returned 21 yards.

LeClair helped anchor a Bengals defense that created seven turnovers and allowed just 72 yards of total offense during a 42–3 rout of the Jets in the 1976 regular-season finale.

LeClair scored the only points of his career when he returned a fumble 27 yards for a touchdown during a 34–10 win over the Steelers on October 14, 1979.

LeClair served as the centerpiece of a defense that allowed just 55 yards rushing and 168 yards of total offense during a 14–0 shutout of the Vikings on October 19, 1980.

LeClair contributed to a 31–17 win over the Los Angeles Raiders on November 28, 1982, by recording a sack and an interception.

Notable Achievements

- Started 90 consecutive games from 1975 to 1980.
- Scored one defensive touchdown.
- Led Bengals in tackles five times.
- Holds Bengals career record for most tackles (1,212).
- Tied for sixth in franchise history with 10 fumble recoveries.
- Three-time division champion (1973, 1981, and 1982).
- 1981 AFC champion.
- 1976 Pro Bowl selection.
- 1982 Second-Team All-AFC selection.
- Named to Bengals 50th Anniversary All-Time Team in 2017.

18

JA'MARR CHASE

Among the finest receivers in the game today, Ja'Marr Chase has excelled for the Bengals at wideout ever since he first arrived in Cincinnati in 2021. A superb pass-catcher who possesses all the qualities desired in a number one receiver, Chase has surpassed 80 receptions and 1,000 receiving yards in each of his three NFL seasons, earning in the process three Pro Bowl selections and one All-Pro nomination. The favorite target of Bengals quarterback Joe Burrow, with whom he shares a special rapport that the two men developed in college, Chase has already set several Bengals single-game and single-season pass-receiving records, with his brilliant play making him a major contributor to teams that have won two division titles and one AFC championship.

Born in Harvey, Louisiana, on March 1, 2000, Ja'Marr Anthony Chase grew up just south of New Orleans, where he got his start in organized football at Archbishop Rummel High School, in the nearby suburb of Metairie. Developing into a star wideout at Archbishop Rummel, Chase ended his high school career with 115 receptions, 2,152 receiving yards, and 30 touchdown catches, with head football coach Jay Roth recalling, "Junior year, first game of the season, we're playing University High out of Baton Rouge. He catches four touchdown passes for over 220 yards."

A four-star recruit who ranked as the nation's 15th best wide receiver prospect coming out of high school, Chase initially committed to the University of Kansas, and, later, the University of Florida, before ultimately choosing to attend Louisiana State University on a football scholarship.

A starter in only eight games as a true freshman in 2018, Chase caught just 23 passes for 313 yards and three touchdowns, before emerging as one of college football's most prolific wideouts his sophomore year, when he finished second in the SEC with 84 receptions and led the nation with 1,780 receiving yards and 20 TD catches. Particularly outstanding in the College Football Playoff championship game, Chase helped lead LSU to a 42–25 victory over Clemson by making nine receptions for 221 yards and

Ja'Marr Chase has led the Bengals in receptions and receiving yards in each of the last three seasons.
Courtesy of All-Pro Reels Photography

two touchdowns, setting in the process a championship game record for most receiving yards. Named a unanimous All-American, Chase also gained recognition as the winner of the Fred Biletnikoff Award, presented annually to the best receiver in college football.

With the COVID-19 pandemic gripping the nation and his agents advising him not to risk illness or injury, Chase elected to sit out his junior year at LSU. Putting his free time to good use, Chase spent the 2020 campaign preparing himself for the rigors of the NFL by following a six-month all-day workout regimen devised by the sports training agency Exos Athletes' Performance Institute, with his personal trainer, Brent Callaway, later claiming that he watched his pupil experience an increase in speed, strength, and flexibility.

Subsequently selected by the Bengals with the fifth overall pick of the 2021 NFL Draft, at the urging of his close friend and former LSU teammate Joe Burrow, Chase entered the league with huge expectations surrounding him. Proving himself worthy of such a high selection, Chase earned Pro Bowl, Second-Team All-Pro, and NFL Offensive Rookie of the Year honors by making 81 receptions, amassing 1,455 receiving yards, and scoring 13 touchdowns for a Bengals team that won the division title for the first time in six years, with his 1,455 yards gained through the air establishing a new single-season franchise record. Continuing his exceptional play in the postseason, Chase set an NFL record for rookies by amassing a total of 368 receiving yards in the playoffs and Super Bowl.

Despite missing four games in 2022 with a hairline fracture in his hip that he sustained during a 30–26 victory over the New Orleans Saints on October 16, Chase posted excellent numbers once again, earning his second straight Pro Bowl nomination by making 87 receptions for 1,046 yards and nine touchdowns, in helping the Bengals capture their second straight division title. Although the Bengals failed to earn a return trip to the Super Bowl, Chase had another outstanding postseason, catching 20 passes, amassing 320 receiving yards, and scoring two touchdowns in their three playoff games.

Blessed with an exceptional skill set, the 6-foot, 201-pound Chase possesses good size, excellent speed, outstanding leaping ability, sure hands, and superb body control, which enable him to gather in virtually anything thrown in his direction. Capable of out-running or out-jumping his defender, Chase also has the ability to use his size and strength to out-fight his man for the football in close quarters. An excellent open-field runner as well, Chase has a knack for either evading would-be tacklers completely or slipping through their fingers, making him a threat to go the distance any time he gains control of the football.

Extremely impressed with Chase after watching him make nine receptions for 116 yards during the Bengals' 26–19 victory over the Raiders in the opening round of the 2021 playoffs, former Cincinnati star wideout Chad Johnson took note of his effortless style of play, saying, "When you look at other guys that are fast, it just looks like they're trying. With Ja'Marr, it doesn't look like he's trying. There's a sense of calmness even though he's playing at full speed."

Commenting on the chemistry between Chase and Joe Burrow, Bengals wide receivers coach Troy Walters offered, "They came into this thing being on the same page, understanding each other. Joe knows exactly what Ja'Marr is going to do in terms of his release, where to throw the ball. Ja'Marr understands where Joe is going to put the ball. It's just uncanny."

In discussing Chase's ability to read his thoughts, Burrow stated, "He knows exactly where the ball is gonna be, depending on the look the corner is presenting."

Meanwhile, Bengals head coach Zac Taylor praised Chase for his strong work ethic, attention to detail, and versatility when he said, "He works as hard as anybody. . . . We ask a lot of him in practice. He runs and he doesn't complain. He doesn't make a mental error due to not paying attention. . . . He's got a great understanding because he switches positions all the time. He plays all three spots. He moves more than anybody. He lines up in the backfield, he motions to the backfield. He's got to know everything, and he does, and he works his tail off in practice. Extra pre-practice. Runs like crazy during practice."

Despite spending almost half of the 2023 campaign playing without an injured Joe Burrow, Chase had another excellent year, earning Pro Bowl honors for the third straight time by making 100 receptions for 1,216 yards and seven touchdowns. Currently on pace to shatter every Bengals pass-receiving record, the 24-year-old Chase will enter the 2024 season with career totals of 268 receptions, 3,717 receiving yards, and 29 touchdown catches.

CAREER HIGHLIGHTS

Best Season

Although Chase caught more passes this past season, he made a slightly greater overall impact as a rookie in 2021, when he helped the Bengals win the division title by making 81 receptions and establishing career-high marks with 1,455 receiving yards and 13 touchdown receptions.

Memorable Moments/Greatest Performances

Chase excelled in his first game as a pro, making five receptions for 101 yards and one touchdown during a 27–24 overtime win over the

Minnesota Vikings in the 2021 regular-season opener, with his TD coming on a 50-yard connection with Joe Burrow.

Chase earned AFC Offensive Player of the Week honors by making eight receptions for 201 yards and one touchdown during a 41–17 victory over the Ravens on October 24, 2021, scoring his TD on an 82-yard hookup with Burrow.

Chase earned that distinction again by making 11 receptions for a franchise-record 266 yards and three touchdowns during a 34–31 win over the Chiefs on January 2, 2022, collaborating with Joe Burrow on scoring plays that covered 72, 18, and 69 yards.

Chase helped lead the Bengals to a 30–26 win over the Saints on October 16, 2022, by making seven receptions for 132 yards and two touchdowns, with his 60-yard TD grab late in the final period providing the margin of victory.

Chase contributed to a 35–17 win over the Atlanta Falcons the following week by making eight receptions for 130 yards and two touchdowns, which came on hookups of 32 and 41 yards with Joe Burrow.

Chase gained recognition as AFC Offensive Player of the Week by making a franchise-record 15 receptions for 192 yards and three touchdowns during a 34–20 win over the Arizona Cardinals on October 8, 2023, with the longest of his TDs coming on a 63-yard connection with Burrow.

Chase helped lead the Bengals to a 34–31 overtime victory over the Jacksonville Jaguars on December 4, 2023, by making 11 receptions for 149 yards and one touchdown, which came on a 76-yard connection with Jake Browning on Cincinnati's opening possession of the second half.

Notable Achievements

- Has surpassed 80 receptions and 1,000 receiving yards three times each.
- Finished second in NFL with an average of 18.0 yards per reception in 2021.
- Finished third in NFL with 13 touchdown receptions in 2021.
- Finished fourth in NFL with 1,455 receiving yards in 2021.
- Has led Bengals in receptions and receiving yards three times each.
- Holds Bengals single-game record for most receptions (15 vs. Arizona on October 8, 2023).
- Holds Bengals single-game record for most receiving yards (266 vs. Kansas City on January 2, 2022).
- Holds Bengals single-season record for most receiving yards (1,455 in 2021).

- Two-time division champion (2021 and 2022).
- 2021 AFC champion.
- Member of 2021 NFL All-Rookie Team.
- Three-time AFC Offensive Player of the Week.
- 2021 NFL Offensive Rookie of the Year.
- 2021 *Sporting News* NFL Rookie of the Year.
- Three-time Pro Bowl selection (2021, 2022, and 2023).
- 2021 Second-Team All-Pro selection.
- 2021 First-Team All-AFC selection.

19

ANDY DALTON

A steady but unspectacular quarterback who often went overlooked due to his inability to significantly raise the level of play of his teammates or overcome their deficiencies, Andy Dalton nevertheless provided the Bengals with consistently strong play behind center during his nine seasons in Cincinnati. The franchise's career leader in pass completions and touchdown passes, Dalton also ranks second in team annals in passing yards, amassing more than 3,000 yards through the air on eight separate occasions. The only QB to lead the Bengals to five consecutive playoff appearances, Dalton also directed them to two division titles, earning in the process three Pro Bowl nominations. Yet Dalton's Bengals legacy will always be tarnished by his failure to deliver a victory in postseason play.

Born in Katy, Texas, on October 29, 1987, Andrew Gregory Dalton grew up some 30 miles west of Houston, where he developed into one of the state's finest quarterbacks at Katy High School. After seeing a limited amount of action as a junior, Dalton emerged as a star his senior year, leading the Tigers to a record of 14–1 that earned them a berth in the state finals by throwing for 2,877 yards and 42 touchdowns, with his outstanding play gaining him recognition from the *Houston Chronicle* as the Greater Houston Area Offensive Player of the Year.

Recruited by three Division I schools, Dalton ultimately chose TCU over UTEP and Memphis after having previously attended two summer camps there. A four-year starter at TCU, Dalton led the Horned Frogs to an overall record of 42–8, two Mountain West Conference championships, and three top-10 finishes in the national rankings by setting then-school records for most passing yards (10,314), pass attempts (1,317), and pass completions (812). Particularly outstanding his senior year, Dalton earned a ninth-place finish in the Heisman Trophy voting by throwing for 2,857 yards and 27 touchdowns, while tossing just six interceptions.

Praising his one-time protégé for his attention to detail and fierce competitive spirit, former TCU quarterbacks coach Justin Fuente said, "You

Andy Dalton led the Bengals to two division titles and five straight playoff appearances.
Courtesy of Keith Allison and All-Pro Reels Photography

had to make sure when you told Andy something you were very precise because he could come back and remind you just what you said. . . . He was as good an individual as you will find off the field, but that's not what he should be known for on the field. He is also the most competitive, team-oriented person you will meet."

Selected by the Bengals in the second round of the 2011 NFL Draft, with the 35th overall pick, Dalton earned the starting quarterback job prior to the start of the regular season, replacing in the process an unhappy

Carson Palmer, who had requested a trade during the offseason. Performing so well the first few weeks of the campaign that ownership granted Palmer's request in mid-October, Dalton ended up leading the Bengals to a 9–7 record and a spot in the playoffs by passing for 3,398 yards, throwing 20 touchdown passes and 13 interceptions, completing 58.1 percent of his passes, and posting a passer rating of 80.4. The first quarterback in NFL history not drafted in the first round to start all 16 games of his rookie season, Dalton earned Pro Bowl honors and a runner-up finish in the NFL Offensive Rookie of the Year voting. But he failed to perform at the same level in his first postseason game, throwing three interceptions during a 31–10 loss to the Houston Texans in the wild card round of the playoffs.

Building on the success he experienced his first year in the league, Dalton led the Bengals to another wild card playoff berth in 2012 by throwing for 3.669 yards and 27 touchdowns, while also completing 62.3 percent of his passes and compiling a passer rating of 87.4. Once again, though, he struggled against Houston in the playoffs, passing for just 127 yards and throwing an interception during a 19–13 loss to the Texans. Dalton followed that up with another strong regular season, helping to lead the Bengals to the division title in 2013 by throwing for 4,293 yards and 33 touchdowns, setting then-single-season franchise records in both categories. However, for the third straight year, Dalton faltered in the playoffs, throwing a pair of interceptions and fumbling on a forward dive during a 27–10 loss to the San Diego Chargers in the opening round of the postseason tournament.

Although Dalton had established himself as one of the NFL's better quarterbacks by the end of his third season, his postseason failures led many to believe that he lacked the ability to lead his team to a deep playoff run. In discussing Dalton, one AFC defensive coordinator said, "The phrase that comes to mind is good enough. He's good enough to win a division, good enough to make you feel like a contender. But good enough to get you all the way (to the Super Bowl)? I'm not so sure."

For his part, Dalton stated, "I'm aware of what people say on Twitter and stuff. Until we win in the playoffs, people can say what they want. We have to take care of business in the regular season first, but we all know that people want more from this team, more from me."

Speaking in defense of Dalton after the team's third straight playoff loss, Bengals head coach Marvin Lewis said, "It isn't just on him. We've had breakdowns in different areas. Dropped passes. Missed blocks. But people want to put all of the blame on the quarterback. He'd be the first to tell you he needs to play better, but the truth is, we haven't performed well as a team the last three playoff games. It's on all of us."

One of the criticisms of the 6'2", 220-pound Dalton was that he lacked superior athletic ability. Although Dalton moved fairly well in the pocket and possessed a strong throwing arm, he lacked the quickness and creativity to make plays when things broke down. Also criticized for being too even-tempered and lacking a killer instinct, Dalton rarely displayed his emotions on the field or chided his teammates when they made mistakes. However, A. J. Green considered that a strength, saying of his QB, "He takes responsibility even when something isn't his fault. If he throws an interception because a receiver runs the wrong route, he doesn't point fingers."

The next two seasons followed a similar script, with the Bengals advancing to the playoffs, only to lose in the opening round. Meanwhile, Dalton earned his second Pro Bowl nomination in 2014 by throwing for 3,398 yards and 19 touchdowns, while also completing 64.2 percent of his passes and posting a passer rating of 83.5. Dalton subsequently led the Bengals to the division title in 2015 by passing for 3,250 yards and 25 touchdowns, throwing only seven interceptions, completing 66.1 percent of his passes, and finishing second in the league with a passer rating of 106.2. But he missed the final three games of the regular season and the Bengals' playoff meeting with the Pittsburgh Steelers with a fractured thumb on his throwing hand. Faring no better in his absence, the Bengals exited the postseason tournament quickly, suffering a heartbreaking 18–16 defeat at the hands of their division rivals with A. J. McCarron starting for them behind center.

Although the Bengals' string of consecutive playoff appearances ended in 2016, Dalton had what Marvin Lewis called "the best campaign of his career." Despite being sacked 41 times and throwing only 18 touchdown passes, Dalton passed for 4,206 yards, tossed just eight interceptions, completed 64.7 percent of his passes, posted a passer rating of 91.8, and ran for four touchdowns. Following another solid performance in 2017, Dalton acquitted himself well over the first 11 weeks of the ensuing campaign, before suffering torn ligaments in his thumb during a 35–20 loss to the Browns in Week 12 that forced him to spend the rest of the year on injured reserve. Dalton subsequently failed to lead the Bengals to victory in any of their first eight games in 2019, prompting new head coach Zac Taylor to bench him in favor of rookie Ryan Finley. But after Finley struggled in his three starts behind center, Dalton started the season's final five contests, leading the Bengals to their only two wins of the season.

With the Bengals owning the first overall pick of the 2020 NFL Draft, they selected Joe Burrow, prompting Dalton to ask for his release. Granting Dalton's request a few days later, the Bengals announced via Twitter: "We have released QB Andy Dalton. Andy has not only been an outstanding player on the field, but a role model in the Cincinnati community for the last nine years. Thank you for everything, Andy."

One day after the Bengals made their announcement, Dalton discussed what his years in Cincinnati meant to him, saying, "I received a lot of support through my career. I felt it ever since yesterday when they announced it. I'm not going to say I was underappreciated, or I think I deserve more than I'm getting. There's been a lot of good stuff that has happened in the last ten years. I think one thing everybody realized. I've given everything to the organization, the city, my family has given so much to the city. We didn't take our position and our platform lightly. To see what has happened since yesterday, it's bigger than football. We understood that. We know that and we're feeling the love, and that's bigger than football."

Dalton, who, with his wife, Jordan, established the Andy & Jordan Dalton Foundation during his time in Cincinnati to help families with special-needs children or children who suffered from chronic illness, added, "One thing that JJ and I can both say is that we poured our heart into the city. It wasn't just the organization, but it was everybody there in different aspects. It's a huge part of our life, the beginning of our marriage, our kids being young and growing up there."

The fans of Cincinnati, in turn, expressed their appreciation to Dalton and his wife for everything they did for the community by donating more than $25,000 to the foundation the day the Bengals released him.

Dalton, who, in his nine years with the Bengals, passed for 31,594 yards and 204 touchdowns, threw 118 interceptions, completed 62 percent of his passes, posted a passer rating of 87.5, and ran for 1,221 yards and 22 touchdowns, subsequently signed with the Dallas Cowboys, for whom he started nine games in 2020 after regular starter Dak Prescott suffered a season-ending injury. Dalton then split the next two seasons between the Chicago Bears and New Orleans Saints, starting a total of 20 games for losing teams, before signing a two-year deal with the Carolina Panthers on March 15, 2023. Appearing in only three games with the Panthers this past season, Dalton threw for just 361 yards and two touchdowns, giving him career totals of 38,511 passing yards, 246 TD passes, and 144 interceptions, a 62.5 pass-completion percentage, and a passer rating of 87.6 heading into the 2024 campaign. Dalton has also run for 1,477 yards and 22 touchdowns.

BENGALS CAREER HIGHLIGHTS

Best Season

Dalton played some of his best ball for the Bengals in 2013 and 2015, passing for 4,293 yards and 33 touchdowns in the first of those campaigns, while posting a career-high passer rating of 106.2 in the second. Nevertheless, we'll go along with Marvin Lewis, who contended that his quarterback had the finest season of his career in 2016. Despite playing behind a porous offensive line, Dalton passed for 4,206 yards, completed 64.7 percent of his passes, and compiled a passer rating of 91.8, while throwing 18 TD passes and only eight picks.

Memorable Moments/Greatest Performances

Dalton led the Bengals to a 34–27 win over the Browns on September 16, 2012, by throwing for 318 yards and three touchdowns, the longest of which came on a 50-yard connection with Andrew Hawkins.

Dalton followed that up with a similarly impressive performance, passing for 328 yards and three touchdowns during a 38–31 win over Washington one week later.

Dalton earned AFC Offensive Player of the Week honors for the first time by throwing for 199 yards and four touchdowns during a 31–13 win over the Giants on November 11, 2012, with the longest of his TD passes going 56 yards to A. J. Green.

Dalton earned that distinction again by throwing for 337 yards and three touchdowns during a 27–24 overtime win over the Bills on October 13, 2013.

Retaining a hot hand the following week, Dalton passed for 372 yards and three touchdowns during a 27–24 win over the Lions on October 20, completing the longest of his TD passes to A. J. Green from 82 yards out.

Dalton subsequently led the Bengals to a 49–9 rout of the Jets on October 27, 2013, by throwing for 325 yards and five touchdowns, connecting four times with Marvin Jones and once with Jermaine Gresham.

Dalton earned AFC Offensive Player of the Week honors by running for one touchdown and passing for three others during a 42–28 win over the Colts on December 8, 2013.

Dalton led the Bengals to a 42–14 dismantling of the Vikings on December 22, 2013, by throwing for 363 yards and four touchdowns.

Dalton turned in a strong performance against the Ravens on September 27, 2015, passing for 383 yards and three touchdowns during a 28–24 Bengals win, with the longest of his TD tosses being an 80-yard connection with A. J. Green.

Dalton led the Bengals to a 31–7 victory over the Browns on October 1, 2017, by completing 25 of 30 passes for 286 yards and four touchdowns, the longest of which came on a 61-yard catch-and-run by Giovani Bernard.

Dalton gave the Bengals a 37–36 win over the Atlanta Falcons on September 30, 2018, when he hit A. J. Green with a 13-yard touchdown pass with just seven seconds left in regulation. Dalton, who completed 29 of 41 passes on the day, finished the game with 337 yards passing and three TD passes.

Although the Bengals lost their 2019 regular-season opener, 21–20, to Seattle, Dalton performed extremely well, throwing for 418 yards and two touchdowns, despite being sacked five times.

Dalton again starred in defeat on December 22, 2019, throwing for 396 yards and four touchdowns during a 38–35 OT loss to Miami, sending the game into overtime by tossing two TD passes in the final 30 seconds of regulation.

Notable Achievements

- Passed for more than 4,000 yards twice, topping 3,000 yards passing six other times.
- Threw more than 30 touchdown passes once, throwing at least 25 TD passes three other times.
- Completed more than 65 percent of passes once.
- Posted touchdown-to-interception ratio of better than 2–1 three times.
- Posted passer rating above 100.0 once.
- Finished second in NFL with passer rating of 106.2 in 2015.
- Finished third in NFL with 33 touchdown passes in 2013.
- Holds Bengals career records for most pass completions (2,757) and touchdown passes (204).
- Ranks among Bengals career leaders with 4,449 pass attempts (2nd), 31,594 passing yards (2nd), and 62.0 pass-completion percentage (3rd).
- Two-time division champion (2013 and 2015).
- Three-time AFC Offensive Player of the Week.
- Two-time AFC Offensive Player of the Month.
- Three-time Pro Bowl selection (2011, 2014, and 2016).

20

JAMES BROOKS

The greatest dual threat in franchise history, James Brooks spent eight seasons in Cincinnati, establishing himself as one of the NFL's finest all-purpose backs. An outstanding runner, Brooks gained more than 1,000 yards on the ground three times, en route to rushing for the second-most yards of any player in team annals. An excellent receiver out of the backfield as well, Brooks caught more than 50 passes and amassed more than 500 receiving yards twice each, enabling him to accumulate more than 1,500 yards from scrimmage on three separate occasions. A major contributor to Bengals teams that won two division titles and one AFC championship, Brooks earned four Pro Bowl selections and four All-AFC nominations, before being further honored following the conclusion of his playing career by being named to the Bengals 40th Anniversary All-Time Team.

Born in Lansing, Michigan, on December 28, 1958, James Robert Brooks moved with his family at an early age to Warner Robins, Georgia, where he starred on the gridiron for Warner Robins High School, setting a then-school record by rushing for a total of 4,700 yards. Offered an athletic scholarship to Auburn University after leading Warner Robins to both the state and national championships as a senior in 1976, Brooks spent the next four years assuming an important role in the Tigers' triple-option offense, gaining 3,524 yards on the ground, amassing 5,596 all-purpose yards, and scoring 30 touchdowns, despite sharing rushing responsibilities with future NFL stars William Andrews and Joe Cribbs at different times.

With Brooks having earned Second-Team All-America honors in each of his final two seasons at Auburn, the San Diego Chargers selected him in the first round of the 1981 NFL Draft, with the 24th overall pick. Joining an offensive juggernaut coached by Don Coryell and directed by quarterback Dan Fouts, Brooks found himself playing second fiddle to star running back Chuck Muncie his first three years in the league, receiving far fewer opportunities to run with the football than the 6'3", 227-pound

James Brooks holds single-season franchise records for most yards from scrimmage and all-purpose yards.
Courtesy of George A. Kitrinos

fullback. Nevertheless, Brooks managed to rush for more than 500 yards and accumulate more than 700 yards from scrimmage twice each, while also performing so well as a punt and kickoff returner that he led the NFL in all-purpose yards on two separate occasions.

Growing increasingly unhappy since he felt that the Chargers failed to take full advantage of his varied skill set, Brooks found particularly objectional the team's practice of occasionally lining up the massive Muncie as a tailback in the I-formation, forcing him to assume the role of fullback. Expressing his dissatisfaction with his deployment by the Chargers some years later, Brooks said, "I didn't want them to put me at fullback. San Diego wanted me to block instead of letting me go one-on-one with linebackers in passing situations."

With Brooks finally airing his grievances to team management after three frustrating seasons, the Chargers completed a trade with the Bengals prior to the start of the 1984 campaign that sent him to Cincinnati for the equally disgruntled Pete Johnson.

Carrying the ball just 103 times his first year in Cincinnati while sharing the workload with Larry Kinnebrew, Charles Alexander, and Stanford Jennings, Brooks rushed for only 396 yards and two touchdowns. But he also made 34 receptions for 268 yards and two TDs, with his 144 kickoff-return yards giving him a total of 808 all-purpose yards. Establishing himself as the Bengals' primary offensive weapon the following year, Brooks rushed for 929 yards, gained another 576 yards on 55 pass receptions, and scored 12 touchdowns, with seven of those coming on the ground and the other five through the air. Performing even better in 1986, Brooks earned Pro Bowl and First-Team All-AFC honors by rushing for 1,087 yards, making 54 receptions for 686 yards, scoring nine touchdowns, finishing third in the league with 1,773 yards from scrimmage, and topping the circuit with an average of 5.3 yards per carry.

Blessed with outstanding speed and quickness, the 5'10", 180-pound Brooks excelled at turning the corner and evading would-be tacklers in the open field. Yet, despite his somewhat smallish frame, Brooks also ran well between the tackles, where he used his toughness and surprising strength to consistently gain additional yardage after being contacted by men much larger than himself. An exceptional pass receiver as well, Brooks proved to be a matchup nightmare for opposing linebackers and safeties, who lacked the ability to stay with him as he navigated his way downfield.

Known also for his tremendous work ethic, Brooks received high praise for his dedication to his profession from former teammate Tom Dinkle, who said, "Some athletes just live on their talent until it runs out, but James was different. He combined his talent with an incredible work ethic and discipline. No one ever wanted to work out with James, he would just run you to death."

Dave Lapham added, "James would do the stadium steps at Riverfront year-round . . . not even Anthony Muñoz did more."

Injured for much of 1987, Brooks appeared in only nine games, limiting him to just 290 yards rushing, 562 yards from scrimmage, and three touchdowns. Healthy again by the start of the 1988 campaign, Brooks helped lead the Bengals to the division title and their second AFC championship by rushing for 931 yards, gaining another 287 yards on 29 pass receptions, and scoring 14 touchdowns, earning in the process Pro Bowl and Second-Team All-AFC honors for the first of three straight times. Continuing his outstanding play the next two seasons, Brooks scored nine touchdowns and ranked among the league leaders with 1,239 yards rushing and 1,545 yards from scrimmage in 1989, before gaining 1,004 yards on the ground, amassing 1,273 yards from scrimmage, and scoring another nine TDs the following year. But after Brooks posted less impressive numbers in 1991, finishing the season with 571 yards rushing, 919 yards from scrimmage, and four touchdowns, the Bengals traded him to the arch-rival Cleveland Browns at the end of the year.

Brooks, who, during his time in Cincinnati, rushed for 6,447 yards and 37 touchdowns, made 297 receptions for 3,012 yards and 27 TDs, amassed 9,459 yards from scrimmage and 9,867 all-purpose yards, scored a total of 64 touchdowns, and posted an average of 4.8 yards per carry that represents the highest career mark in team annals, subsequently split the first six games of the 1992 season between the Browns and Tampa Bay Buccaneers, gaining a total of only 44 yards on the ground while serving as a backup for both teams, before announcing his retirement midway through the campaign after sustaining a minor injury. Over parts of 12 NFL seasons, Brooks rushed for 7,962 yards, gained another 3,621 yards on 383 pass receptions, amassed 11,583 yards from scrimmage and 14,910 all-purpose yards, and scored 79 touchdowns.

After retiring from football, Brooks ran afoul of the law in 1999, when police arrested him for owing $110,000 in back child support. Subsequently found to be functionally illiterate during his trial, Brooks revealed that he never had to attend class while in college. Soon after news of Brooks's illiteracy broke, Auburn offered to pay for his education. Meanwhile, Brooks had to serve the first three months of a six-month sentence, before being assigned to a work-release program.

When asked about his former teammate's ability to read and communicate, Dave Lapham said, "James was never much of a conversationalist, he had a problem with his diction, so he was so tough to interview. But he was always a key performer, so you wanted to talk with him. He was a very smart guy, but you could tell it was the field where he learned the playbook. If James had to rely solely on the Bengals written playbook, he would have had difficulty knowing his assignments. We all knew James struggled, but it wasn't something we ever talked about. . . . He knew enough to get by."

BENGALS CAREER HIGHLIGHTS

Best Season

Brooks had a tremendous year for the Bengals in 1989, scoring nine touchdowns and ranking among the league leaders with 1,239 yards rushing, 1,545 yards from scrimmage, and a career-high average of 5.6 yards per carry. But Brooks posted slightly better overall numbers in 1986, when, in addition to scoring nine TDs, he led the NFL with an average of 5.3 yards per carry and set a single-season franchise record that still stands by amassing 1,773 yards from scrimmage, gaining 1,087 of those yards on the ground and the other 686 through the air.

Memorable Moments/Greatest Performances

Brooks helped lead the Bengals to a 37–24 win over the Steelers on September 30, 1985, by rushing for 133 yards and two touchdowns, which came on runs of 14 and 32 yards.

Brooks earned AFC Offensive Player of the Week honors by making six receptions for 62 yards and carrying the ball 18 times for 133 yards and two touchdowns during a 31–28 win over the Houston Oilers on October 19, 1986, with his 21-yard TD run late in the fourth quarter providing the margin of victory.

Brooks again earned AFC Offensive Player of the Week honors by amassing 264 yards from scrimmage and scoring a touchdown on a 56-yard run during a 31–7 win over the Patriots on December 7, 1986, gaining 163 yards on the ground and another 101 yards on six pass receptions.

Brooks contributed to a 44–21 victory over the Oilers on October 23, 1988, by rushing for 102 yards and three touchdowns, the longest of which came on an 18-yard run.

Brooks led the Bengals to a 38–24 win over the Cowboys on November 20, 1988, by carrying the ball 16 times for 148 yards and two touchdowns, earning in the process his third AFC Offensive Player of the Week nomination.

Brooks proved to be the difference in a 26–16 win over the Steelers on October 8, 1989, rushing for 127 yards and two touchdowns, with his 65-yard TD run in the final period sealing the victory.

Brooks earned AFC Offensive Player of the Week honors by rushing for 201 yards and one touchdown during a 40–20 win over the Oilers on December 23, 1990, scoring his TD on a 56-yard run just before halftime.

Notable Achievements

- Rushed for more than 1,000 yards three times.
- Surpassed 50 receptions and 500 receiving yards twice each.
- Amassed more than 1,000 yards from scrimmage five times, topping 1,500 yards three times.
- Amassed more than 1,000 all-purpose yards six times.
- Scored more than 10 touchdowns twice.
- Averaged more than 5 yards per carry four times.
- Led NFL with rushing average of 5.3 yards per carry in 1986.
- Finished second in NFL in average yards per carry twice.
- Finished third in NFL with 1,773 yards from scrimmage in 1986.
- Led Bengals in rushing four times.
- Holds Bengals career record for highest rushing average (4.8 yards per carry).
- Holds Bengals single-season records for most yards from scrimmage (1,773 in 1986), most all-purpose yards (1,773 in 1986), and highest rushing average (5.6 yards per carry in 1989).
- Ranks among Bengals career leaders with 1,344 rushing attempts (5th), 6,447 rushing yards (2nd), 9,459 yards from scrimmage (4th), 9,867 all-purpose yards (2nd), 37 rushing touchdowns (tied for 5th), 64 touchdowns (tied for 4th), and 384 points (11th).
- Two-time division champion (1988 and 1990).
- 1988 AFC champion.
- Four-time AFC Offensive Player of the Week.
- Two-time NFL Offensive Player of the Week.
- Four-time Pro Bowl selection (1986, 1988, 1989, and 1990).
- 1986 First-Team All-AFC selection.
- Three-time Second-Team All-AFC selection (1988, 1989, and 1990).
- Named to Bengals 40th Anniversary All-Time Team in 2007.

21

CARLOS DUNLAP

An outstanding defensive end who combined with Geno Atkins for a decade to give the Bengals a formidable twosome on their defensive front, Carlos Dunlap spent parts of 11 seasons in Cincinnati, recording the second-most sacks of any player in franchise history. A member of the Bengals from 2010 to 2020, Dunlap proved to be a significant contributor to teams that won two division titles and made five consecutive playoff appearances, recording at least eight sacks on six separate occasions. A solid run-defender as well, Dunlap forced more fumbles than any other player in team annals, with his strong all-around play earning him two Pro Bowl selections.

Born in North Charleston, South Carolina, on February 28, 1989, Carlos Dunlap grew up having the importance of education stressed to him by his mother, Dr. Diane Ross, a teacher who eventually returned to school to earn her doctoral degree. While Dunlap always did well in the classroom, he also proved to be an excellent all-around athlete, starring in multiple sports at Fort Dorchester High School. Particularly outstanding on the gridiron, Dunlap was listed as the number one weakside defensive end in the nation in 2007 after registering 105 tackles, 35 tackles for loss, and 24 sacks his senior year.

Offered athletic scholarships to several major colleges, Dunlap narrowed his choices down to a select few with the help of his parents, recalling, "During recruiting, my mom always looked at the schools for education, and my dad always looked at them for the competition in athletics."

Ultimately choosing the University of Florida over Clemson, South Carolina, Auburn, and Tennessee, Dunlap spent three seasons playing for head coach Urban Meyer. A two-year starter for the Gators, Dunlap earned Second-Team All-SEC honors as a sophomore by recording 39 tackles and 9 1/2 sacks, before gaining consensus First-Team All-SEC recognition his junior year by making 38 tackles and registering nine sacks.

Carlos Dunlap's 82 1/2 sacks represent the second-highest total in franchise history.
Courtesy of Jeffrey Beall

Electing to forgo his senior year, Dunlap declared himself eligible for the 2010 NFL Draft, which he entered with high expectations. But, with Dunlap having suffered a one-game suspension during his final season at Florida after being arrested for driving under the influence of alcohol, he ended up slipping to the second round, where the Bengals selected him with the 54th overall pick.

Following his arrival in Cincinnati, Dunlap spent his first pro season serving the Bengals primarily as a situational pass-rusher, earning a spot on the NFL All-Rookie Team by recording 9 1/2 sacks, despite missing four games with a hamstring injury. Assuming a similar role in 2011 and 2012, Dunlap helped the Bengals earn a wild card playoff berth each season by registering a total of 10 1/2 sacks, while also making 64 tackles and scoring one touchdown on defense. Named the Bengals starting left defensive end prior to the start of the 2013 campaign, Dunlap remained the full-time starter at that post for the next seven seasons, establishing himself as one of the NFL's most consistent edge-rushers by averaging just under nine sacks per season. Performing especially well in 2015 and 2016, Dunlap earned consecutive Pro Bowl nominations by finishing fourth in the league with 13 1/2 sacks and recording 55 tackles in the first of those campaigns, before registering eight sacks, 49 tackles, and 15 passes defensed in the second, with the last figure representing the highest total by any non–defensive back in the league.

Standing 6'6" and weighing 285 pounds, Dunlap possessed good size and strength. Extremely quick as well, Dunlap often beat his blocker to the outside or outmaneuvered him when he chose to employ an inside pass-rush. And when Dunlap failed to get to the opposing quarterback, he did an excellent job of using his size and athleticism to bat down passes, annually ranking among the league's top linemen in passes defensed.

Displaying a nose for the football throughout his career, Dunlap also excelled at stripping the ball from opposing ball-carriers and recovering it once it hit the ground, recording the most forced fumbles and the 10th-most fumble recoveries of any player in team annals. Extremely durable as well, Dunlap appeared in all but two games the Bengals played from 2013 to 2019, at one point starting 101 consecutive contests.

In addition to his contributions on the playing field, Dunlap, who the Bengals nominated for the NFL Walter Payton Man of the Year Award twice, gave back to the community through the Dunlap Rewards Scholars program that he founded, with the help of his mother. In discussing the program, which offers incentives to inner-city athletes in Cincinnati to succeed in school and eventually attend college, Dunlap said, "We try and keep them motivated. We also work with them as mentors. The reason why I really wanted to go back and make an impact in my community was because, early on in high school, I wasn't exactly the best athlete on my team. For me to be the first one to go to a big college and go to the NFL, I wanted to leave that door open for the next."

Dunlap added, "It's not just the Bengals that I'm grateful to, but the city of Cincinnati. They were very welcoming. I bought my first home here. I was barely 21 when I first came here. I pretty much had a lot of growing pains here, more great times than bad times. It's been a journey. It's been a battle. It's been a test. It's been fun. I'm grateful for the experiences."

Unfortunately, Dunlap's time in the Queen City came to an end shortly after Zac Taylor assumed head coaching duties and Lou Anarumo became defensive coordinator in 2019. After recording nine sacks and 63 tackles under both men the previous season, Dunlap found himself lower on the depth chart when he reported to training camp in 2020. Dunlap subsequently received a limited amount of playing time over the first two months of the regular season, appearing in just four of the Bengals' first seven games, prompting him to voice his displeasure. In response, the Bengals completed a trade with the Seahawks on October 28, 2020, that sent Dunlap to Seattle for center B. J. Finney and a seventh-round pick in the 2021 NFL Draft.

Upon completion of the deal, Zac Taylor told reporters, "Carlos has done a lot of great things for this organization and the community. He deserves to go out the right way. He's being sent to a team that's really a great organization. They're in the hunt right now. They've got a great record, and he'll have a chance to help."

Expressing his appreciation to Dunlap for the way he treated him during their two-plus years together, Bengals safety Jessie Bates III said, "I think the biggest thing Carlos has taught me is learn from other guys. Obviously, Carlos has been in the league for a long time. He's a really good player. He's taught me a lot. More than just football. Off the field, just knowing the city of Cincinnati and knowing the business of the NFL. I have nothing but good things to say about Carlos. I know things didn't work out for him here at the end, but I'm sure he'll have a lot of success in Seattle. May God be with him."

Meanwhile, when asked about his final weeks in Cincinnati, Dunlap told Zach Gelb on CBS Sports Radio, "I had a million and one fans asking me why I wasn't playing, and this, that, and the third. One of my friends made me aware of an article that just came out where the coaches said I was frustrated and not handling the demotion and/or new role properly, and I just wanted to give people a clear picture of what they were asking me to do. I don't think they (people) understood how low I was on the depth chart."

Dunlap continued, "Obviously, it's not the way I would have liked to go about things, but there's a lot of love and respect still for Cincinnati. And the front office team, they still communicate and reach out from time to time. I always think I'll be welcome back one day in like the ring of honor, or whatever it is that they might invite me for, possibly for holding the records. Obviously, I'm still a Bengals fan until I play them, and I support my guys on the team."

Dunlap, who left Cincinnati with career totals of 82 1/2 sacks, 472 tackles (315 solo), 20 forced fumbles, nine fumble recoveries, two interceptions, and three touchdowns, ended up spending the rest of 2020 and all of 2021 in Seattle, recording a total of 13 1/2 sacks, before being released by the Seahawks on March 18, 2022. Subsequently signed by Kansas City, Dunlap registered four sacks in a backup role for a Chiefs team that went on to win Super Bowl LVII, after defeating the Bengals in the AFC Championship Game. A free agent again at the end of the year, Dunlap failed to hook up with another team, causing him to sit out the entire 2023 campaign. Dunlap, who, as of this writing, has yet to announce whether he plans to retire or attempt a comeback in 2024, currently boasts career totals of 100 sacks, 578 tackles (384 solo), 22 forced fumbles, nine fumble recoveries, two interceptions, and three touchdowns, compiling the vast majority of those numbers during his time in Cincinnati.

BENGALS CAREER HIGHLIGHTS

Best Season

Although Dunlap earned Pro Bowl honors for the second straight time in 2016 by batting down 15 passes and recording eight sacks, 49 tackles, and three forced fumbles, he performed slightly better the previous season, when he recorded a career-high 13 1/2 sacks, registered 55 tackles, 16 of which resulted in a loss, forced two fumbles, and recovered another.

Memorable Moments/Greatest Performances

Dunlap sealed a 27–17 victory over the Indianapolis Colts on October 16, 2011, when he recovered a fumble and ran 35 yards for a touchdown with 2:22 left in the final period.

Dunlap earned AFC Defensive Player of the Week honors by recording two strip-sacks of Philip Rivers and recovering a fumble during a 20–13 win over the Chargers on December 2, 2012.

Dunlap helped lead the Bengals to a 23–17 victory over the Ravens in the final game of the 2012 regular season by recording a sack and returning the first of his two career interceptions 14 yards for a touchdown.

Dunlap gained recognition as AFC Defensive Player of the Week for a second time by recording a sack and returning his interception of a Jacoby

Brissett pass 16 yards for a touchdown during a 24–23 win over the Colts on October 29, 2017.

Dunlap's three sacks and seven tackles during a 22–6 victory over the Jets on December 1, 2019, garnered him AFC Defensive Player of the Week honors for a third time.

Dunlap earned that honor for the fourth and final time by registering 2 1/2 sacks, making five tackles, and forcing a fumble during a 33–23 win over the Browns in the 2019 regular-season finale.

Notable Achievements

- Started 101 consecutive games from 2013 to 2019.
- Scored three defensive touchdowns.
- Finished fourth in NFL with 13 1/2 sacks in 2015.
- Led Bengals in sacks five times.
- Holds Bengals career record for most forced fumbles (20).
- Ranks among Bengals career leaders with 82 1/2 sacks (2nd) and nine fumble recoveries (tied for 10th).
- Two-time division champion (2013 and 2015).
- Member of 2010 NFL All-Rookie Team.
- Four-time AFC Defensive Player of the Week.
- 2015 Week 15 AFC Special Teams Player of the Week.
- Two-time Pro Bowl selection (2015 and 2016).

22

ANDREW WHITWORTH

Known for his longevity, tremendous leadership ability, and compassion for his fellow man, Andrew Whitworth spent 11 seasons in Cincinnati impacting the Bengals both on and off the playing field. A starter on the left side of the Bengals offensive line from 2006 to 2016, primarily at tackle, Whitworth provided superior run-blocking and pass protection for teams that made six playoff appearances and won three division titles. A three-time Pro Bowler and two-time All-Pro who missed a total of just eight games his entire time in the Queen City, Whitworth also earned three All-AFC nominations, before departing for Los Angeles, where he helped lead the Rams to two NFC titles and one world championship over the course of the next five seasons.

Born in Monroe, Louisiana, on December 12, 1981, Andrew James Whitworth began his career in football at West Monroe High School, where he served as a key member of three Louisiana Class 5A State Championship teams under head coach Don Shows. An excellent all-around athlete, Whitworth also won a junior tennis championship as a child and pitched for West Monroe High's freshman baseball team.

Ranked by CNNSI.com as the sixth-best offensive line prospect in the nation, Whitworth received a football scholarship to Louisiana State University, where, after redshirting his freshman year, he helped lead the Tigers to a 13–1 record and a BCS national title as a sophomore in 2003. Whitworth subsequently earned All-SEC First-Team honors in each of his final two seasons by going 22 straight games without allowing a sack.

Impressed with Whitworth's exceptional play at LSU, the Bengals made him the 55th overall pick of the 2006 NFL Draft when they selected him in the second round. Named the team's starting left tackle during the early stages of his rookie campaign, Whitworth performed well his first year in the league, before moving to left guard for the next two seasons. Shifted back to his more natural position of left tackle in 2009, Whitworth began an eight-year stint as the Bengals' starter at that post, missing just two

Andrew Whitworth earned three Pro Bowl selections and two All-Pro nominations during his time in Cincinnati.
Courtesy of Navin Rajagopalan

games that entire time. Meanwhile, with Whitworth serving as offensive captain for much of the period, the Bengals won three division titles and missed the playoffs just twice, advancing to the postseason tournament five consecutive seasons at one point.

An excellent run-blocker, the 6'7", 330-pound Whitworth helped a Bengals running back gain more than 1,000 yards on the ground a total of six times, with Cedric Benson (three times), Rudi Johnson (once), BenJarvus Green-Ellis (once), and Jeremy Hill (once) all surpassing that magical mark at different times. Equally proficient in pass protection, Whitworth did a magnificent job of protecting the blind side of quarterbacks Carson Palmer and Andy Dalton, surrendering no sacks and just one hit on the latter one year. Remarkably durable as well, Whitworth started 126 out of 128 contests from 2009 to 2016.

Perhaps Whitworth's greatest strength, though, lay in his extraordinary leadership ability, which caused him to accept responsibility not only for his own performance, but for the play of others as well. In discussing the burden he placed on himself, Whitworth said, "Part of my job being a leader and captain of the team is not just to play well and lead well but find a way to make everybody around me better."

Whitworth continued, "Leadership is a position where you want to create the opportunity to inspire people to walk along beside you, not listen to what you say."

An honorable man, Whitworth said on another occasion, "I've got two contracts in my life: One with my wife because we're married. And two, I've got a contract to protect Andy Dalton. I'll do both of those to the best of my ability."

A devout Christian, Whitworth found himself being driven by his faith that he rediscovered after his second NFL season, when he attended church for the first time in years. Admitting that, after growing up in a Christian home, he strayed from his beliefs, Whitworth stated, "I had lots of success as an athlete, but my personal life was a wreck. I was unfaithful to women, my family, and most importantly, to God. I thought I was strong and had everything together, but I was only fooling myself. I allowed guilt to control my life and cause me to make huge mistakes."

Recommitting to his faith after going to church one day, Whitworth recalled, "I fell to my knees and told God I was tired of running. I was ready to live the way He called me to. . . . I now live life with a new clear mind, whole heart, and a burning passion to spread Christ's love."

A true humanitarian who became involved in several charitable causes during his time in Cincinnati, Whitworth expressed his desire to help those less fortunate than himself when he said, "I think the greatest value there is in life, to me, is to be there for someone else when they need you. And I think, to me, there's no greater thing than to have the opportunity to be there, stand up for, fight for, protect someone when they need those things. . . . At the end of the day, who you are as a man is more important than who you are as a football player."

Whitworth's strong moral fiber gave him a sense of loyalty that prompted him to tell Jim Owczarski of the *Cincinnati Enquirer* after he signed a one-year contract extension with the Bengals in September 2015, "I've always wanted to be a Cincinnati Bengal, and that's still the case right now, and that's always where I wanted to play and where I wanted to finish playing. And it's the only helmet I ever wanted to wear. So, that stays true to this point, so I'm very happy."

However, Whitworth ultimately chose to leave Cincinnati and sign with the Los Angeles Rams when they offered him a three-year contract worth $11 million per season in March 2017. In explaining his decision to leave the Queen City, Whitworth admitted that the Bengals' unwillingness to offer him more than a one-year deal factored into the equation. But he added, "At one point, it was just pure loyalty, all you know is Cincinnati, and you just need to go back there because that's all you know. But then I started to really open my eyes to man, what a challenge, and a new place, that would be something that invigorates me and makes me want to push even harder and do even more, find some other part of me that I don't know exists that I can challenge myself to become. And that's what really intrigued me about the move. . . . And then when I realized I was open to moving on to a new challenge, I really wanted to be away from Cincinnati's situation. I wanted to go far away and kind of have a fresh start."

Whitworth ended up spending five seasons in Los Angeles, helping the Rams win three division titles, two NFC championships, and one NFL championship, which they claimed with a 23–20 victory over the Bengals in Super Bowl LVI.

Choosing to go out on top, the 40-year-old Whitworth announced his retirement a little over one month later, saying at the time, "The warrior in me wants to go again, but the body just doesn't. The body is tired. As driven as I am . . . it's just time to realize, while I still have the spirit and the fighting attitude, that maybe there's new people and new things, new ways that I can fight."

Whitworth added, "Over time, I started to feel that I didn't want to be a disservice to my teammates with starting to lose the ability to truly be out there, giving them what they deserve. I would never want that for them. I want them to be successful, and I want every dream they ever had to come true. If I'm in the way of that at all, that would be one of the worst things I could ever be a part of. It was just realizing it was time from a body standpoint."

Expressing his admiration for Whitworth, who won the 2021 Walter Payton NFL Man of the Year award in his final season for his extensive charitable work, mentorship of younger teammates, and strong play, Rams head coach Sean McVay called him "one of the best leaders, one of the best people, players, check the box," and added, "He changed the trajectory of this organization when he got here. . . . You want to feel real inadequate, start looking at what Andrew Whitworth has accomplished. I can't think of anything that epitomizes our team better than the way Andrew leads. He's the kind of guy that you want to be better for, because of the way he treats everyone he comes in contact with."

Since retiring from football, Whitworth, who, during his five seasons in Los Angeles, contributed to several charitable causes that included launching the "Big Whit Homes for LA Families" program, donating $50,000 to Black-owned Inglewood restaurant, The Serving Spoon, to help it stay afloat during the COVID-19 pandemic, donating $250,000 to the Los Angeles Regional Food Bank, and contributing $215,000 to the players' social justice fund, has continued to give back to his community, hosting a fundraising golf tournament in Louisiana and serving as a motivational speaker to youth groups in both his home state and Greater Cincinnati. Whitworth also serves as an analyst on Amazon Prime's *Thursday Night Football* telecasts.

BENGALS CAREER HIGHLIGHTS

Best Season

Whitworth gained First-Team All-Pro recognition for the only time as a member of the Bengals in 2015, when he helped them compile a regular-season record of 12–4 that enabled them to capture the division title. However, he committed 10 penalties, with officials flagging him for holding his opponent six times. On the other hand, when Whitworth earned Second-Team All-Pro honors the previous season for a Bengals team that advanced to the playoffs as a wild card, he committed just three penalties. Furthermore, Whitworth allowed no sacks and only one hit on quarterback Andy Dalton all year. All things considered, Whitworth turned in his most dominant performance for the Bengals in 2014.

Memorable Moments/Greatest Performances

Whitworth helped the Bengals amass season-high totals of 215 yards rushing and 448 yards of offense during a 45–10 manhandling of the Chicago Bears on October 25, 2009.

Whitworth scored the only touchdown the Bengals managed during a 23–7 loss to the Steelers on December 12, 2010, when he caught a 1-yard TD pass from Carson Palmer.

Whitworth provided ample protection for Andy Dalton during a 38–31 win over Washington on September 23, 2012, with the Bengals QB throwing for 385 yards and three touchdowns.

Whitworth's strong blocking at the point of attack helped the Bengals amass 559 yards of total offense during a 31–17 win over the Browns on October 23, 2016.

Notable Achievements

- Missed just two games from 2009 to 2016, starting 126 of 128 contests.
- Three-time division champion (2009, 2013, and 2015).
- Three-time Pro Bowl selection (2012, 2015, and 2016).
- 2015 First-Team All-Pro selection.
- 2014 Second-Team All-Pro selection.
- Two-time First-Team All-AFC selection (2014 and 2015).
- 2010 Second-Team All-AFC selection.
- Pro Football Reference All-2010s Second Team.

23

CARL PICKENS

One of the most productive wide receivers in franchise history, Carl Pickens spent eight of his nine NFL seasons in Cincinnati, amassing the third most receptions and the fourth most receiving yards in team annals during that time. The first Bengals player to catch as many as 100 passes in a season, Pickens also set a single-season franchise record that still stands when he scored 17 touchdowns in 1995. A two-time Pro Bowler and two-time All-Pro, Pickens led the Bengals in receptions and receiving yards four times each, before his criticism of the team's coaching staff bought him a ticket out of Cincinnati.

Born in the small town of Murphy, North Carolina, on March 23, 1970, Carl McNally Pickens grew up in the Smoky Mountains, some 100 miles southeast of Knoxville, Tennessee. An outstanding all-around athlete, Pickens starred in multiple sports at Murphy High School, excelling as both a wide receiver and free safety in football, a guard in basketball, and a sprinter and high jumper in track, once leaping over seven feet. Performing especially well on the gridiron, Pickens helped lead the Bulldogs to a pair of undefeated seasons and consecutive 1A state championships by recording a total of 15 interceptions, while also gaining All-America recognition from *Parade* magazine as a senior by making 71 receptions for 1,536 yards and 24 touchdowns.

Ranked by the *Atlanta Journal-Constitution* as the seventh-best high school football prospect in the country, Pickens, who also averaged 27 points per game on the court during his time at Murphy High, found himself being recruited by several major college programs in both sports as graduation neared. But, after electing to focus on football and narrowing his choices down to a few schools, Pickens decided to remain close to home and attend the University of Tennessee on a football scholarship, saying at the time, "Tennessee has a reputation for very good receivers, and I wanted to challenge myself to see if I could play here."

Carl Pickens's league-leading 17 touchdown catches in 1995 remain a single-season franchise record.

After redshirting as a freshman in 1988, Pickens played on both sides of the ball for Vols head coach Johnny Majors the following year, earning All-SEC honors by intercepting four passes on defense, catching seven passes, amassing 81 receiving yards, and scoring two touchdowns on offense, and scoring a third TD on a 93-yard kickoff return. Used exclusively at wide receiver in 1990, Pickens gained First-Team All-SEC recognition by making 53 receptions for 917 yards and six touchdowns, prompting Coach Majors to say prior to the start of the ensuing campaign, "Pickens is an exceptional athlete, probably as fine an all-around athlete as I've ever had the pleasure to coach."

Excelling once again as a junior in 1991, Pickens helped lead the Vols to a 9–3 record by making 49 receptions for 877 yards and five touchdowns, earning in the process First-Team All-America and First-Team All-SEC honors. Commenting on Pickens after watching him play against Notre Dame during an NBC telecast, former 49ers head coach turned broadcaster Bill Walsh called him "as fine a receiver as I've ever seen."

Feeling that he had nothing else to prove at the collegiate level, Pickens chose to forgo his senior year and enter the 1992 NFL Draft, where the Bengals ended up taking him in the second round, with the 31st overall pick. Starting opposite Tim McGee his first year in Cincinnati, Pickens earned NFL Offensive Rookie of the Year honors by making 26 receptions for 326 yards and one touchdown, while gaining another 229 yards and scoring a second TD returning punts. Improving upon those numbers the following year, Pickens caught 43 passes, amassed 565 receiving yards, and scored six touchdowns, despite missing three games due to injury.

Yet, even as he began to establish himself as the Bengals' top wideout, Pickens, who became known during his time at Tennessee as the "Dude with the 'Tude" because of his frequent clashes with Johnny Majors and the rest of the Vols coaching staff, occasionally displayed his volatile temperament and argumentative nature. After a middle-aged man accused him of grabbing him by the throat and throwing him against a car following a traffic mishap prior to the start of a Bengals game earlier in 1993, Pickens scuffled with Rod Woodson during a game against the Steelers after he reportedly made a mocking reference to the cornerback's interracial marriage.

Nevertheless, with Pickens performing well on the field, Bengals management chose to look the other way, especially after he began an outstanding three-year run in 1994 that saw him produce the following numbers:

YEAR	RECS	REC YDS	TD RECS
1994	71	1,127	11
1995	99	1,234	17
1996	100	1,180	12

In addition to leading the NFL with a franchise-record 17 touchdown receptions in 1995, Pickens finished third in the league in that category in each of the other two seasons. Pickens also placed third in the circuit with 100 receptions in 1996, breaking in the process his own team mark that he set one year earlier. Accorded Pro Bowl and Second-Team All-Pro honors in both 1995 and 1996, Pickens also gained All-AFC recognition all three years.

Big and strong at 6'2" and 206 pounds, Pickens knew how to use his body to ward off opposing defenders, making him extremely effective at catching balls in traffic. Also blessed with outstanding speed, Pickens possessed the ability to stretch the field and beat his man deep. Known for his competitiveness as well, Pickens received high praise from Bengals owner Mike Brown, who said, "We've never had anybody here who was more of a competitor."

Although Pickens described himself as "very low-key," he cautioned others not to misinterpret that aspect of his personality, adding, "I think a lot of people take that the wrong way. My job is to play football, and I take that very seriously. That's what I concentrate on a lot of the time."

Continuing to post solid numbers for the Bengals from 1997 to 1999, Pickens averaged 64 receptions, 818 receiving yards, and five touchdowns over that three-year stretch, performing especially well in 1998, when he caught 82 passes, amassed 1,023 receiving yards, and scored five TDs. However, with the Bengals finishing well below .500 almost every year, Pickens grew increasingly dissatisfied with the situation in Cincinnati.

Also unhappy over the fact that the Bengals' failures as a team prevented him from receiving much national exposure, Pickens stated at one point during the 1998 campaign, "You rarely see me on TV. I'm rarely asked to do stuff like that. No commercials, no endorsements or posters, and stuff like that. You just don't see it. It has been frustrating. You don't get as much notoriety. This is a team game, and when the team does well, everybody benefits from that."

Things finally came to a head between Pickens and team management in 1999, when, with the Bengals in the middle of a 4–12 season and the temperamental receiver upset over the uninspired play calling of head coach Bruce Coslet, he openly questioned why the team's coaching staff remained in place. Subsequently informed by Mike Brown that he intended to add a clause to his contract before giving him his $3.5 million signing bonus stipulating that he needed to discontinue his practice of disparaging the organization in the media if he wished to receive his bonus, Pickens remained silent for the rest of the season, before being released by the Bengals during training camp the following year.

Pickens, who left Cincinnati with career totals of 530 receptions, 6,887 receiving yards, 307 punt-return yards, 7,200 all-purpose yards, 63 touchdown receptions, and 64 TDs, signed a new five-year deal with the Tennessee Titans shortly after the Bengals waived him. However, plagued by a torn hamstring he suffered during the latter stages of the previous campaign, Pickens made just 10 receptions for 242 yards in nine games with the Titans in 2000, before being released. Following an unsuccessful attempt to earn a spot on the Dallas Cowboys roster in 2001, Pickens announced his retirement, with his agent, Steve Zucker, subsequently saying, "He had no choice. He hasn't been able to run more than 10 yards. He just can't accelerate at all."

Moving to Lawrenceville, Georgia, following his retirement from football, Pickens has remained mostly out of the spotlight the past two decades, although his name appeared in the news in 2014, when police arrested him on charges of misdemeanor battery for allegedly attacking his wife after a movie date.

BENGALS CAREER HIGHLIGHTS

Best Season

Pickens had a big year for the Bengals in 1996, placing near the top of the league rankings with 100 receptions, 1,180 receiving yards, and 12 TD catches. But he posted slightly better overall numbers the previous season, when, in addition to making 99 receptions, he established career-high marks with 1,234 receiving yards and a league-leading 17 touchdown receptions.

Memorable Moments/Greatest Performances

Although the Bengals suffered a 24–23 defeat at the hands of the Packers on September 20, 1992, Pickens scored the first touchdown of his career on a 95-yard punt return.

Pickens helped lead the Bengals to a 34–31 win over the Houston Oilers on November 13, 1994, by making 11 receptions for 188 yards and three touchdowns, which came on connections of 21, 50, and 21 yards with Jeff Blake.

Pickens gave the Bengals a 17–13 victory over Jacksonville on November 26, 1995, when he gathered in a 5-yard touchdown pass from Jeff Blake with just 17 seconds left in regulation.

Pickens earned AFC Offensive Player of the Week honors by making 11 receptions for 176 yards and three touchdowns during a 41–31 win over

Atlanta on November 24, 1996, with the longest of his TDs coming on a 61-yard connection with Jeff Blake.

Pickens and Blake combined to give the Bengals a 24–21 win over the Arizona Cardinals in the opening game of the 1997 regular season when the latter hit his favorite receiver with a 7-yard touchdown pass with just 38 seconds left on the clock.

Pickens earned his second AFC Offensive Player of the Week nomination by making 13 receptions for 204 yards and one touchdown during a 25–20 win over the Steelers on October 11, 1998, with his TD coming on a 25-yard connection with Neil O'Donnell that put the Bengals ahead to stay with less than one minute left in regulation.

Pickens gave the Bengals an 18–17 win over the Browns on October 10, 1999, when he gathered in a 2-yard TD pass from Akili Smith with just five seconds remaining in the game.

Notable Achievements

- Finished third in NFL with 100 receptions in 1996.
- Surpassed 80 receptions two other times.
- Surpassed 1,000 receiving yards four times.
- Recorded more than 10 touchdown receptions three times, leading NFL with 17 TD catches in 1995.
- Returned one punt for a touchdown.
- Led Bengals in receptions and receiving yards four times each.
- Holds Bengals single-season record for most touchdowns scored (17 in 1995).
- Ranks among Bengals career leaders with 530 receptions (3rd), 6,887 receiving yards (4th), 6,893 yards from scrimmage (7th), 7,200 all-purpose yards (6th), 388 points scored (10th), 64 touchdowns (tied for 4th), and 63 touchdown receptions (3rd).
- Member of 1992 NFL All-Rookie Team.
- 1992 NFL Offensive Rookie of the Year.
- Two-time AFC Offensive Player of the Week.
- Two-time Pro Bowl selection (1995 and 1996).
- Two-time Second-Team All-Pro selection (1995 and 1996).
- Two-time First-Team All-AFC selection (1995 and 1996).
- 1994 Second-Team All-AFC selection.

24

CRIS COLLINSWORTH

Although he is better known to younger fans of the game for his work as a color commentator on NFL football telecasts, Cris Collinsworth previously spent eight seasons in Cincinnati excelling for the Bengals at wide receiver. A tall, lanky wideout who surpassed 60 receptions five times and 1,000 receiving yards on four separate occasions, Collinsworth contributed significantly to teams that won three division titles and two AFC championships by serving as the favorite target of Ken Anderson and Boomer Esiason at different times. A three-time Pro Bowler and three-time All-Pro who ranks among the franchise's career leaders in every major pass-receiving category, Collinsworth later received the additional honor of being named to the Bengals 50th Anniversary All-Time Team.

Born in Dayton, Ohio, on January 27, 1959, Anthony Cris Collinsworth moved with his family at the age of four to Melbourne, Florida, before relocating again nine years later to Titusville, Florida. A four-sport athlete at Astronaut High School, Collinsworth earned letters in baseball, basketball, football, and track, proving to be especially proficient in the last two sports. A three-year letterman in track, Collinsworth won the Florida High School Athletic Association Class 3A 100-yard dash state championship as a senior in 1976. Meanwhile, Collinsworth gained High School All-America recognition that same year for his exceptional play at quarterback.

Recruited by several major colleges as graduation neared, Collinsworth ultimately accepted an athletic scholarship to the University of Florida, where he spent most of his collegiate career playing for head coach Doug Dickey. However, after spending his first season in Gainesville assuming the role of a run-first quarterback in the Gators' run-heavy option system, Collinsworth moved to wide receiver when Dickey switched to a pro set offense prior to the start of his sophomore year.

Making a seamless transition to his new post, Collinsworth gained First-Team All-SEC recognition in each of his final three seasons and earned

Cris Collinsworth surpassed 1,000 receiving yards four times as a member of the Bengals.

All-America honors as a senior in 1980, when he caught 40 passes, amassed 599 receiving yards, and scored three touchdowns. Collinsworth, who, in his last three years with the Gators, made 120 receptions for 1,977 yards and 14 touchdowns, rushed for 210 yards, and gained another 791 yards and scored one touchdown on special teams, excelled in the classroom as well, earning Academic All-America honors three straight times from 1978 to 1980.

Praising his team's top wideout, Charlie Pell, who served as head coach at Florida in Collinsworth's senior year, said, "There are guys who can run as fast, leap as high, and catch as well. But to give 100 percent all the time, that's unique. Even in practice, if the play calls for him to go 35 yards and break at a 30-degree angle, that's precisely what he does. All out, all the time."

Selected by the Bengals in the second round of the 1981 NFL Draft, with the 37th overall pick, one round after they made David Verser of Kansas the first receiver to hear his name called, Collinsworth remembered how he felt about going to Cincinnati: "I was more scared about making the team than anything else. They picked Verser, and they already had Isaac Curtis, Pat McInally, and Steve Kreider. There weren't many openings left. I think the fear of being rejected helped me a lot. I was geared up. One day in camp I must have done something good, because they put me at No. 1. I said to myself, 'Well, you've gone and done it now. You'll have to kill me to get me out of here.'"

Although the 6'5", 192-pound Collinsworth hardly looked the part of an NFL player, he proved himself worthy of a second-round selection his first year in the league, earning a spot on the 1981 NFL All-Rookie Team, a trip to the Pro Bowl, and a Second-Team All-Pro nomination by making 67 receptions for 1,009 yards and eight touchdowns, with his outstanding play helping the Bengals win their first AFC championship.

Surprising many NFL scouts with his exceptional performance, Collinsworth recalled, "One of the scouting reports said I might not be physical enough to play in the NFL. I could understand that. My skinny ol' body won't win any prizes. When I took the physicals, I couldn't believe some of those linemen. The receivers were ashamed to take off their shirts. But if the guy who said that would like to line up across from me, I'd be glad to show him how physical I can be."

Collinsworth even forced Bengals head coach Forrest Gregg to change his opinion of him, with Gregg, who initially had concerns over the gangly receiver's ability to be effective against the bump-and-run technique employed by many NFL defensive backs at the time, saying at one point during the 1981 season, "I was wrong. After the first preseason game, I knew he was tough enough. He gets laid out, but he bounces back up. . . . He's far ahead of any rookie I've ever coached. I don't think there's a limit on how good he can be."

Bengals backup quarterback Jack Thompson added, "He'll [Collinsworth] sell out his body to get the ball."

Meanwhile, Bengals GM Paul Brown likened Collinsworth to former NFL receiver Dub Jones, whom he previously coached in Cleveland, saying, "He's built like Jones, he's intelligent, and he's a sprinter."

Adding that he considered Collinsworth to be "a natural," Brown stated, "He plays like he's been here five years."

Continuing to perform well during the strike-shortened 1982 campaign, Collinsworth again earned Pro Bowl and Second-Team All-Pro honors by ranking among the league leaders with 49 receptions and 700 receiving yards. A Pro Bowler and Second-Team All-Pro for the third straight time in 1983, Collinsworth made 66 receptions for 1,130 yards and five touchdowns, before gathering in 64 passes, amassing 989 receiving yards, and scoring six TDs the following year.

As Collinsworth established himself as one of the NFL's top wideouts, he continued to make believers out of those who previously doubted him, with Anthony Muñoz saying, "Right away, I learned it didn't matter how lean, how skinny; the guy is one of the toughest guys I've ever seen play the game."

Meanwhile, Boomer Esiason spoke of his former teammate's intelligence and calm demeanor, stating, "He always had a nice communication way about him on the sideline that was calming. Probably to this day, the smartest football player that I've ever played with on the field."

Collinsworth remained a force-to-be-reckoned-with for two more seasons, making 65 receptions for 1,125 yards and five touchdowns in 1985, before catching 62 passes, amassing 1,024 receiving yards, and scoring a career-high 10 TDs the following year. But, after Collinsworth received less playing time in each of the next two seasons, the Bengals cut him just prior to the start of the 1989 campaign. In explaining the team's decision, head coach Sam Wyche said, "Cris has been an important part of the franchise over the years, but there comes a time when cold, hard, tough decisions have to be made, and you make them. Cris has taken a lot of hits, and we thought some younger guys could hold up better."

Announcing his retirement shortly thereafter, Collinsworth, who ended his playing career with 417 receptions, 6,698 receiving yards, and 36 touchdown catches, moved directly into broadcasting, becoming one of the co-hosts of HBO's *Inside the NFL*, a position he retained for nearly two decades. While still serving in that capacity in 1998, Collinsworth joined the *NFL on Fox* team, with whom he spent the next several years doing color commentary and hosting the network's NFL Sunday pregame show. Eventually moving to NBC, Collinsworth replaced John Madden as the color commentator on NBC's *Sunday Night Football* telecasts following the latter's retirement in 2009. Praised by his longtime broadcast partner Al Michaels for his knowledge and dedication to his profession, Collinsworth, said Michaels, "understands the game so thoroughly, and he's done such an enormous amount of homework. He sees things that I don't think any other analyst does."

In addition to his work as a broadcaster, Collinsworth, who currently lives with his wife, Holly, in Fort Thomas, Kentucky, is majority owner of Pro Football Focus, which, utilizing a complicated formula, evaluates the performance of every NFL and college player. Collinsworth also participates in several charitable causes, including the Cris Collinsworth ProScan Fund, which helps promote breast cancer awareness, provides breast cancer services, and supplies unique opportunities for children to enhance their intellectual development.

CAREER HIGHLIGHTS

Best Season

Although Collinsworth amassed more receiving yards (1,130) in 1983 and scored more touchdowns (10) in 1986, he made his greatest overall impact as a rookie in 1981, when he helped lead the Bengals to their first division title in nearly a decade and a date with the San Francisco 49ers in Super Bowl XVI by making 67 receptions for 1,009 yards and eight TDs, earning in the process a runner-up finish to New Orleans Saints running back George Rogers in the NFL Offensive Rookie of the Year voting.

Memorable Moments/Greatest Performances

Collinsworth went over 100 receiving yards for the first time in his career during a 27–24 overtime victory over the Bills on September 27, 1981, finishing the game with 10 catches for 111 yards and one touchdown.

Collinsworth contributed to a 30–28 win over the Atlanta Falcons in the 1981 regular-season opener by making five receptions for 128 yards and one touchdown, which came on a career-long 74-yard connection with Ken Anderson.

Collinsworth scored what proved to be the game-winning touchdown of a 28–21 victory over the Bills in the divisional round of the 1981 playoffs when he gathered in a 16-yard TD pass from Ken Anderson in the fourth quarter.

Collinsworth starred in defeat on October 2, 1983, making eight receptions for a career-high 206 yards and one touchdown during a 34–31 loss to the Baltimore Colts.

Collinsworth helped lead the Bengals to a 35–14 win over Atlanta on November 25, 1984, by making six receptions for 134 yards and two touchdowns, the longest of which covered 57 yards.

Although the Bengals lost to the Chargers, 44–41, on September 22, 1985, Collinsworth had a huge game, making 10 receptions for 161 yards and two touchdowns.

Collinsworth contributed to a 55–21 blowout of the Jets in the final game of the 1986 regular season by making five receptions for 95 yards and three touchdowns, collaborating with Boomer Esiason on scoring plays of 12, 42, and 21 yards.

Notable Achievements

- Surpassed 60 receptions five times.
- Surpassed 1,000 receiving yards four times.
- Scored 10 touchdowns in 1986.
- Finished fourth in NFL with 49 receptions and 700 receiving yards in 1982.
- Led Bengals in receptions five times and receiving yards six times.
- Ranks among Bengals career leaders with 417 receptions (6th), 6,698 receiving yards (5th), 6,683 yards from scrimmage (9th), 6,683 all-purpose yards (11th), and 36 touchdown receptions (tied for 7th).
- Three-time division champion (1981, 1982, and 1988).
- Two-time AFC champion (1981 and 1988).
- Member of 1981 NFL All-Rookie Team.
- Finished second in 1981 NFL Offensive Rookie of the Year voting.
- Three-time Pro Bowl selection (1981, 1982, and 1983).
- Three-time Second-Team All-Pro selection (1981, 1982, and 1983).
- 1983 First-Team All-AFC selection.
- Three-time Second-Team All-AFC selection (1981, 1982, and 1985).
- Named to Bengals 50th Anniversary All-Time Team in 2017.

25

BOB TRUMPY

The only Bengals player to earn both AFL All-Star and NFL Pro Bowl honors on multiple occasions, Bob Trumpy helped to redefine the position of tight end with his ability to make big plays downfield. Joining the Bengals in their inaugural season of 1968, Trumpy spent his entire 10-year career in Cincinnati, leading the team in receptions and receiving yards twice each, while also posting the second-highest single-season yards per catch average in franchise history. A major contributor to the Bengals' first two division championship teams, Trumpy appeared in four All-Star/Pro Bowl games and earned one All-AFL selection and one All-AFC nomination, before being further honored by being named to the Bengals 50th Anniversary All-Time Team.

Born in Springfield, Illinois, on March 6, 1945, Robert Theodore Trumpy Jr. starred in multiple sports at Springfield High School, excelling in football, basketball, and track-and-field. Competing in four different state tournaments while in high school, Trumpy started for head basketball coach Ray Page's 1959 state championship team, won the 1963 state meet in the long jump, and tied for fifth in that year's high jump.

Choosing to focus more on football after he enrolled at the University of Illinois, Trumpy spent just one season playing wide receiver for the Fighting Illini, before transferring to the University of Utah. Forced to sit out the 1965 season, Trumpy subsequently moved to tight end when he returned to action the following year, catching only nine passes for 159 yards and two touchdowns in an offense that relied heavily on its running game.

Drafted into the US Navy following his graduation in 1966, Trumpy spent six months serving in the military during the Vietnam War, before being discharged early in 1967. Trumpy then moved to Southern California, where he worked as a bill collector until the Bengals selected him in the 12th round of the 1968 NFL/AFL Common Draft, with the 301st overall pick.

Bob Trumpy excelled for the Bengals at tight end both prior to and following the AFL/NFL merger.

Recalling that period in his life, Trumpy said, "At the time I was drafted, I was collecting bills for Beneficial Finance out of 607 Hill Street in downtown Los Angeles. . . . The disadvantage was I was a 12th-round draft pick. The advantage was I went to a team that had no roster."

Although Trumpy had yet to fully develop his pass-receiving skills, he gained confidence as a pass-catcher prior to the start of his first pro training camp with the help of NFL quarterback Zeke Bratkowski. Revealing that he and Bratkowski formed a bond after he discovered the veteran signal-caller working out with several other players at a junior college one day, Trumpy remembered, "I stopped one day, and the workout was being run by Bart Starr's backup, Zeke Bratkowski. We worked out six days a week, and I ran the Green Bay Packers' patterns. I was really the only receiver Zeke had to throw to, so we became buds."

Trumpy continued, "The last day we worked out together, he said, 'You know, I gotta tell you, we like big receivers,' and on their team at the time was Max McGee, Boyd Dowler, and (tight end) Marv Fleming. He said, 'You know, you could make our team. I'm going to tell those scouts, if your name shows up on the waiver wire, give this kid a chance.'"

Recalling the confidence that Bratkowski's words instilled in him, Trumpy said, "Here's Bart Starr's backup telling me I could make the (defending Super Bowl champion) Green Bay Packers. I show up in Cincinnati in great condition with an emotional feeling that, 'Wait a minute, I've got as good of a chance as anyone else to make this team.' I did and played 10 years."

Arriving at his first training camp weighing just 208 pounds, the 6'6" Trumpy, who eventually added some 20 pounds onto his frame, fooled the team's coaching staff at weigh-in by sneaking a 10-pound weight onto the scale with him under a towel, remembering, "I was actually 208, I weighed in at 218."

After laying claim to the starting tight end job, Trumpy quickly developed into one of the league's top players at his position, earning a trip to the AFL All-Star game as a rookie by making 37 receptions for 639 yards and three touchdowns. Even more productive in 1969, Trumpy caught 37 passes and ranked among the league leaders with 835 receiving yards and nine TD catches, earning in the process First-Team All-AFL honors and his second AFL All-Star nomination.

Crediting his early success to then-Bengals receivers coach Bill Walsh, the architect of the West Coast offense he later popularized in San Francisco, Trumpy said, "I had speed for a guy who was, at that time, 6 foot 6, maybe 215 (pounds); I could get down the field. I give all the credit in the world to Bill Walsh for recognizing and realizing that I shouldn't just line up next to a tackle on every down. I followed his orders; he moved me all over the place, and it blew up defenses all over the American Football League."

Unlike most other tight ends of the day, Trumpy did not merely serve as an extension of the offensive line. Although he proved to be a willing blocker despite his somewhat slender frame, Trumpy made his greatest contributions to the Bengals with his ability to stretch the field. Too quick for opposing linebackers to guard, and too big and strong for opposing defensive backs to cover one-on-one, Trumpy proved to be a matchup nightmare, often beating his man deep downfield, outmuscling his smaller defender for the football, or turning short passes into long gains. As a result, Trumpy became very much the prototype for the modern-day tight end, even though the style of play employed at the time limited him to relatively modest numbers.

Continuing to perform well following the merger of the two leagues, Trumpy earned Pro Bowl and First-Team All-AFC honors in 1970 by making 29 receptions for 480 yards and two touchdowns for the AFC Central Division champions. Trumpy followed that up with two more solid seasons, totaling 84 receptions, 1,031 receiving yards, and five TD catches from 1971 to 1972, before being named to his final Pro Bowl in 1973 after catching 29 passes, amassing 435 receiving yards, and making five touchdown receptions. Trumpy remained with the Bengals for four more years, assuming a somewhat diminished role on offense after Isaac Curtis established himself as the team's top receiving threat, before announcing his retirement following the conclusion of the 1977 campaign with career totals of 298 receptions, 4,600 receiving yards, and 35 touchdown catches.

Transitioning seamlessly into a career in broadcasting following his playing days, Trumpy became a color analyst for telecasts of AFC games at NBC, where he spent the next 11 years teaming up at different times with play-by-play announcers Sam Nover (1978–1980), Bob Costas (1981–1983), and Don Criqui (1984–1988), while also hosting a weeknight sports talk show on WLW-AM in Cincinnati. Replacing Bill Walsh as the lead NFL analyst at NBC in 1992, Trumpy worked alongside Dick Enberg for the next four years, during which time he helped call Super Bowls XXVII and XXVIII. Trumpy remained with NBC until 1997, when the station lost the AFC package to CBS. After two years off, Trumpy became an analyst for *Sunday Night Football* on Westwood One radio, where he remained until 2007, when he retired to private life. The father of two sons and grandfather to six grandchildren, the 79-year-old Trumpy currently lives with his wife, Pat, in the Cincinnati suburb of Glendale, Ohio.

CAREER HIGHLIGHTS

Best Season

Although Trumpy made a few more receptions in 1971 and 1972, he had his finest all-around season in 1969, when he gained consensus All-AFL recognition by catching 37 passes and establishing career-high marks with 835 receiving yards and nine touchdown receptions, while also posting an average of 22.6 yards per catch that ranks as the second-highest single-season mark in franchise history (Eddie Brown averaged 24.0 yards per reception in 1988).

Memorable Moments/Greatest Performances

Trumpy contributed to a 24–10 win over the Denver Broncos on September 15, 1968, by making four receptions for 114 yards and scoring the first touchdown of his career on a 58-yard connection with quarterback John Stofa that also represented the first TD pass in franchise history.

Although Trumpy made just one reception during a 38–21 win over the Dolphins on November 17, 1968, it went for an 80-yard touchdown.

Trumpy helped the Bengals earn a 34–20 victory over the Chargers on September 21, 1969, by making three receptions for 118 yards and one TD, which came on a 78-yard catch-and-run.

Trumpy contributed to a 24–19 victory over the Chiefs on September 28, 1969, by making four receptions for 100 yards and one touchdown, which came on an 80-yard connection with Sam Wyche early in the fourth quarter that put the Bengals ahead to stay.

Trumpy helped the Bengals forge a 31–31 tie with the Houston Oilers on November 9, 1969, by making five receptions for 159 yards and three touchdowns, hooking up with Greg Cook on scoring plays of 44, 70, and 14 yards.

Notable Achievements

- Ranked among AFL leaders with 835 receiving yards (6th), nine touchdowns (5th), and an average of 22.6 yards per reception (3rd) in 1969.
- Led Bengals in receptions and receiving yards twice each.
- Ranks among Bengals career leaders with 4,600 receiving yards (11th) and 35 touchdown receptions (9th).
- Two-time division champion (1970 and 1973).

- Two-time AFL All-Star selection (1968 and 1969).
- Two-time Pro Bowl selection (1970 and 1973).
- 1969 First-Team All-AFL selection.
- 1970 First-Team All-AFC selection.
- Named to Bengals 50th Anniversary All-Time Team in 2017.

26

DAVID FULCHER

A hard-hitting defensive back who helped revolutionize the safety position during the late 1980s and early 1990s with the unique role he played in defensive coordinator Dick LeBeau's innovative zone blitz scheme, David Fulcher spent seven seasons in Cincinnati excelling at strong safety for the Bengals. Often referred to as "a safety in a linebacker's body," Fulcher roamed the secondary with abandon, delivering vicious hits to opposing receivers and running backs, while also doing an outstanding job of tracking the football. A member of teams that won two division titles and one AFC championship, Fulcher led the Bengals in interceptions four times and tackles twice, ending his career with the third most picks in franchise history. A three-time Pro Bowler and three-time All-Pro, Fulcher later received the additional honor of being named to the Bengals 50th Anniversary All-Time Team.

Born in Los Angeles, California, on September 28, 1964, David Dwayne Fulcher grew up on the city's south side, where he starred in multiple sports while attending John C. Fremont High School. Excelling on the gridiron at wide receiver and the diamond at both catcher and first base, Fulcher had an opportunity to pursue a career in baseball when the Atlanta Braves drafted him in 1982. But, after learning of Atlanta's plans to put him behind the plate, Fulcher chose not to sign with the Braves, recalling, "When I became a senior, after I got out of high school, I got drafted by Atlanta to play catcher, and I didn't want to catch. In high school, I had this big growing pain from 5'10" to 6'2", and my knees were killing me. So, I played first base my senior year in high school, and they still drafted me as a catcher, and I didn't want to play catcher, and my dad wanted me to play baseball. But, fortunate for me, Arizona State said, 'We'll give you an opportunity to play football,' and I got a scholarship to go there and play."

Choosing Arizona State over USC and UCLA because both California schools wanted him to play defensive back, Fulcher remembered, "I'd been

David Fulcher earned Pro Bowl and All-Pro honors three times each during his time in Cincinnati with his outstanding play at safety.

a wide receiver my whole life. Arizona State was the only school who was recruiting me as a receiver."

However, with the ASU coaching staff seeing something special in him, Fulcher ended up moving to the secondary shortly after he arrived in Tempe, later admitting, "I wasn't too happy about the move. It meant I had to hit people."

Before long, though, Fulcher came to enjoy his new position, saying, "Once I started hitting people, I started liking it. . . . It turned out to be for the best. Sometimes you have to look at a player and put him in a position to best succeed . . . and ASU did just that for me."

After earning Second-Team All-America honors as a freshman, Fulcher gained consensus First-Team recognition in each of the next two seasons, becoming known during his college career for his punishing tackles and superior cover skills. Earning the nickname "Fo-Rock" after tackling an opposing wide receiver in a game against New Mexico State University, Fulcher explained how he acquired his moniker: "The guy laid there for a while, then got up and was dizzy. Then he said, 'Man, I feel like I ran into a rock.' My teammates started calling me 'Rock.' A lot of people, when they pronounce my last name, say 'Fo-cher.' So, I just put the 'Fo' in front of Rock."

Commenting on Fulcher's exceptional play for the Sun Devils, Edward Beaudet, a high school football standout in Mesa, Arizona, during the former's time at ASU, remembered, "The guy just seemed to be all over the field. Wherever the ball was, Fulcher was certainly nearby, and he hit people like no one else."

Declaring himself eligible for the 1986 NFL Draft at the end of his junior year after recording 12 interceptions and 293 total tackles in his three seasons at ASU, Fulcher saw his name come off the board in the third round, when the Bengals selected him with the 78th overall pick. While many NFL observers anticipated a move to inside linebacker for the 6'3", 236-pound Fulcher, Bengals defensive coordinator Dick LeBeau instead decided to take advantage of his size and speed in the secondary by creating the zone blitz—a defensive scheme that has since become extremely popular throughout the league.

Functioning very much like a combination linebacker/safety, Fulcher usually lined up close to the line of scrimmage, where he had the option of either defending against the run, rushing the opposing quarterback, or dropping into pass coverage. Displaying an affinity for his new role his first year in the league, Fulcher earned a spot on the 1986 NFL All-Rookie Team by intercepting four passes, recovering one fumble, and recording two sacks. After picking off another three passes and registering three more sacks the following year, Fulcher helped lead the Bengals to the AFC championship in 1988 by recording five interceptions and scoring one touchdown, earning in the process Pro Bowl, All-Pro, and All-AFC honors for the first of three straight times. Although the Bengals subsequently lost Super Bowl XXIII to the San Francisco 49ers in the closing moments, Fulcher acquitted himself extremely well during the contest, making several key tackles, registering a sack, and forcing a fumble that his team recovered.

Later saying that he experienced his most memorable NFL moment prior to the start of the game, Fulcher stated, "It was the time they called my name during the introductions at the Super Bowl. Walking out of the tunnel at Joe Robbie Stadium, making sure I did not trip on the turf and fall down."

Despite a rather mediocre 8–8 showing by the Bengals in 1989, Fulcher turned in the finest all-around performance of his career, finishing second in the NFL with eight interceptions, while also recovering four fumbles and leading the team with 107 tackles. Fulcher then helped the Bengals return to the playoffs the following year by picking off four passes, forcing three fumbles, and recording 53 solo tackles.

Although Fulcher became better known for his ability to deliver hard hits to the opposition, he proved to be an outstanding ball-hawk as well, recording at least three interceptions in each of his seven seasons in Cincinnati. In discussing his propensity for picking off passes, Fulcher said, "I just found a way. As Dick LeBeau used to tell me, 'You just gotta' make plays,' and I made plays."

Fulcher continued, "I played basketball on the football field. I went up for a rebound, and, when the ball was up, I was gonna' get the rebound, and that's how I did what I did. . . . It was just having a knack for where the ball was going . . . being in the right place at the right time, and I credit a lot of that to Dick LeBeau because of the zone blitz and just the defense."

While Fulcher credited LeBeau for much of his success, Cincinnati's former defensive coordinator deflected praise to his one-time protégé, saying, "David Fulcher was a unique athlete. Very big for his position, but also very talented. Blitzing with him was one of the ways we expanded the possibilities of the fire zone, and it was very effective."

Fulcher spent two more seasons in Cincinnati, recording four interceptions, leading the team with 68 solo tackles, forcing four fumbles (three of which he recovered), and scoring a touchdown in 1991, before signing with the Los Angeles Raiders as a free agent after he intercepted another three passes the following year. Injured for most of 1993, Fulcher appeared in only three games with the Raiders, before announcing his retirement at the end of the year with career totals of 31 interceptions, 246 interception-return yards, 10 forced fumbles, nine fumble recoveries, 8 1/2 sacks, and two touchdowns, compiling all those numbers as a member of the Bengals.

Following his playing days, Fulcher remained in Cincinnati, where he founded the nonprofit organization, Mentoring Against Negative Actions, which seeks to teach prison inmates life skills and raises awareness of the fight against multiple sclerosis. Fulcher also later became the alumni president for the Walter Camp Football Foundation, served as head football coach at Cincinnati Christian High School from 2011 to 2015, and assumed the same role at Cincinnati Christian University for two years. Fulcher has spent the last few years serving as campus coordinator at Mason High School, where he does everything from helping in the classroom to traffic control.

Looking back on his playing career, Fulcher said, "I think my career was really good. I had fun—I just wish I could have played longer. I was one of the first juniors to get drafted and go to the NFL. Back then, you didn't really want to get drafted and play for Cincinnati. I was shocked when they drafted me. But they gave me an opportunity, and it worked out very well for me."

BENGALS CAREER HIGHLIGHTS

Best Season

Although Fulcher had several outstanding seasons, he reached the apex of his career in 1989, when he earned his lone First-Team All-Pro nomination by establishing career-high marks with eight interceptions, 87 interception-return yards, 107 tackles, and four fumble recoveries.

Memorable Moments/Greatest Performances

Fulcher recorded the first two interceptions of his career during a 31–28 win over the Houston Oilers on October 19, 1986.

Although the Bengals lost to the Browns, 23–16, on October 30, 1988, Fulcher scored the first of his two career touchdowns when he returned his pick of a Bernie Kosar pass 16 yards for a TD.

Fulcher earned AFC Defensive Player of the Week honors for the first of four times by recording three interceptions during a 21–17 win over the Kansas City Chiefs on October 1, 1989.

In addition to recording an interception during a 21–0 shutout of the Browns on December 3, 1989, Fulcher helped limit Cleveland to just 88 yards rushing, earning in the process his second AFC Defensive Player of the Week nomination.

Fulcher received that honor again just two weeks later after picking off Warren Moon twice and Cody Carlson once during a 61–7 rout of the Oilers on December 17, 1989.

Fulcher earned AFC Defensive Player of the Week honors for the final time by recording an interception and sacking quarterback Ken O'Brien in the end zone for a safety during a 25–20 win over the Jets in the 1990 regular-season opener.

Fulcher scored the only touchdown the Bengals managed during a 17–10 loss to the Steelers on December 15, 1991, when he ran 27 yards to pay dirt after picking off a Bubby Brister pass.

Notable Achievements

- Scored two defensive touchdowns.
- Recorded three interceptions in one game twice.
- Recorded 107 tackles in 1989.
- Finished second in NFL with eight interceptions in 1989.
- Led Bengals in interceptions four times and tackles twice.
- Ranks among Bengals career leaders with 31 interceptions (3rd), 246 interception-return yards (9th), and nine fumble recoveries (tied for 10th).
- Two-time division champion (1988 and 1990).
- 1988 AFC champion.
- Member of 1986 NFL All-Rookie Team.
- Four-time AFC Defensive Player of the Week.
- Two-time NFL Defensive Player of the Week.
- December 1989 AFC Defensive Player of the Month.
- Three-time Pro Bowl selection (1988, 1989, and 1990).
- 1989 First-Team All-Pro selection.
- Two-time Second-Team All-Pro selection (1988 and 1990).
- Three-time First-Team All-AFC selection (1988, 1989, and 1990).
- Named to Bengals 40th Anniversary All-Time Team in 2007.
- Named to Bengals 50th Anniversary All-Time Team in 2017.

27

LOUIS BREEDEN

An outstanding cover-corner who spent his entire 10-year NFL career in Cincinnati, Louis Breeden combined with Ken Riley much of that time to give the Bengals one of the league's finest cornerback tandems. Second only to Riley in franchise history in interceptions and interception-return yards, Breeden led the Bengals in picks three times, intercepting seven passes in a season twice. A sure tackler as well, Breeden brought down opposing ball-carriers more times than any other Bengals defensive back on three separate occasions, with his stellar all-around play making him a significant contributor to teams that won two division titles and one AFC championship.

Born in Hamlet, North Carolina, on October 26, 1953, Louis Everett Breeden attended Hamlet High School, where he starred in multiple sports, excelling in football, basketball, and track. Particularly outstanding on the gridiron, Breeden performed well enough on both sides of the ball to earn an athletic scholarship to North Carolina Central University, a small, historically Black college located some 90 miles north, in Durham, North Carolina. A four-year starter for the Eagles at safety, Breeden recorded a total of 17 interceptions, earning in the process All–Mid-Eastern Athletic Conference (MEAC) honors three times. Named to the second team in 1974 and the first team in each of the next two seasons, Breeden also excelled on special teams, averaging 20.2 yards per punt return during his college career.

Selected by the Bengals in the seventh round of the 1977 NFL Draft, with the 187th overall pick, Breeden ended up spending the entire 1977 season on injured reserve, during which time starting cornerbacks Ken Riley and Lemar Parrish counseled him on the art of playing corner. Recalling the mentorship that he received from Riley and Parrish, Breeden, who never played any position other than safety in college, said, "Our defensive backs coach then in Cincinnati was a former head coach—he knew the game but didn't know much about the position. Lemar Parrish

Louis Breeden ranks second in franchise history in both interceptions and interception-return yards.

and Kenny—they taught me most of what I learned. I watched Kenny, and he'd talk to me a lot about the position."

Named the starter at left cornerback the following year after the Bengals traded Parrish to Washington, Breeden described how he landed the starting job: "The first season I was hurt, but my second season I came back and there were rumors I was going to replace Riley—but he wasn't going anywhere. Parrish was gone, and they were looking to replace him with Mel Morgan. I remember in practice I was covering Isaac (Curtis), and he ran by our defensive coach, and as he did, he yelled to the coach, 'You got your two best defensive backs on the same side!' I was on the same side behind Riley then. Well, the next day they moved me over to the other side, and I started the next 10 years."

Performing well in his first full season at his new position, Breeden picked off three passes, recorded a sack, recovered a fumble, and led all Bengals defensive backs with 69 tackles and 12 passes defended. Plagued by injuries in 1979, Breeden took a step backward, failing to intercept a single pass in the 10 games he started. But he rebounded nicely the following year, recording a team-high seven interceptions, which he returned a total of 91 yards. Breeden had another solid season in 1981, intercepting four passes, amassing 145 interception-return yards, recovering a fumble, and scoring the first of his two career touchdowns for the AFC champions, before earning First-Team All-Pro honors during the strike-shortened 1982 campaign by picking off two passes, registering a sack, and ranking among the team leaders in tackles.

Although Breeden stood just 5'11" and weighed only 185 pounds, he proved to be a hard hitter and a sure tackler, rarely allowing ball-carriers to escape once he got his hands on them. Blessed with good speed and superior ball-tracking abilities, Breeden also excelled in pass coverage, performing equally well in a zone scheme or as a man-to-man defender. Registering a total of 33 interceptions over the course of his career, Breeden did an excellent job of creating turnovers. Yet, he felt that he should have recorded many more picks, saying jokingly when asked about the discrepancy in the number of interceptions recorded by him and Ken Riley (65), "Kenny caught his. I dropped 300. If I would have caught 70 percent of the ones that hit my hands, I would have beaten Ken Riley by 50 [interceptions]. Ken Riley would pick at me all the time about the balls that I dropped. I would get to balls, and I'd drop so many interceptions, but Ken Riley had a remarkable ability to track the football and catch it and bring it in, and bring it over to the sideline, and I had a great knack for knocking it down or letting it hit me in the helmet."

Breeden remained one of the league's better corners for four more years, recording a total of 15 interceptions for the Bengals from 1983 to 1986, with his seven picks in the last of those campaigns matching his single-season high. But after being limited by injuries to just eight games and two starts in 1987, Breeden chose to announce his retirement, ending his career with 33 interceptions, 558 interception-return yards, three fumble recoveries, four sacks, two touchdowns, and an unknown number of tackles.

Following his playing days, Breeden remained in Cincinnati, where he became a part-time broadcaster and the owner of an advertising company he named Louis Breeden Promotions, saying during a 2022 interview, "I retired about nine years ago. After I was out of football, I did the Bengals pre- and post-game shows on the radio and was a TV analyst for Louisville's football games. At the same time, I had an advertising company that I ran for over 10 years."

In discussing his health, Breeden stated, "I had some challenges over the past few years. I have atrial fibrillation and had two unsuccessful cardiac ablations. I had the third a few months ago, and I've felt the best I have in years—knock on wood. A lot of people have atrial fibrillation—I had mine for the last 30 years—after football. I had an irregular heartbeat but no symptoms until recently, when it started to really bother me—that's when it can be really dangerous. . . . I feel now like I did when I was nearsighted and got glasses—I remember looking outside and thinking, 'Wow, this is what the world looks like!' I feel good now."

CAREER HIGHLIGHTS

Best Season

Although Breeden earned his lone All-Pro nomination in 1982, he appeared in only six games due to a players' strike. That being the case, Breeden made more of an impact in 1980, 1981, and 1986, compiling better overall numbers in each of those campaigns. Even though Breeden picked off seven passes in both 1980 and 1986, we'll opt for 1981 since he returned his four interceptions for a total of 145 yards and one touchdown, with his 145 interception-return yards representing the second-highest single-season total in franchise history.

Memorable Moments/Greatest Performances

Breeden helped lead the Bengals to a 17–14 overtime victory over the Bears on December 14, 1980, by recording three interceptions, which he returned a total of 70 yards.

Breeden starred again during a 40–17 rout of the San Diego Chargers on November 8, 1981, earning NFL Defensive Player of the Week honors by recovering a fumble and recording two interceptions, one of which he returned 102 yards for a touchdown. Breeden's 102-yard pick-six remained the longest play in Bengals history until safety Brandon Williams returned a kickoff 103 yards for a touchdown 39 years later.

Breeden contributed to a 24–10 win over the Los Angeles Rams on November 15, 1981, by picking off another two passes.

Breeden recorded another pair of interceptions during a 22–20 win over the Steelers on November 11, 1984, returning his two picks a total of 70 yards.

Breeden earned AFC Defensive Player of the Week honors by returning one of his two interceptions 36 yards for a touchdown during a 34–7 win over Seattle on November 16, 1986.

Notable Achievements

- Scored two defensive touchdowns.
- Recorded seven interceptions in a season twice.
- Amassed 145 interception-return yards in 1981.
- Led Bengals in interceptions three times.
- Ranks second in franchise history with 33 interceptions and 558 interception-return yards.
- Two-time division champion (1981 and 1982).
- 1981 AFC champion.
- 1981 Week 10 NFL Defensive Player of the Week.
- 1986 Week 11 AFC Defensive Player of the Week.
- 1982 First-Team All-Pro selection.

28

CARSON PALMER

The first quarterback in NFL history to throw for more than 4,000 yards in a season with three different teams, Carson Palmer accomplished the feat twice during his time in Cincinnati, where he spent the first half of his professional career. Starting behind center for the Bengals from 2004 to 2010, Palmer amassed more than 3,800 yards through the air in four of those seven seasons, earning in the process two Pro Bowl selections and one top-five finish in the league MVP voting. The central figure on teams that won two division titles, Palmer ranks among the franchise's all-time leaders in every major passing category. Nevertheless, the former Heisman Trophy winner left Cincinnati a hated man after threatening to retire due to his dissatisfaction with the way upper management ran the organization.

Born in Fresno, California, on December 27, 1979, Carson Hilton Palmer grew up some 110 miles southwest, in the city of Santa Margarita, where his father enrolled him in private classes for aspiring young quarterbacks after he displayed tremendous arm strength during his early teenage years. Continuing to hone his skills at Santa Margarita Catholic High School, Palmer performed so well for the freshman team that members of the varsity squad often halted practice to watch him play.

Approached by several major colleges at the end of his junior year, Palmer received scholarship offers from, among others, the University of Southern California, Notre Dame, Colorado, and Miami (Florida). Ultimately deciding to attend USC after he earned First-Team All-League honors in his final season by leading Santa Margarita to its second straight CIF (California Interscholastic Federation) championship, Palmer ended up starting behind center for the Trojans for four years, during which time he set or tied 33 Pac-10 and USC total offense and passing records. Particularly outstanding his senior year, Palmer finished first in the Heisman Trophy balloting and gained consensus First-Team All-America recognition by throwing for 3,942 yards and 33 touchdowns, in leading USC to an 11–2 record and a fourth-place finish in the national rankings.

Carson Palmer passed for more than 4,000 yards twice during his time in Cincinnati.
Courtesy of Keith Allison

Subsequently selected by the Bengals with the first overall pick of the 2003 NFL Draft, Palmer spent his entire rookie campaign sitting on the bench, watching veteran signal-caller Jon Kitna direct the team to a surprising 8–8 record (the Bengals finished just 2–14 the previous season). Replacing Kitna behind center the following year, Palmer passed for 2,897 yards and 18 touchdowns, threw 18 interceptions, completed 60.9 percent of his passes, and posted a passer rating of 77.3 for a Bengals team that once again finished 8–8.

Displaying tremendous growth in his second season as a starter in 2005, Palmer led the Bengals to an 11–5 record and their first division title in 15 years by ranking among the league leaders with 3,836 passing yards and a passer rating of 101.1, while also topping the circuit with 32 touchdown passes and a pass-completion percentage of 67.8, with his outstanding play earning him Pro Bowl honors and a fifth-place finish in the NFL MVP voting.

Praising his young quarterback at one point during the campaign for the confidence with which he carried himself, Bengals head coach Marvin Lewis said, "He feels like he's invincible, but right now he knows he can go win it on the next play. He doesn't have to win it on every play. And I think that says a lot for how he is and how important he is to this football team."

Also extremely confident in the 6'5", 235-pound Palmer's abilities, the Bengals signed him to a six-year contract extension worth $118.75 million just days before the final game of the regular season, prompting the 26-year-old signal-caller to say, "Hopefully, this is the last place I'll end up playing. That's so rare in this league these days. It's so rare to see a person have a 5-, 8-, 10-, 12-year career in one place. And I feel very fortunate that it looks like that's going to be my future."

However, Palmer and the Bengals suffered a major setback a little over one week later, when, during the team's January 8, 2006, meeting with the Pittsburgh Steelers in the opening round of the playoffs, the quarterback sustained a serious knee injury on Cincinnati's second play from scrimmage. Although Palmer completed a 66-yard pass to receiver Chris Henry, Pittsburgh defensive tackle Kimo von Oelhoffen delivered a blow to his left knee that tore both the anterior cruciate and medial collateral ligaments, damaged cartilage and his meniscus, and dislocated his kneecap.

After undergoing reconstructive surgery on his injured knee two days later, Palmer returned in time for the start of the 2006 campaign. And even though he appeared somewhat less mobile, Palmer acquitted himself extremely well, earning his second straight Pro Bowl nomination and a third-place finish in the NFL Comeback Player of the Year voting by ranking among the league leaders with 4,035 passing yards, 28 touchdown passes, and a passer rating of 93.9. Palmer followed that up with another strong season, throwing for 4,131 yards and 26 touchdowns in 2007, despite leading the league with 20 interceptions.

But with the Bengals, who ended up losing to the Steelers by 14 points in their 2005 postseason matchup after Palmer left the game, failing to come close to earning another playoff berth in either of the next two seasons, the hometown fans and media often made their team's quarterback the scapegoat. The situation grew even worse in 2008, when, after getting off to an 0–4 start, the Bengals lost Palmer for the year when he suffered a torn UCL in his right (throwing) elbow during a game against the Giants. While the Bengals went on to finish the season with a record of 4-11-1, Palmer, having lost some of his arm strength and mobility, appeared somewhat unsure of himself in the pocket when he returned to action the following year. Nevertheless, he still managed to post decent numbers in 2009, leading the Bengals to a 10–6 record and another division title by passing for almost 3,100 yards, throwing 21 TD passes and 13 interceptions, completing 60.5 percent of his passes, and compiling a passer rating of 83.6.

Even though Palmer improved upon his performance slightly in 2010, concluding the campaign with 3,970 passing yards, 26 touchdown passes, a 61.8 pass-completion percentage, and a passer rating of 82.4, the Bengals finished just 4–12, prompting him to request a trade to another team. With Bengals owner Mike Brown turning down his request, Palmer threatened to retire, with a local television station reporting that he told a friend, "I will never set foot in Paul Brown Stadium again. I have $80 million in the bank. . . . I don't have to play football for money. I'll play it for the love of the game, but that would have to be elsewhere."

Meanwhile, Palmer's agent stated, "Because of the lack of success that Carson and the Bengals have experienced together, Carson strongly feels that a separation between him and the Bengals would be in the best interest of both parties."

In response, the Bengals selected TCU quarterback Andy Dalton in the second round of the 2011 NFL Draft. Three months later, Mike Brown held a press conference during which he said that he did not expect Palmer to return to the Bengals for the 2011 season, that the organization wished him well, and that he had no plans to trade him. When asked why he did not intend to trade his disgruntled quarterback, Brown answered: "Carson signed a contract. He made a commitment. He gave his word. We relied on his word. We relied on his commitment. We expected him to perform here. He's going to walk away from his commitment. We aren't going to reward him for doing it."

With Palmer choosing not to report to training camp or participate in the team's workouts, Brown forced him to sit out the first six weeks of the regular season, before finally dealing him to the Oakland Raiders for a pair of high draft picks just prior to the trade deadline. After completing the trade, Brown said in a statement, "Several factors made us believe that trading Carson to Oakland was the best move for the Bengals at this time. The principal development has been Andy Dalton, who has shown himself to be one of the best and most exciting young quarterbacks in the NFL. We have a good, young football team, and Andy can be the cornerstone of that team for a long time."

Palmer, who left Cincinnati having passed for 22,694 yards, thrown 154 touchdown passes and 100 interceptions, completed 62.9 percent of his passes, compiled a passer rating of 86.9, and rushed for 316 yards and five touchdowns, ended up spending two seasons in Oakland, leading the Raiders to a total of just eight victories, although he threw for more than 4,000 yards (4,018) for the third time in 2012. Dealt to the Arizona Cardinals prior to the start of the 2013 campaign, Palmer spent five years starting behind center for the Cardinals, having the finest season of his career in 2015, when he led Arizona to an appearance in the NFC Championship Game by placing near the top of the league rankings with 4,671 passing yards, 35 touchdown passes, and a passer rating of 104.6, earning in the process a runner-up finish in the NFL MVP voting and both Pro Bowl and Second-Team All-Pro honors.

Expressing his regret over the unfortunate circumstances surrounding Palmer's departure from Cincinnati a few years earlier, Mike Brown stated before the Bengals' meeting with the Cardinals during the latter stages of the 2015 season, "I like Carson Palmer personally. I did when he was here. I regret it broke apart the way it did. I don't want him to beat us any more than he wants us to beat him. I'm sure that will be in the back of his mind. But other than that, I wish him well. He's a special passer, very accurate. I look at him play and I see the player that we had when he was here. When he's on and playing the way he can play, he is a big-time winning quarterback."

Palmer remained in Arizona for two more years, before announcing his retirement at the end of 2017 with career totals of 46,247 passing yards, 294 touchdown passes, and 187 interceptions, a pass-completion percentage of 62.5, and a passer rating of 87.9.

Although it had been quite some time since he donned a Bengals uniform, Palmer, who currently resides with his wife, Shaelyn, in Sun Valley, Idaho, remained somewhat critical of the organization as of 2020. During an interview with Damon Amendolara of CBS Sports Radio prior to that year's draft, Palmer discussed the perception that others held toward the Bengals when he came out of USC, and the things Joe Burrow might be hearing prior to his impending selection by the team: "Everybody I was talking to along the way said, 'You can't go to Cincinnati. You got to go somewhere else. You can't play for the Bengals. You can't play for the Bengals.'"

Palmer continued, "I, at the time, was going, 'This is awesome.' I was arrogant. I was a young, arrogant kid. 'I'm good enough. I'm going to change the whole thing around. I'm going to change the narrative.' Obviously, I wasn't able to change that narrative and flip that."

Adding that he never felt the organization seriously committed itself to winning a Super Bowl during his time in Cincinnati, Palmer stated, "No, that's why I wanted out. I never felt like the organization was really trying to win a Super Bowl and really chasing a Super Bowl. That's what today's day and age is. You can't just hope you draft well and not go after free agents and you end up in the Super Bowl. You got to go get it."

While Palmer's remarks unquestionably further antagonized a Bengals fanbase that has often criticized him for the way he handled his departure from Cincinnati, he praised the hometown fans for their loyalty, passion, and knowledge prior to the team's appearance in Super Bowl LVI, saying, "That fanbase understands football. They know it. They know when to be loud in stadiums, they know when to be quiet. . . . They understand all the nuances of the game. So, it's a great place to play from a player's perspective because the fanbase is so knowledgeable. . . . They watch every game. They read the press clippings; they follow the team on the Internet. So, to see them finally get a chance to be celebrated in that city, and in a place like LA, and around the world, is more than I expected. I'm just happy for that fanbase."

BENGALS CAREER HIGHLIGHTS

Best Season

Although Palmer threw for more yards in each of the next two seasons, he played his best ball for the Bengals in 2005, when he led them to the division title by passing for 3,836 yards, posting a passer rating of 101.1, and leading the league with 32 touchdown passes and a pass-completion percentage of 67.8, while also throwing just 12 interceptions.

Memorable Moments/Greatest Performances

Palmer earned AFC Offensive Player of the Week honors by completing 29 of 36 passes for 382 yards and three touchdowns during a 27–26 victory over the Baltimore Ravens on December 5, 2004, that the Bengals won on a last-second field goal by Shayne Graham.

Palmer led the Bengals to a lopsided 37–8 victory over the Vikings on September 18, 2005, by throwing for 337 yards and three TDs, the longest of which went 70 yards to Chad Johnson.

Although Palmer lost a 49–41 shootout with San Diego's Philip Rivers on November 12, 2006, he threw for 440 yards and three TDs, the longest of which came on a 74-yard connection with Chad Johnson.

Palmer starred in defeat once again on September 16, 2007, throwing for 401 yards and six touchdowns during a 51–45 loss to the Browns.

Palmer helped the Bengals overcome a 20–9 fourth-quarter deficit by leading them on two late scoring drives, giving them a 23–20 victory over the Steelers on September 27, 2009, by tossing a game-winning 4-yard TD pass to Andre Caldwell with just 14 seconds left in regulation.

Palmer provided further heroics on October 11, 2009, when he gave the Bengals a 17–14 win over the Ravens by hitting Caldwell with a 20-yard TD pass with just 22 ticks left on the clock.

Palmer earned AFC Offensive Player of the Week honors by completing 20 of 24 passes for 233 yards and five touchdowns during a 45–10 rout of the Chicago Bears on October 25, 2009.

Although the Bengals lost to the Falcons, 39–32, on October 24, 2010, Palmer had a big game, throwing for 412 yards and three touchdowns.

Palmer led the Bengals to a 34–20 win over the Chargers on December 26, 2010, by completing 16 of 21 passes for 269 yards and four touchdowns, the longest of which came on a 59-yard connection with Jerome Simpson.

Notable Achievements

- Passed for more than 3,000 yards five times, topping 4,000 yards twice.
- Threw more than 30 touchdown passes once.
- Completed more than 65 percent of passes once.
- Posted touchdown-to-interception ratio of better than 2–1 twice.
- Posted passer rating above 100.0 once.
- Led NFL with 32 touchdown passes and 67.8 pass-completion percentage in 2005.
- Finished second in NFL in pass completions, touchdown passes, and passer rating once each.
- Ranks among Bengals career leaders with 3,217 pass attempts (4th), 2,024 pass completions (3rd), 22,694 passing yards (4th), 154 TD passes (4th), and 62.9 pass-completion percentage (2nd).
- Two-time division champion (2005 and 2009).

- Two-time AFC Offensive Player of the Week.
- 2009 Week 7 NFL Offensive Player of the Week.
- September 2005 AFC Offensive Player of the Month.
- Finished fifth in 2005 NFL MVP voting.
- Two-time Pro Bowl selection (2005 and 2006).
- Named to Bengals 40th Anniversary All-Time Team in 2007.

29

EDDIE EDWARDS

A versatile player who started for the Bengals at every defensive line position at one time or another, Eddie Edwards spent his entire 12-year NFL career in Cincinnati, recording more sacks during that time than any other player in franchise history. The Bengals starting left defensive end for nearly a decade, Edwards finished in double digits in sacks three times, leading the team in that category on four separate occasions. A stout run-defender as well, Edwards did an excellent job of forcing opposing ball-carriers inside and pursuing them from sideline to sideline, with his strong all-around play helping the Bengals win three division titles and two AFC championships. Extremely durable, Edwards started 133 of 137 non-strike games over a nine-year period, earning a spot on the Bengals 50th Anniversary All-Time Team with his overall contributions to the success of the organization.

Born in Sumter, South Carolina, on April 25, 1954, Eddie Lee Edwards moved with his family at an early age to Fort Pierce, Florida, where he established himself as a star on the gridiron at Fort Pierce Central High School, which he helped lead to the state championship in 1971. In discussing Edwards, former Fort Pierce head coach Lewis Rice said, "He was quick and mean."

Meanwhile, former Cobras trainer Terry Mosely stated, "Eddie was very quiet. He did his talking on the field. He would get after you."

Offered an athletic scholarship to the University of Miami, Edwards spent three seasons terrorizing opposing quarterbacks and running backs from his defensive end position, recording over 50 tackles in each of his first two seasons, before gaining consensus First-Team All-America recognition as a senior in 1976 by averaging more than 13 stops and two quarterback sacks per game. Named the winner of the Jack Harding Memorial Award as the most valuable player for the Hurricanes in his final season, Edwards received high praise from Miami head coach Carl Selmer, who described him as "the best defensive football player in the country."

Eddie Edwards recorded more sacks than anyone else in team annals.

Former Hurricanes assistant coach Harold Allen also spoke glowingly of Edwards, stating, "Eddie just had it all, great size, speed, quickness, and a hard-working attitude that you rarely see in a player of his pure natural ability."

Selected by the Bengals with the third overall pick of the 1977 NFL Draft, Edwards moved inside to left defensive tackle following his arrival in Cincinnati, earning a spot on the NFL All-Rookie Team by recording 4 1/2 sacks and recovering one fumble. Splitting the next two seasons between left and right tackle, Edwards totaled 10 1/2 sacks and four fumble recoveries, before emerging as one of the league's better pass-rushers in 1980 under new head coach Forrest Gregg. With Gregg switching to a 3–4 defense, he moved Edwards back outside to his more natural position of defensive end, where he recorded an unofficial total of 12 sacks that made him the team leader in that category for the first of four times. Performing extremely well again in 1981, Edwards helped lead the Bengals to the division title and their first AFC championship by recording 10 sacks, earning in the process Second-Team All-AFC honors.

The 6'5" Edwards, who spent most of his career playing at somewhere between 250 and 255 pounds, possessed great strength, allowing him to make good use of the "bull rush" when trying to apply pressure to opposing quarterbacks. Also blessed with tremendous agility and superior instincts, Edwards proved to be exceptionally quick off the ball and did an excellent job of diagnosing plays at the line of scrimmage.

Beginning a string of 73 consecutive starts during the strike-shortened 1982 campaign, Edwards registered six sacks in just nine games, before amassing a career-high 13 sacks the following year. Continuing to perform well for the Bengals the next three seasons, Edwards recorded a total of 24 sacks and scored the only touchdown of his career when he recovered a fumble in the end zone. But, after seeing his production fall off somewhat in 1987, Edwards lost his starting job to Skip McClendon the following year, prompting him to announce his retirement shortly after the Bengals suffered a heartbreaking 20–16 defeat at the hands of the San Francisco 49ers in Super Bowl XXIII.

Although Edwards would have preferred a different outcome to his final game, in which he only played a few snaps, he looked back fondly at Super Bowl XXIII at the 1988 team's 30th anniversary reunion, saying of the contest played at Miami's Joe Robbie Stadium, "I started my career at the University of Miami, so it was like the end to a good story—why not finish there? Last Super Bowl, 1988, going home. All your family and friends get a chance to see you play your final game. That was special. It would have been better if we won, but I just can't believe it's been 30 years."

Although Edwards ended his career with a franchise-record 84 1/2 sacks (only 47 1/2 of which are considered "official" since the NFL did not begin keeping an official record of that statistic until 1982), he believes that circumstances prevented him from registering many more, saying during a team reunion held in 2020, "I played in a 3–4. If I played in a 4–3, I would have had about 100 sacks."

Agreeing with his former teammate, Cris Collinsworth stated, "He's probably right. . . . Oh yeah, he was good. If he played today, he would have been more famous. Sacks were just starting to become a stat."

In addition to his 84 1/2 sacks, Edwards recorded 17 fumble recoveries, which represents the third-highest total in team annals.

Following his playing days, Edwards retired to his home state of Florida, where he currently lives.

CAREER HIGHLIGHTS

Best Season

Although Edwards recorded three more sacks two years later, he made his greatest overall impact in 1981, when he earned his lone All-AFC nomination by registering 10 sacks and making 47 tackles for the AFC champion Bengals.

Memorable Moments/Greatest Performances

Edwards contributed to a 37–7 win over the Atlanta Falcons on December 3, 1978, by recording the only interception of his career.

Although the Bengals lost the 1980 regular-season finale, 27–24, to the Browns, Edwards tied the franchise record for most sacks in one game by bringing down quarterback Brian Sipe behind the line of scrimmage five times. Recalling his extraordinary effort, Edwards said, "To tell you the truth, I wanted to hurry up and play the game and get back to Florida; It was just too cold. Sipe ran around a lot, like Fran Tarkenton, and everything I did that day worked. I did swim moves where I'd head butt (the tackle) and go over the guy's shoulder or do a rip move and go underneath him. That day, everything our line coach (Dick Modzelewski) told me worked."

Edwards recorded one of the two sacks the Bengals registered against Dan Fouts during a 27–7 victory over the San Diego Chargers in the 1981 AFC Championship Game.

Edwards sacked Jim Zorn twice during a 24–10 win over the Seattle Seahawks on December 26, 1982.

Edwards recorded another two sacks during a 23–17 win over the Tampa Bay Buccaneers on September 25, 1983.

Edwards scored the only touchdown of his career when he recovered a fumble in the end zone during a 34–7 victory over the Seahawks on November 16, 1986.

Notable Achievements

- Missed just four non-strike games from 1978 to 1986, starting 133 of 137 contests.
- Scored one defensive touchdown.
- Finished in double digits in sacks three times.
- Led Bengals in sacks four times.
- Holds Bengals career record for most sacks (84 1/2).
- Ranks third in franchise history with 17 fumble recoveries.
- Three-time division champion (1981, 1982, and 1988).
- Two-time AFC champion (1981 and 1988).
- Member of 1977 NFL All-Rookie Team.
- 1981 Second-Team All-AFC selection.
- Named to Bengals 50th Anniversary All-Time Team in 2017.

30

BILL BERGEY

Although Bill Bergey is remembered more for his time in Philadelphia, he previously spent five seasons in Cincinnati excelling for the Bengals at middle linebacker. The cornerstone of the Bengals defense during their formative years, Bergey led the team in tackles five straight times, earning in the process one trip to the Pro Bowl and a spot on the Bengals 50th Anniversary All-Time Team. Receiving even greater acclaim after he left Cincinnati, Bergey went on to earn four Pro Bowl selections and five All-Pro nominations as a member of the Eagles, whom he helped lead to three playoff appearances and one NFC championship.

Born in South Dayton, New York, on February 9, 1945, William Earl Bergey got his start in organized football at South Dayton High School, recalling, "I started in the ninth grade. I played playground football before that."

Despite starring as both a fullback and linebacker at South Dayton, Bergey failed to receive any scholarship offers as graduation neared, remembering, "I played football at a Class C school. There were 47 in our graduating class. We barely had enough guys to play football. So, we never even had any films for our football games. I had my guidance director when I was a senior write to maybe eight or ten colleges, and two of them responded. One was the University of New Mexico, and the other was Arkansas State University."

Bergey continued, "Now, I was from western New York, between Buffalo and Jamestown. So, I got my map out and saw where Arkansas State was closer than New Mexico, so I decided to go ahead and pursue Arkansas State."

After contacting Arkansas State coaches Bennie Ellender and Wayne Armstrong, who happened to be in New York City for a coaches' convention, Bergey received an invitation to meet them, remembering years later, "I said 'Yes.' Unbeknownst to me, from where I was in New York, it was about 425 miles away. We went to New York City. We packed up a couple

Bill Bergey excelled for the Bengals at middle linebacker during their formative years.

of scrapbooks that I had put together and I just pleaded for any kind of scholarship help that they could give to me, because I didn't have any money at all. They gave me a partial scholarship."

Recalling his days at the university, Bergey said, "I went down to Arkansas State and red-shirted my first year. Then, I started four years in a row. I didn't start at linebacker. It was kind of a platoon system that we had. I was an offensive guard and a nose guard. After a couple of plays, that whole unit would go out and another unit would come in. My junior year, they moved me to linebacker. I was standing up and could see everything. Things just started to click for me."

Bergey, who led the team in tackles three times, ended up setting school records for most fumble recoveries in a season, most tackles in a game, most tackles in a season, and most career tackles, earning in the process All–Southland Conference honors three times and gaining First-Team College Division All-America recognition as a senior in 1968. Commenting on his performance at the collegiate level, Bergey stated, "I was a pretty good athlete. I could run real fast. I was big enough. I started out at linebacker in college around 232 or 234 (pounds). I made All-American."

Subsequently selected by the Bengals in the second round of the 1969 NFL Draft, with the 31st overall pick, Bergey immediately laid claim to the team's starting middle linebacker job, recalling, "Cincinnati was in the second year of their franchise, and they needed a linebacker. I was about two weeks late getting to the Bengals, and I looked at the two linebackers they had, and I said, 'If you don't beat out one of those guys, you don't belong in the game of pro football.'"

Acquitting himself extremely well his first year in the league, Bergey earned Pro Bowl and *Sporting News* NFL Defensive Rookie of the Year honors by intercepting two passes and registering more than 100 tackles. Continuing to perform at an elite level the next four seasons, Bergey helped lead the Bengals to two division titles by recording well over 100 tackles each year.

The centerpiece of one of the league's better defenses in Cincinnati, the 6'3", 245-pound Bergey did an exceptional job of pursuing opposing ball-carriers all over the field, while also discouraging opposing receivers from crossing over the middle. Almost maniacal in the level of intensity he displayed on the playing field, Bergey proved to be one of the NFL's surest tacklers and hardest hitters over the course of his career, with Walt Michaels, who served as his defensive coordinator in Philadelphia from 1973 to 1975, once saying, "Bill reminds me of Rocky Marciano. He knows how to gather himself. Some boxers are always on their toes, never in balance to deliver a blow. Bill delivers with his whole body. He explodes. Boom! You can't teach that. A guy has it or he doesn't."

Also blessed with good speed and soft hands, Bergey excelled at covering running backs and tight ends downfield, recording nine interceptions for the Bengals and 27 career picks.

In discussing everything Bergey brought to the Bengals, current team owner and president Mike Brown said, "Bergey was big for his time, 250-some. He was [Vontaze] Burfict who could run 4.6. He had range. He could 'nub em'—meaning, when he hit 'em, they stopped. They didn't carry him. He knocked 'em over backwards. He was a tremendous player for us."

Brown added, "He was, if I were listing all our linebackers over 50 years—there are different times, and a lot goes into it—but the really good ones could play in any time, and Bergey would be at the top of the list."

Revealing that he loved playing for Brown's dad, legendary head coach Paul Brown, Bergey stated, "Paul Brown was a great guy. I loved him. I really liked his values. He loved his players being married. He loved his players having kids. He wanted to see his players have responsibilities off the field, too. He encouraged us to go to church on Sunday morning before we played football Sunday afternoon."

However, Bergey's relationship with Brown soured after he signed a futures contract to play with Orlando in the upstart World Football League following the conclusion of the 1973 campaign. Recalling the events that transpired at the time, Bergey stated, "It was strictly the money. I will make no bones about it. I was making $37,500 with Paul Brown. The World Football League came along and offered me, I think it was $625,000 for three years, guaranteed, no cut, no trade. I think you can do the math on that. I was strictly in it for the cash."

Bergey continued: "Paul Brown took me to court, stating that 'It impairs the integrity of any professional athlete to play for one ball club and to be compensated by another.' I had already received an $80,000 bonus from the World Football League, and that was more than twice my salary. I had one more year under Paul Brown. I had said that 'I would honor that one year and then I was going on to the World Football League.' We had the biggest, most unbelievable court battle you can imagine in Philadelphia. . . . I won the court battle. I won the appeal, and I pretty much pissed Paul Brown off, and he was not going to have anything to do with me."

With the WFL folding shortly thereafter and Brown seeking to rid himself of Bergey, the Bengals traded him to the Eagles for first-round draft picks in 1977 and 1978, along with a second rounder in 1978. Revealing years later that he initially had reservations about joining the Eagles, Bergey said, "At first, I wasn't sure that I wanted to go to Philadelphia. I knew it was the home of the Liberty Bell and they had something called soft pretzels and losing football. Plus, Mike McCormack, the coach, had testified against me in court as a favor to Paul Brown. But Leonard Tose was very, very persistent about me coming to the Philadelphia Eagles. He honestly thought that all he needed to win the Super Bowl was a middle linebacker."

Bergey, who, in addition to his nine interceptions, registered 4 1/2 sacks, six fumble recoveries, and a countless number of unrecorded tackles during his time in Cincinnati, ended up playing arguably the best ball of his career for the Eagles over the course of the next seven seasons, earning a spot on Pro Football Reference's All-1970s Second Team by helping to transform his new club into perennial contenders for the NFC title. Performing especially well in 1974 and 1976, Bergey gained consensus First-Team All-Pro recognitions and earned a runner-up finish in the NFL Defensive Player of the Year voting in the first of those campaigns by recording a career-high five interceptions and leading the Eagles in tackles for the first of six times, before establishing a single-season franchise record that still stands by registering 233 tackles in the second.

However, after sustaining a serious knee injury in 1979 that limited him to just three games, Bergey failed to reach the same level of excellence when he returned to action the following year, later saying, "If I was at one time a 100 percent football player, after my knee injury, I don't think I got past 65 percent. When I was on top of my game, I could diagnose a play and get to a spot to almost wait for a ball carrier. After the knee injury, I could still diagnose a play, but by the time I could get to that spot, the ball carrier was gone."

Bergey added, "Nobody had to tell me that it was my time. I would always be up in the 200s, as far as tackles go. I think that the year we went to the Super Bowl [1980], I played in every game and played on every play. I think that I was around 135 tackles. It was just dreadful. I used to watch film, and I would remember, 'Gosh, I used to be able to make that play, and it was so easy to make that play.' I just couldn't make it anymore. That's when it was time for me to hang up the old strap."

Choosing to announce his retirement after the Eagles lost Super Bowl XV to the Oakland Raiders by a score of 27–10, Bergey ended his career with 27 interceptions, 397 interception-return yards, 21 fumble recoveries, 18 1/2 sacks, and an unknown number of tackles that likely approached 2,000 (he made close to 1,200 stops as a member of the Eagles).

Since retiring as an active player, the now 79-year-old Bergey has remained close to the Eagles, first serving as a color commentator on the team's radio broadcasts from 1982 to 1983, before eventually doing pregame and postgame radio and television commentary for the team during the season. He also spent many years in the hospitality business, owning a few hotels and restaurants in the Philadelphia area.

Looking back on his playing career, Bergey said, "Personally, I think the thing that makes me the proudest is I know that I left everything on the field. I played as hard as I could all the time. I wasn't one of those players that takes plays off, or anything like that. I've had an awful lot of pats on the back and a lot of awards, and all of that, but just knowing that I gave everything I had on every play, that's pretty rewarding."

Meanwhile, in reminiscing on his time in Cincinnati, Bergey stated, "I enjoyed playing with the Bengals. I remember much more about playing for the Bengals than I did with the Eagles, if you believe it or not. I got married. I had kids. I had three sons. Nobody got paid a lot of money. On an off day, a lot of players would get together and play cards or have a pot-luck supper, or something like that. All of that stuff was pretty cool."

BENGALS CAREER HIGHLIGHTS

Best Season

Although Bergey earned his only Pro Bowl nomination as a member of the Bengals in his rookie campaign of 1969, his final season in Cincinnati proved to be his most impactful, as he helped lead the Bengals to a 10–4 record and their second division title in 1973 by picking off three passes, recovering three fumbles, registering 1 1/2 sacks, and recording an unofficial total of 152 tackles.

Memorable Moments/Greatest Performances

Bergey made an impact in his very first game as a pro, helping to set up a Bengals score by returning his interception of a Bob Griese pass 58 yards during a 27–21 win over the Miami Dolphins in the 1969 regular-season opener.

Although the Bengals lost to the Houston Oilers, 20–13, on October 4, 1970, Bergey picked off two passes in one game for the only time in his career.

In addition to recording an interception during a 31–0 shutout of the San Diego Chargers on November 28, 1971, Bergey helped anchor a defense that created six turnovers and allowed just 130 yards of total offense.

Notable Achievements

• Recorded more than 100 tackles five times.

- Led Bengals in tackles five times.
- Two-time division champion (1970 and 1973).
- 1969 AFL Defensive Rookie of the Year.
- 1969 Pro Bowl selection.
- 1970 Bengals team MVP.
- Named to Bengals 50th Anniversary All-Time Team in 2017.

31
TOMMY CASANOVA

A versatile defender who excelled at both safety positions for the Bengals, Tommy Casanova spent six seasons in Cincinnati, establishing himself as one of the finest defensive backs in the game. A starter in the Bengals defensive secondary from 1972 to 1977, Casanova proved to be a huge contributor to teams that made two playoff appearances and won one division title, recording five interceptions twice and scoring four touchdowns, en route to earning one All-Pro nomination, three trips to the Pro Bowl, and four All-AFC selections. One of the franchise's career leaders in interceptions and interception-return yards despite his relatively brief stay in Cincinnati, Casanova later received the additional honor of being named to the Bengals 50th Anniversary All-Time Team.

Born in New Orleans, Louisiana, on August 29, 1950, Thomas Henry Casanova III moved with his family some 155 miles west, to Crowley, Louisiana, when his father, Dr. Thomas H. Casanova Jr., returned to the United States after serving in the Korean War. Following his graduation from the Roman Catholic Notre Dame High School in Crowley, Casanova attended Louisiana State University in Baton Rouge, where he became known for his extraordinary all-around ability on the football field.

After excelling on both sides of the ball for the freshman team his first year at LSU, Casanova spent the next three seasons starring for the varsity squad as a cornerback and return-man, earning three straight All-SEC nominations and gaining consensus All-America recognition in each of his final two seasons despite missing nearly half his senior year with a pulled right hamstring. Casanova's most memorable performance as a collegiate player came in the final game of his junior year, when he returned two punts for touchdowns during a 61–17 rout of Ole Miss, prompting *Sports Illustrated* to feature him on its front cover just prior to the start of the ensuing campaign with a headline that read, "Tommy Casanova of LSU, Best Player in the Nation."

Tommy Casanova earned All-AFC honors in four of his six seasons in Cincinnati.
Courtesy of RMYAuctions.com

In expressing his admiration for Casanova, who also occasionally carried the ball his sophomore and junior years at LSU, then-Tigers head coach Charles McClendon said, "Tommy was one of the most gifted athletes I ever coached. We needed him more on defense, but there's no question in my mind he could've been an All-American running back. He could really have jazzed up our offense."

Meanwhile, Casanova recalled, "I wanted to play both ways. Just about everybody who ever played football fancies themselves as a running back. But I knew if I had a pro career, it would be as a defensive back."

Selected by the Bengals in the second round of the 1972 NFL Draft, with the 29th overall pick, Casanova briefly considered an offer from the Canadian Football League's Ottawa Rough Riders, before choosing to remain in the States. Laying claim to the starting free safety job immediately upon his arrival in Cincinnati, Casanova performed exceptionally well his first year as a pro, earning Second-Team All-AFC honors and a runner-up finish in the NFL Defensive Rookie of the Year voting by recording five interceptions, which he returned for a total of 108 yards, and scoring the first touchdown of his career on a 66-yard punt return. Remaining at free safety the next two seasons, Casanova picked off four passes in 1973, before earning his first Pro Bowl nomination the following year by recording two interceptions and amassing 313 yards on special teams. Moving to strong safety in 1975, Casanova continued to perform at an elite level, gaining First-Team All-AFC recognition, despite missing three games due to injury.

Equally effective at both safety positions, the 6'2", 202-pound Casanova had the physical tools to play anywhere in the defensive secondary. In addition to his size and strength, Casanova, who posted personal-best times of 9.6 seconds in the 100-yard dash and 4.5 seconds in the 40, possessed great speed and quickness. Also blessed with superior instincts and tremendous anticipation, Casanova played both the run and the pass extremely well, doing an outstanding job of tracking down opposing ball-carriers, while also excelling as a man-to-man defender downfield. And, once he got his hands on the football, Casanova, who averaged 8.6 yards per punt return over the course of his career, proved to be an elusive runner, scoring three times on defense and once on special teams.

Praising Casanova for his exceptional all-around play, Bengals head coach Paul Brown called him, "Just plain Special. We never had anyone else like him. On defense, he played the ball like a center fielder. On punt returns, he was excellent. A very good football player, and always a gentleman."

Casanova had two more excellent years for the Bengals, earning Pro Bowl and First-Team All-Pro honors in 1976 by picking off five passes and scoring three touchdowns, before gaining Pro Bowl recognition for the third and final time the following season. But with Casanova having missed three games in each of the previous three seasons due to knee problems, he decided to announce his retirement following the conclusion of the 1977 campaign, later saying, "I could have kept playing. I could have got by. But I couldn't play at the level I wanted to play. I didn't think it was fair to me or my teammates, and I knew I had something to fall back on. It just wore out."

Retiring at only 27 years of age, Casanova ended his career with 17 interceptions, 276 interception-return yards, three fumble recoveries, 2 1/2 sacks, 784 punt-return yards, 1,190 all-purpose yards, and four touchdowns.

Following his retirement from football, Casanova, who obtained a medical degree from the University of Cincinnati while playing for the Bengals, did a residency in New Orleans and an ophthalmic plastic surgery fellowship at the University of Utah, before returning to his hometown of Crowley, Louisiana, where he joined his father's practice and exercised his surgical skills at American Legion Hospital.

Recalling the support that he received from Paul Brown and the Bengals during his playing days, Casanova said, "Brown was behind me. They let me miss a lot of training camp my second year when I got started in med school. They made a lot of concessions. I stayed in pretty good shape all year and, once I got there and began playing, after a couple of seasons you know what you're doing, and you just go out and do it."

Specializing in eye surgery and eyelid reconstruction, Casanova eventually earned a seat on the board of trustees for colleges and universities in Louisiana, worked with an environmental society, and helped improve the vision of lepers in Louisiana. Later choosing to enter the world of politics, Casanova ran for and won a four-year term in the state senate as a Republican in 1995. However, he served just one term before his disillusionment with the political system prompted him to return full-time to his medical practice in 1999.

CAREER HIGHLIGHTS

Best Season

Although Casanova picked off five passes, scored a touchdown, and amassed a career-high 431 all-purpose yards as a rookie in 1972, he made a slightly greater overall impact in 1976, when he earned First-Team All-AFC honors and his lone All-Pro nomination by recording five interceptions, two of which he returned for touchdowns, and scoring a third time when he returned a fumble recovery 25 yards for a TD.

Memorable Moments/Greatest Performances

Casanova scored the first points of his career when he returned a punt 66 yards for a touchdown during a 21–10 win over the Denver Broncos on October 8, 1972.

Casanova recorded his first interception as a pro one week later, when he picked off a pass thrown by Len Dawson during a 23–16 victory over the Kansas City Chiefs on October 15, 1972.

Casanova starred in defeat on October 28, 1973, intercepting two passes in one game for the only time in his career during a 20–13 loss to the Steelers.

Although the Bengals lost to the Colts, 28–27, on September 19, 1976, Casanova scored his first touchdown on defense when he ran 31 yards to pay dirt after picking off a Bert Jones pass.

Casanova put the finishing touches on a 28–7 win over the Packers on September 26, 1976, when he returned his interception of a Carlos Brown pass 33 yards for a TD in the fourth quarter.

Casanova lit the scoreboard again on October 10, 1976, when he returned a fumble 25 yards for a touchdown during a 21–0 victory over Tampa Bay.

NOTABLE ACHIEVEMENTS

- Scored three defensive touchdowns.
- Returned one punt for a touchdown.
- Recorded five interceptions twice.
- Amassed more than 100 interception-return yards twice.
- Finished second in NFL in total punt-return yards and average yards per punt return once each.
- Led Bengals in interceptions twice.
- Ranks among Bengals career leaders with 17 interceptions (8th) and 276 interception-return yards (7th).
- 1973 division champion.
- Finished second in 1972 NFL Defensive Rookie of the Year voting.
- 1972 Bengals team MVP.
- Three-time Pro Bowl selection (1974, 1976, and 1977).
- 1976 First-Team All-Pro selection.

- Three-time First-Team All-AFC selection (1975, 1976, and 1977).
- 1972 Second-Team All-AFC selection.
- Named to Bengals 50th Anniversary All-Time Team in 2017.

32

PETE JOHNSON

Once identified by Pittsburgh Steelers Hall of Fame middle linebacker Jack Lambert as the most difficult player in the NFL to tackle, Pete Johnson spent seven seasons in Cincinnati, leading the Bengals in rushing in each of those. A powerful back who intimidated opposing defenders with his size, strength, and aggressive running style, Johnson proved to be particularly effective in short-yardage and goal-line situations, scoring more touchdowns than anyone else in franchise history, while also amassing the fourth-most rushing yards. A capable receiver as well, Johnson gained more than 1,000 yards through the air during his time in Cincinnati, with his total body of work earning him a place on the Bengals 50th Anniversary All-Time Team.

Born in Fort Valley, Georgia, on March 2, 1954, William James Hammock acquired the nickname "Pete" at an early age, recalling, "My Uncle James started calling me that when I was five. On hot summer days, I'd chase the Peter Pan ice cream truck."

Raised by his great-grandparents on a farm in Fort Valley after his teenage mother moved to Long Beach, New York, to live with her mother, young Pete experienced tragedy at the age of nine, when his younger brother slipped off a rope under a bridge and drowned in Long Island Sound. Remembering how the loss of his brother affected him, Johnson said, "It set me to thinking. Life is a lot shorter than people realize. They work so hard they never have time to enjoy life. All they have to look forward to is dying. When I go, I don't want anyone to say I haven't lived."

Beginning his career on the gridiron at the age of 12 after catching the eye of Hunt High's football coach, the 5'5", 155-pound Johnson, who began using his more familiar name right around that time, soon found himself starting for the varsity squad, even though he later admitted, "The school frowned on 12-year-olds playing on the varsity."

Eventually establishing himself as a star running back at Peach County High School, Johnson recalled being recruited in the 10th grade by Auburn

Pete Johnson scored more touchdowns than anyone else in franchise history.

representatives, who believed him to be much older. After three years at Peach County, Johnson moved to New York to live with his mother following the death of his great-grandfather. Continuing to excel on the gridiron his senior year at Long Beach High School, Johnson performed well enough to receive a scholarship offer from West Virginia University. However, after initially signing a letter of intent to play for the Mountaineers, Johnson chose instead to enroll at Ohio State University at the urging of head football coach Woody Hayes.

Developing into a classic power fullback at OSU, Johnson combined with future Bengals teammate Archie Griffin to give the Buckeyes the top backfield tandem in the nation. While Griffin gained far more recognition, becoming the only two-time Heisman Trophy winner, Johnson set a Big Ten record by scoring 58 touchdowns in his four years at Columbus. Particularly outstanding as a junior in 1975, Johnson rushed for 1,059 yards and set OSU single-season records for most rushing touchdowns (25) and most points scored (156).

Selected by the Bengals in the second round of the 1977 NFL Draft, with the 49th overall pick, Johnson arrived in Cincinnati with his new team underestimating him to some degree, recalling, "When I came here, it was said that I couldn't catch the ball. It was kind of like being stereotyped. Archie (Griffin) had the same problem: 'Well, you know, he can't catch the ball.' The quarterbacks we had; they would think twice before they threw to me. Then they found out I can catch the ball."

Johnson continued, "They said they drafted me for short yardage. I knew I could do more than that."

Starting alongside his former Buckeyes teammate as a rookie in 1977, Johnson ended up rushing for more yards (585) and scoring more touchdowns (4) than Griffin. Emerging as the team's top offensive weapon the following year, Johnson gained 762 yards on the ground, amassed 998 yards from scrimmage, and scored seven TDs. Posting excellent numbers again in 1979, Johnson rushed for 865 yards, accumulated 1,019 yards from scrimmage, and placed near the top of the league rankings with 14 rushing touchdowns and 15 total TDs.

One of the biggest running backs in the game, the 6-foot Johnson, whose weight fluctuated from 245 to 265 pounds, and whose thighs measured 38 inches, presented a huge challenge to any defender seeking to take him off his feet, with Steelers linebacker Jack Ham saying, "As a defender, you're taught to hit and wrap your arms around a ball carrier and run through him. I couldn't wrap my arms around Pete Johnson if my hands were at his calves."

Former Bengals guard Dave Lapham commented, "We could tell that he'd just wear on defenses, you know? People didn't want any part of tackling him in cold weather in the fourth quarter of games. He just was so thick you couldn't get your arms around him."

Lapham continued, "He'd just hammer it, man. Just hammer it in there. As a lineman, Pete would just lower his head and just run right up your back. You better make sure you're doing your thing and getting out of the way because he'll just run up your backside. Guys didn't want that happening. I can vividly remember linebackers mumbling hitting him, mumbling like, 'Holy s--- I don't want any part of that!' If the Red Sea parted and they were one-on-one in the hole with him—nightmare."

Virtually impossible to stop in short-yardage situations, Johnson drew praise for his proficiency in that area from Houston Oilers linebacker Greg Bingham, who said, "It's hard to stop Pete in his tracks. No, impossible. Particularly on third-and-one. It's a matter of physics."

Adding to the woes of opposing defenders, Johnson took a nasty temperament with him to the playing field, with Jack Ham stating, "Every time he plays us, he appears to be snarling."

In discussing his on-field mentality, Johnson, who ran low to the ground, with his head bowed, looking for someone to hit, said, "I go into a trance. If someone's going to bother to tackle me, I want him to feel it more than I do. I want to make him pay."

Johnson added, "I kind of use the defensive player. When I can get a full head of steam going and I can find the crack, I can get my head in. You get between two defensive players, and they kind of hold you up. . . . I protect myself, believe me. You've got to run low, and know when you can run up, and know when you can take a block on with your shoulder or your head. You've got to know how to use the ball to protect yourself when you're falling."

Although Johnson, who possessed surprising speed for a man of his proportions, enjoyed running between the tackles, he considered himself to be a multidimensional back, saying, "I get letters. They love it when it's third-and-two and everybody in the stadium knows you're going to get the ball. Sometimes you hear them say the Bengals need a back who can get to the outside and go 30 yards, go 50 yards. I've done all that. But it still doesn't register in people's minds. I know what I can do."

Extremely productive again in 1980, Johnson rushed for 747 yards, amassed 919 yards from scrimmage, and scored seven touchdowns, before earning his lone Pro Bowl nomination the following year by gaining 1,077 yards on the ground, accumulating 1,397 yards from scrimmage, and scoring 16 touchdowns for the AFC champion Bengals.

Expressing his appreciation to Johnson for everything he brought to the team, Forrest Gregg, who assumed head coaching duties in Cincinnati in 1980, said, "Pete Johnson is the type of fullback that I like, and, when you give him the football, and when you give him any type of daylight, he's going to make yardage. He's going to make that tough yardage for you. . . . When Pete gets rolling, he can intimidate the opponent by just his sheer power. I know that defensive backs, once he gets in the open, don't like to tackle him. When you measure his size against theirs, I can certainly understand that."

Meanwhile, Bengals punter Pat McInally defended his teammate's practice of rarely speaking to the press, saying, "Pete's just Pete. Most athletes I know get lost within the system and become conscious of their images as pro football players. But Pete just uses football; it gives him the freedom to be himself. It's not that he's rude; he really is in his own world. You gotta love Pete."

Johnson had two more solid seasons for the Bengals, rushing for 622 yards, amassing 889 yards from scrimmage, and scoring seven touchdowns in 1982, before gaining 763 yards on the ground, accumulating 892 yards from scrimmage, and finishing third in the league with 14 touchdowns the following year, despite being suspended for the first four games of the campaign for using cocaine. Seeking a salary increase the following offseason, Johnson became disenchanted with team management when it refused to renegotiate his contract. After threatening to jump to the newly formed USFL, Johnson found himself headed to San Diego when the Bengals completed a trade with the Chargers on May 29, 1984, that sent him to the West Coast for equally disgruntled running back James Brooks.

Johnson, who left Cincinnati with career totals of 5,421 rushing yards, 173 receptions, 1,327 receiving yards, 6,748 yards from scrimmage, 64 rushing touchdowns, and 70 TDs, ended up playing just three games for the Chargers, before being dealt to the Dolphins. After finishing out the season in Miami, Johnson announced his retirement, ending his career with 5,626 yards rushing, 6,960 yards from scrimmage, and 82 touchdowns, 76 of which came on the ground.

Following his playing days, Johnson remained in Miami, where he became a car salesman. While working in that capacity in 1987, Johnson was indicted by a federal grand jury on four cocaine-related charges. Although eventually cleared of those charges, Johnson again ran into trouble some 20 years later, when, after relocating to Columbus, Illinois, a Champaign County grand jury indicted him on December 17, 2007, on one count of passing bad checks and another of grand theft auto. Although acquitted of the second charge, Johnson received a sentence of 60 hours of community service and three years of probation after a jury found him guilty of writing a bad check when purchasing a pickup truck from a car dealership.

BENGALS CAREER HIGHLIGHTS

Best Season

Although Johnson also performed extremely well two years earlier, he made his greatest overall impact in 1981, when he helped lead the Bengals to their first AFC championship by establishing career-high marks with 1,077 rushing yards, 46 receptions, 320 receiving yards, 1,397 yards from scrimmage, and 16 touchdowns.

Memorable Moments/Greatest Performances

Johnson contributed to a convincing 48–16 victory over the Browns in the final game of the 1978 regular season by carrying the ball 27 times for 160 yards and one touchdown, which came on a 12-yard run.

Johnson helped lead the Bengals to a 14–0 win over Minnesota on October 19, 1980, by making five receptions for 38 yards and running for 115 yards and one touchdown.

Johnson led the Bengals to a 20–6 win over the Chiefs on November 30, 1980, by rushing for 112 yards and one TD, which came on a 57-yard run in the fourth quarter that sealed the victory.

Johnson followed that up by rushing for 118 yards and two touchdowns during a 34–33 win over the Baltimore Colts on December 7, 1980.

Johnson proved to be the difference in a 24–10 win over the Los Angeles Rams on November 15, 1981, scoring all three Bengals TDs on a pair of short runs and a 3-yard pass reception.

Johnson contributed to a 31–17 victory over the Los Angeles Raiders on November 28, 1982, by carrying the ball 23 times for 129 yards and one touchdown.

Johnson helped lead the Bengals to a 34–14 win over Green Bay on October 30, 1983, by rushing for 112 yards, gaining another 53 yards on five pass receptions, and scoring two touchdowns.

Johnson led the Bengals to a 38–10 victory over the Houston Oilers on November 20, 1983, by rushing for 137 yards and two touchdowns, which came on runs of 12 and 10 yards.

Notable Achievements

- Rushed for 1,077 yards in 1981.
- Amassed more than 1,000 yards from scrimmage twice.

- Scored more than 10 touchdowns four times.
- Finished third in NFL in touchdowns three times.
- Led Bengals in rushing seven times.
- Holds Bengals career records for most rushing touchdowns (64) and most touchdowns (70).
- Ranks among Bengals career leaders with 1,402 rushing attempts (4th), 5,421 rushing yards (5th), 6,748 yards from scrimmage (8th), 6,757 all-purpose yards (9th), and 420 points scored (6th).
- Two-time division champion (1981 and 1982).
- 1981 AFC champion.
- 1981 Pro Bowl selection.
- 1981 Second-Team All-AFC selection.
- Named to Bengals 50th Anniversary All-Time Team in 2017.

33
MIKE REID

An excellent player who proved to be one of the game's finest defensive tackles during his relatively brief professional career, Mike Reid competed in the NFL for just five seasons, all of which he spent in Cincinnati. Yet, over the course of those five seasons, Reid made an enormous impact, helping the Bengals win two division titles with his dominant play up front. A two-time Pro Bowler who also earned two All-Pro nominations and four All-AFC selections, Reid performed so well during his brief stint in Cincinnati that he eventually landed a spot on the Bengals 50th Anniversary All-Time Team even though he chose to retire from football at a very young age to pursue a career in music.

Born in Altoona, Pennsylvania, on May 24, 1947, Michael Barry Reid starred in football and wrestling at Altoona Area High School, before excelling in both sports at Penn State University as well. Electing to focus more on further developing his skills on the gridiron after winning the Eastern heavyweight wrestling title as a sophomore in 1967, Reid became a team captain and a two-time All-America defensive tackle for the Nittany Lions, whom he helped lead to consecutive undefeated seasons in 1968 and 1969. Particularly outstanding his senior year, Reid gained unanimous First-Team All-America recognition, won the Outland Trophy as the nation's top interior lineman and the Maxwell Trophy as college football's most outstanding player, and finished fifth in the Heisman Trophy balloting. Meanwhile, Reid spent every possible moment away from the football field and classroom playing piano, which brought him more joy than anything else.

Subsequently selected by the Bengals in the first round of the 1970 NFL Draft, with the seventh overall pick, Reid became an immediate starter at left defensive tackle, earning a third-place finish in the NFL Defensive Rookie of the Year voting by recording unofficial totals of five sacks and 29 tackles, despite missing the season's final five games with a left knee injury. Taking his game up a notch in 1971, Reid gained consensus

Before retiring from football to pursue a career in music, Mike Reid starred for the Bengals at defensive tackle for five seasons.

First-Team All-AFC recognition by making 54 tackles and ranking among the league leaders with 12 1/2 sacks. Reid followed that up with two more outstanding seasons, earning consecutive Pro Bowl and First-Team All-AFC nominations in 1972 and 1973 by recording 13 sacks each year, while also bringing down opposing ball-carriers a total of 104 times.

A First-Team All-Pro as well in 1972, Reid joined fellow defensive tackle "Mean" Joe Greene on the squad, finishing just ahead of Hall of Famers Bob Lilly and Alan Page in the balloting. Similar to Page in that he possessed extraordinary quickness, Reid had a knack for synchronizing his charge toward the offensive backfield with the snap of the football, allowing him to often gain an advantage over his blocker.

In comparing Reid to Page, writer Jim Klobuchar stated in his newspaper column, "Reid and Alan Page are probably the two best defensive tackles in the game." Klobuchar then quoted a Vikings offensive lineman, who said, "Put it this way, I think Page is the best lineman in football. I would never want to go a full game against him. But this Reid may be quicker in his movements at the line. We saw one play against Dallas, I think, where he went past the guard and center practically without getting touched, on a straight charge. And you don't do that without a rocket booster."

Although, at 6'3¼" and just over 250 pounds, Reid did not possess ideal size for an NFL defensive tackle, he made up for whatever he lacked in that area with his exceptional quickness, superior instincts, and outstanding technique, to which his background in wrestling contributed.

Once told by most pro scouts that they considered him three-quarters of an inch too short and 15 pounds too light to excel at defensive tackle in the NFL, Reid played the game with great passion, spending his entire career trying to prove his doubters wrong. Expressing his annoyance with those who initially expressed concerns over his size, or lack thereof, Reid once asked, rhetorically, "Can you tell me what difference three-fourths of an inch makes?"

However, even though Reid earned Second-Team All-AFC honors in 1974 by recording six sacks and 50 tackles, his passion began to leave him as the pain in his knees and ankles grew worse. Having undergone surgery on both knees in college, Reid spent his entire time in Cincinnati playing in discomfort. And, after suffering several other injuries during his pro career, Reid found it increasingly difficult to muster the same enthusiasm for the game he once loved, remembering, "I had been through five knee operations, cracked a vertebrae, and had a shoulder problem. The life of an athlete was no longer the life I wanted to lead."

Further troubled by the business of football, Reid recalled, "By the time I quit, the World Football League had come into existence, and they were drafting a lot of our players. We were called into court to testify. I became somewhat discouraged with the rout professional sports were taking."

Suffering from depression, Reid began to seriously consider leaving the game, making his final decision with the help of his father, Bill, a railroad worker in their hometown of Altoona, Pennsylvania. Recalling how his dad helped him find his true calling, Reid told the *Windsor Star*, "He was probably the most supportive person of my decision to leave football. He hated his job, and he could see that music was what I loved."

Informing head coach Paul Brown of his decision to retire from football early in 1975, Reid left the game with career totals of 49 1/2 sacks, 237 tackles, two fumble recoveries, and one forced fumble. Stating years later that he made the right choice, Reid said, "I never felt that football defined me too much. I came into pro football more or less curious to see if I could compete at that level."

Adding that his choice of occupations came as something of a surprise to even him, Reid said, "I had studied music and earned my degree in music from college, but I never thought I would get into it professionally."

Although Reid stated, "I didn't really quit football to go into music . . . I just kind of drifted into it," he devoted himself completely to his new profession following his retirement from sports, eventually moving to Nashville and signing with country singer Ronnie Milsap's publishing company. A successful pianist and songwriter in the years that followed, Reid played with the Utah, Dallas, and Cincinnati Symphony Orchestras, wrote for artists such as Milsap and Larry Gatlin, won a Grammy in 1984, and entered the Nashville Songwriters Hall of Fame in 2005.

CAREER HIGHLIGHTS

Best Season

Although Reid posted comparable numbers in 1971 and 1973, he had his finest all-around season in 1972, when he earned his lone First-Team All-Pro nomination by finishing third in the league with 13 sacks and recording a career-high 56 tackles.

Memorable Moments/Greatest Performances

Reid helped anchor a Bengals defense that allowed just 142 yards of total offense during a 45–7 rout of the Boston Patriots in the final game of the 1970 regular season, with the Pats gaining only 82 yards through the air and 67 yards on the ground.

Reid set a single-game franchise record (later tied) by sacking Len Dawson five times during a 23–16 win over the Kansas City Chiefs on October 15, 1972, earning in the process NFL Defensive Player of the Week honors.

Reid led the defensive charge when the Bengals recorded four sacks of Terry Bradshaw and yielded just 138 yards of total offense during a 19–7 win over the Steelers on October 14, 1973.

Notable Achievements

- Finished in double digits in sacks three times.
- Finished in top five in NFL in sacks three times.
- Led Bengals in sacks three times.
- Holds share of franchise record for most sacks in one game (5).
- Ranks sixth in franchise history with 49 1/2 career sacks.
- Two-time division champion (1970 and 1973).
- 1972 Week 5 NFL Defensive Player of the Week.
- Two-time Pro Bowl selection (1972 and 1973).
- 1972 First-Team All-Pro selection.
- 1973 Second-Team All-Pro selection.
- Three-time First-Team All-AFC selection (1971, 1972, and 1973). 1974 Second-Team All-AFC selection.
- Named to Bengals 40th Anniversary All-Time Team in 2007.
- Named to Bengals 50th Anniversary All-Time Team in 2017.

34

RUDI JOHNSON

A punishing runner who helped the Bengals end their 15-year playoff drought in 2005 by setting a single-season franchise record for most yards gained on the ground, Rudi Johnson spent seven seasons in Cincinnati, rushing for the third-most yards of any player in team annals during that time. The Bengals' leading rusher for four straight seasons, Johnson ran for more than 1,000 yards in three of those, while also amassing more than 1,000 yards from scrimmage on four separate occasions. A fan favorite during his time in the Queen City, Johnson earned one Pro Bowl nomination, before joining the Detroit Lions, with whom he spent his final NFL season.

Born in Ettrick, Virginia, on October 1, 1979, Burudi Ali Johnson grew up some 30 miles south of Richmond, where he became more commonly known during his childhood as "Rudi"—a derivative of his given name, which means "cool" in Swahili. Meanwhile, Johnson's middle name, "Ali," serves as a tribute to former world heavyweight boxing champion Muhammad Ali.

Raised by his divorced mother, Johnson began playing football at the age of six with the Ettrick Trojans of the Chesterfield Quarterback League. Developing into a standout two-way player in high school, Johnson performed well on both sides of the ball for the Thomas Dale Knights. Proving to be especially proficient on offense, Johnson broke the school's career rushing record, which had previously been held by his friend, mentor, and coach, Henry Jefferson.

Failing to receive any scholarship offers, Johnson enrolled at Butler Community College, in El Dorado, Kansas, where he helped lead the Grizzlies to consecutive National Junior College Athletic Association (NJCAA) championships in 1998 and 1999 by rushing for close to 4,000 yards and scoring 46 touchdowns. Particularly outstanding in the second of those campaigns, Johnson earned First-Team All-America and NJCAA Player of

Rudi Johnson's 1,458 yards gained on the ground in 2005 set a single-season franchise record that still stands.

the Year honors by setting school records for most rushing yards (2,310) and touchdowns scored (31).

While in El Dorado, Johnson also made a lasting impression on Bill and Betty Kirkpatrick, a middle-aged couple that became his host family. Later identifying Johnson as her favorite of all the players for whom she has cared through the years, Betty, who never had any children of her own, said, "There was just something special about Rudi. He was the only player I ever kept a scrapbook for."

Ms. Kirkpatrick continued, "Reporters crowded around Rudi after the game, but he would always excuse himself and come over and talk to Bill. I'd give him a hug, and then he would go back and talk about the game. . . . If I had a son, I'd want him to be just like Rudi."

With Johnson having performed so well in his two seasons at Butler, he received a scholarship to Auburn University. Continuing to excel at the NCAA Division I level, Johnson gained SEC Player of the Year recognition as a junior by rushing for 1,567 yards and 13 touchdowns. Choosing to forgo his senior year, Johnson declared himself eligible for the 2001 NFL Draft, where the Bengals selected him in the fourth round, with the 100th overall pick.

Johnson subsequently received very little playing time his first two seasons in Cincinnati, amassing a total of just 457 all-purpose yards while serving the Bengals primarily as a kickoff returner and cover man on special teams. However, with Pro Bowl running back Corey Dillon being plagued by injuries for much of 2003, Johnson assumed a far more prominent role on offense, rushing for 957 yards, amassing 1,103 yards from scrimmage, and scoring nine touchdowns. Taking on an even bigger share of the workload after the Bengals traded Dillon to the New England Patriots following the conclusion of the 2003 campaign, Johnson began an outstanding three-year run during which he posted the following numbers:

YEAR	YDS RUSHING	RECS	REC YDS	YDS FROM SCRIMMAGE	TDS
2004	1,454	15	84	1,538	12
2005	1,458	23	90	1,548	12
2006	1,309	23	124	1,433	12

Placing near the top of the league rankings in rushing yards and rushing touchdowns all three years, Johnson became just the second player in team annals to gain more than 1,000 yards on the ground three straight times (Corey Dillon accomplished the feat in six consecutive seasons). After earning his lone Pro Bowl nomination in the first of those campaigns by setting a single-season franchise record for most rushing yards, Johnson broke his own mark the following year. Of greater importance, the Bengals captured their first division title in 15 years in 2005 by compiling a regular-season record of 11–5.

Part of an outstanding Bengals offense that also featured quarterback Carson Palmer and wide receivers Chad Johnson and T. J. Houshmandzadeh, Johnson served as the perfect complement to the team's potent aerial assault. Running in a brutal and aggressive manner that earned him the nickname the "Auburn Rambler," the 5'10", 228-pound Johnson followed his blockers well and did most of his best work between the tackles, often outmaneuvering or shrugging off defenders near the line of scrimmage. However, Johnson also possessed the speed to break his runs to the outside, with the home crowd at Paul Brown Stadium serenading him with a chant of "Rudi! Rudi! Rudi!" every time he made a big play.

Recalling how the support of the hometown fans affected him and his teammates, Johnson told Geoff Hobson of Bengals.com in December 2016, "It's always nice to hear. Music to my ears. That always got me through, and it got my teammates through. That's how we closed out games."

Johnson added, "The culture was changing. There were new times. Me and Chad and Carson and T. J. were in the middle of it as far as turning the tide."

One of the team's most popular players during his heyday, Johnson endeared himself to his teammates with his genuine and unpretentious nature, with Chad Johnson describing him as "Quiet, into his job. Whatever you ask him, he gets it done. He doesn't say much."

A pillar within the community as well, Johnson established in 2005 the Rudi Johnson Foundation, which assists families and children in becoming self-sufficient and self-reliant by incorporating several community-based programs. The foundation, which helped fund the formation of the first football team for Clark Montessori High School in Cincinnati, has also collaborated with the National Bone Marrow Registry the past two decades and regularly organizes and conducts donor drives to recruit minorities.

Hampered by a nagging hamstring injury that sidelined him for five games in 2007, Johnson rushed for only 497 yards and scored just four touchdowns, before being waived by the Bengals just prior to the start of the ensuing campaign. Expressing little surprise upon learning of his release, Johnson stated, "The word got out last month that the Bengals were trying to trade me, so I knew this was coming. I had a great run in Cincinnati, but now it's time to move on."

Johnson, who left Cincinnati with career totals of 5,742 rushing yards, 101 receptions, 588 receiving yards, 6,330 yards from scrimmage, 6,709 all-purpose yards, 48 rushing touchdowns, and 49 TDs, subsequently signed with the Detroit Lions, with whom he gained 237 yards on the ground, amassed 325 yards from scrimmage, and scored two touchdowns in a backup role in 2008, before announcing his retirement at the end of the year. Following his playing days, Johnson moved to Miami, Florida, where he became a real estate investor and boxing promoter. Johnson, who has always had a passion for cars, also co-manages the Warren Henry Auto Group in Fort Lauderdale, Florida.

BENGALS CAREER HIGHLIGHTS

Best Season

Johnson posted extremely comparable numbers in 2004 and 2005, gaining Pro Bowl recognition for the only time in the first of those campaigns. But with the Bengals winning the division title the following year, we'll identify the 2005 season as the most impactful of Johnson's career.

Memorable Moments/Greatest Performances

Johnson went over 100 yards rushing for the first time as a pro during a 27–24 win over Seattle on October 26, 2003, carrying the ball 27 times for 101 yards and one touchdown, which came on an 18-yard run.

Johnson helped lead the Bengals to a 34–27 victory over the Houston Texans on November 9, 2003, by rushing for 182 yards and two touchdowns.

Johnson followed that up by carrying the ball 22 times for 165 yards during a 24–19 win over the Chiefs on November 16, with his longest run of the day being a 54-yard scamper.

Johnson contributed to a 41–38 victory over the 49ers on December 14, 2003, by rushing for 174 yards and two touchdowns, the longest of which covered 49 yards.

Johnson led the Bengals to a 58–48 win over the Browns on November 28, 2004, by rushing for a career-high 202 yards and two touchdowns, both of which came on 7-yard runs.

Johnson had another big game against the Browns on December 11, 2005, carrying the ball 30 times for 169 yards and one touchdown during a 23–20 Bengals win.

Johnson continued to torment the Browns on September 17, 2006, rushing for 145 yards and two touchdowns during a 34–17 Bengals win.

Notable Achievements

- Rushed for more than 1,000 yards three times, topping 1,400 yards twice.

- Amassed more than 1,000 yards from scrimmage four times, surpassing 1,500 yards twice.
- Scored 12 touchdowns three times.
- Led Bengals in rushing four times.
- Holds Bengals single-season record for most rushing yards (1,458 in 2005).
- Ranks among Bengals career leaders with 1,441 rushing attempts (3rd), 5,742 rushing yards (4th), 6,330 yards from scrimmage (11th), 6,709 all-purpose yards (10th), 48 rushing touchdowns (3rd), and 49 touchdowns (9th).
- 2005 division champion.
- 2004 Pro Bowl selection.

35

T. J. HOUSHMANDZADEH

An outstanding possession receiver who did an excellent job of finding the "soft spot" in opposing defenses, T. J. Houshmandzadeh spent eight seasons in Cincinnati, combining with Chad Johnson much of that time to give the Bengals one of the top wide receiver pairings in all of football. Houshmandzadeh, who ranks among the franchise's all-time leaders in every major pass receiving category, caught more than 90 passes three times and amassed more than 1,000 receiving yards twice, with his 112 receptions in 2007 representing the highest single-season total in team annals. And even though Houshmandzadeh often found himself being overshadowed by Johnson, he led the Bengals in receptions three times and receiving yards once, earning in the process one Pro Bowl selection.

Born in Victorville, California, on September 26, 1977, Touraj Houshmandzadeh Jr. grew up in the San Bernardino County region of Southern California, just west of the Mohave Desert. Born to an African American mother and an Iranian American father whom he has never met and only communicated with by telephone from the latter's home in Iran, Houshmandzadeh owes his surname to a Persian compound name meaning "son of wisdom or intelligence."

Raised in a single-parent household, Houshmandzadeh lacked proper guidance as a youth, causing him to often roam the streets and neglect his studies. After dropping out of Barstow High School, Houshmandzadeh later returned to school and eventually enrolled at Cerritos College, a public community college located in Norwalk, California. Emerging as a star wide receiver and kickoff returner for the Cerritos College football team, Houshmandzadeh earned consecutive First-Team Mission Conference selections, prompting Oregon State University to offer him an athletic scholarship after his sophomore year. Houshmandzadeh subsequently spent his final two years of college playing for head coach Dennis Erickson, starting for the Beavers as a senior in 2000, when he caught 48 passes,

T. J. Houshmandzadeh set a single-season franchise record by gathering in 112 passes in 2007.
Courtesy of Keith Allison and All-Pro Reels Photography

amassed 730 receiving yards, scored seven touchdowns, and gained another 298 yards on special teams.

Selected by the Bengals in the seventh round of the 2001 NFL Draft, with the 204th overall pick, Houshmandzadeh received a limited amount of playing time on offense his first year in Cincinnati, making just 21 receptions for 228 yards and no touchdowns. However, he amassed another 348 yards as a punt- and kickoff-returner, giving him a total of 576 all-purpose yards. Seeing a bit more action on offense the following year, Houshmandzadeh caught 41 passes, amassed 492 receiving yards, accumulated 897 all-purpose yards, and scored one touchdown.

Houshmandzadeh subsequently missed virtually the entire 2003 campaign with a severe hamstring injury. But upon his return to action the following year, Houshmandzadeh replaced an injured Peter Warrick as the starter opposite Chad Johnson. Acquitting himself extremely well in his first season as a full-time starter, Houshmandzadeh earned consideration for NFL Comeback Player of the Year honors by catching 73 passes, amassing 978 receiving yards, accumulating 1,029 yards from scrimmage and 1,344 all-purpose yards, and scoring four touchdowns. Continuing to perform at an elite level the next four seasons, Houshmandzadeh posted the following numbers from 2005 to 2008:

YEAR	RECS	REC YDS	TD RECS
2005	78	956	7
2006	90	1,081	9
2007	112	1,143	12
2008	92	904	4

After helping the Bengals win the division title in 2005 by making 78 receptions for 956 yards despite being hampered by an injury to his right hand that limited his effectiveness for several games, Houshmandzadeh earned Pro Bowl honors two years later by becoming the first player in franchise history to lead the NFL in receptions. Houshmandzadeh also placed near the top of the league rankings in that category in two of the other three seasons and ranked among the leaders in touchdown receptions twice. Meanwhile, after combining with Chad Johnson in 2006 to become the first Bengals teammates ever to surpass 1,000 receiving yards in the same season, Houshmandzadeh joined his cohort in accomplishing the feat again the following year.

Arguably the league's best number two receiver throughout the period, Houshmandzadeh used his soft hands and superior route-running ability to serve as an excellent safety net for quarterback Carson Palmer, who often looked for him in third-down situations. Although not as much of a threat deep downfield as Chad Johnson, Houshmandzadeh possessed enough speed and quickness to evade tacklers in the open field. And, at 6'2" and 200 pounds, he had the size and strength to drag defenders for additional yardage after gathering in the football. One of the league's most physical wideouts, Houshmandzadeh also excelled as a downfield blocker.

When asked to compare Houshmandzadeh and Johnson, Carson Palmer said, "They're both unique. They do completely different things well and complement each other perfectly. T. J.'s a physical guy; a physical blocker, physical when he gets the ball. He's like [Pittsburgh Steelers wideout] Hines Ward."

Two things Houshmandzadeh and Johnson had in common, though, were their outgoing personalities and constant craving for media attention. But Houshmandzadeh's failure to speak to the media on one occasion led to a controversial incident that remains something of a blot on his record. After Houshmandzadeh failed to make a scheduled appearance on Andy Furman's Cincinnati-based sports-talk show on October 5, 2006, Furman criticized him on the air. The following evening, Furman alleged that he heard from another source that Houshmandzadeh called him a "punk-ass white boy" for criticizing his no-show. Although Houshmandzadeh subsequently denied making the comment, Furman remained firm in his beliefs, referring to his adversary on the air as a racist, which resulted in him being relieved of his duties less than one month later.

With Houshmandzadeh coming off his outstanding four-year run, the Seattle Seahawks offered him a five-year, $40 million contract when he became a free agent following the conclusion of the 2008 campaign. Choosing to sign with Seattle rather than return to Cincinnati for less money, Houshmandzadeh stated at the time, "If Cincinnati wanted, they could have had me. They wanted me, but at their convenience. . . . Cincinnati's offer wasn't enough for me to consider to play there. I think I should be able to start fresh."

Houshmandzadeh then took a jab at the Bengals organization by saying, "I want to win some games for once."

Expressing his satisfaction with the signing of Houshmandzadeh, Seahawks general manager Tim Ruskell said, "We made the bolstering of our wide receiver corps one of our top priorities in the offseason, and obviously this move goes a long way toward doing that."

Meanwhile, Seattle head coach Jim Mora said of his team's new wideout, "He is what we are looking for in a Seattle Seahawk. . . . He brings a physical presence to the field. He adds toughness to our team. A swagger. And, as we all know, a load of productivity. . . . He gives teams huge matchup problems. And he is known as one of the finest route runners in the NFL."

Houshmandzadeh, who left Cincinnati having caught 507 passes, amassed 5,782 receiving yards, 5,924 yards from scrimmage, and 7,068 all-purpose yards, and scored 38 touchdowns, 37 of which came through the air, ended up spending just one year in Seattle, making 79 receptions, accumulating 911 receiving yards, and scoring three touchdowns for a Seahawks team that won just five games in 2009. Meanwhile, the Bengals captured the division title with a record of 10–6, giving them the last laugh.

Released by the Seahawks just prior to the start of the 2010 campaign, Houshmandzadeh split the next two seasons between the Baltimore Ravens and Oakland Raiders, assuming a backup role with both teams, before announcing his retirement at the end of 2011 with career totals of 627 receptions, 7,237 receiving yards, 7,379 yards from scrimmage, 8,253 all-purpose yards, and 45 touchdowns.

After retiring as an active player, Houshmandzadeh joined the coaching staff of Long Beach Poly High School, in Long Beach, California, where he spent two seasons coaching the school's wide receivers, before being elevated to varsity offensive coordinator in 2018. He also works as a football analyst for FS1.

BENGALS CAREER HIGHLIGHTS

Best Season

Although Houshmandzadeh's work on special teams enabled him to amass a career-best 1,344 all-purpose yards in 2004, he had his finest season in 2007, when he earned his lone Pro Bowl nomination by establishing career-high marks with 112 receptions, 1,143 receiving yards, and 12 touchdown receptions, with his league-leading 112 catches setting a single-season franchise record that still stands.

Memorable Moments/Greatest Performances

Although the Bengals lost to the Browns, 18–0, on November 25, 2001, Houshmandzadeh set a single-game franchise record by amassing a total of 126 yards on five punt returns.

Houshmandzadeh proved to be a huge factor in a 27–26 win over the Baltimore Ravens on December 5, 2004, making 10 receptions for 171 yards and one touchdown.

Houshmandzadeh again riddled Baltimore's defensive secondary on November 27, 2005, catching nine passes for 147 yards and one touchdown during a 42–29 Bengals win.

Houshmandzadeh earned AFC Offensive Player of the Week honors by making nine receptions for 94 yards and two touchdowns during a 28–20 win over the Steelers on September 24, 2006, with the longest of his TDs covering 30 yards.

Houshmandzadeh starred in defeat on September 21, 2008, making 12 receptions for 146 yards and one touchdown during a 26–23 overtime loss to the Giants.

Houshmandzadeh posted nearly identical numbers during a 13–13 tie with the Eagles on November 16, 2008, finishing the game with 12 catches for 149 yards and one touchdown, which came on a 26-yard connection with Ryan Fitzpatrick.

Notable Achievements

- Surpassed 100 receptions once, topping 90 catches two other times.
- Amassed more than 1,000 receiving yards twice.
- Amassed more than 1,000 yards from scrimmage four times.
- Caught 12 touchdown passes in 2007.
- Led NFL with 112 receptions in 2007.
- Led Bengals in receptions three times and receiving yards once.
- Holds Bengals single-game record for most punt-return yards (126 vs. Cleveland on November 25, 2001).
- Holds Bengals single-season record for most receptions (112 in 2007).
- Ranks among Bengals career leaders with 507 receptions (5th), 5,782 receiving yards (9th), 7,068 all-purpose yards (8th), and 37 touchdown receptions (6th).
- 2005 division champion.
- 2006 Week 3 AFC Offensive Player of the Week.
- 2007 Pro Bowl selection.
- Named to Bengals 40th Anniversary All-Time Team in 2007.

36

JIM BREECH

The Bengals' all-time leading scorer, Jim Breech spent 13 seasons in Cincinnati, establishing himself as one of the greatest clutch performers in team annals. The only kicker in NFL history to attempt nine or more field goals in overtime and make them all, Breech scored more than 100 points four times and successfully converted at least 80 percent of his field goal attempts on three separate occasions, in helping the Bengals win four division titles and two AFC championships. One of the few men who served as a member of each of the Bengals' first two Super Bowl teams, Breech also ranks among the franchise's all-time leaders in games played and seasons played, with his many years of service and contributions to the success of the organization earning him a spot on the Bengals 50th Anniversary All-Time Team.

Born in Sacramento, California, on April 11, 1956, James Thomas Breech got his start in organized sports in the local Pop Warner Football league. Eventually emerging as a star athlete at Sacramento High School, Breech earned All-City honors in football as a quarterback and placekicker, while also being named to the All–Metro League team in baseball. Offered an athletic scholarship to the University of California–Berkeley, Breech spent two seasons excelling on the gridiron for the Golden Bears, gaining All–Pac-8 Conference recognition his senior year by leading the conference in scoring and field goals made.

Selected by Detroit in the eighth round of the 1978 NFL Draft, with the 206th overall pick, Breech failed to earn a roster spot with the Lions, who cut him before the opening game of the regular season. Subsequently signed by Oakland, Breech ended up spending the 1979 season with the Raiders, successfully converting 18 of his 27 field goal attempts, before being waived by them prior to the start of the ensuing campaign. Asked by Cleveland Browns personnel director Paul Warfield shortly thereafter if he had any interest in temporarily replacing an injured Don Cockroft, Breech responded in the affirmative. However, while waiting to hear back from the

Jim Breech scored more points than anyone else in team annals.

Browns, Breech received a phone call from Cincinnati's assistant personnel director Frank Smouse, who offered him an opportunity to sign with the Bengals.

After sharing placekicking duties with Ian Sunter in 1980, Breech began a 12-year stint as the Bengals' sole kicker the following season. Proving to be one of the NFL's more reliable kickers throughout the period, Breech consistently placed well above the league average in field goal percentage, which typically ranged somewhere between 65 and 72 percent. Successfully converting more than 80 percent of his field goal attempts on three separate occasions, Breech posted a career-best mark of 85.7 percent in 1989 that represented the second-highest figure in the league. Breech also consistently ranked among the NFL leaders in points scored, finishing third in the league and first in the AFC in that category twice.

A soccer-style kicker who became known more for his accuracy than the strength of his leg, the 5'6", 160-pound Breech rarely attempted anything from more than 50 yards out, hitting on only 6 of 26 attempts from beyond 50 over the course of his career. But he proved to be extremely accurate on kicks of less than 40 yards, successfully converting 87 percent of his attempts from within that range.

Also known for his ability to perform well under pressure, Breech placed a premium on delivering in the clutch, saying, "Reggie Williams once told me that the way for a kicker to gain respect from the team was to make the kicks that mattered. I took it to heart because you never want to let the guys down. It's one way we can really help the team."

Breech added, "I always thought the big game type kicks were fun. Heck, why play the game if you don't want to be in that situation? I finally learned I could control only one thing, and that was the kick. When I stopped worrying about everything around me, good things started to happen. Control what you can control."

Displaying his ability to perform well when it mattered most, Breech successfully converted nine of his 11 field goal attempts in postseason play, including all three of his tries in Super Bowl XXIII.

Notable as well for wearing a different size cleat on his kicking foot, Breech, who normally wore a size 7 shoe, sported a size 5 cleat on his right (kicking) foot because he felt it gave him more control and stability when addressing the football. In discussing his unusual practice, Breech said, "I would stick my foot in some water and get the shoe wet, and I'd just wear it around like that until it dried on my foot and kind of formed on my foot like a slipper. Now, it was a tight slipper in the toes, but I'd loosen the laces and walk around with it not fully tied until I had to tie it back up, and it was good. I liked having it nice and tight. I would imagine most guys today go at least one size or a size-and-a-half smaller than their normal shoes."

Breech remained with the Bengals until the end of 1992, when, after 13 seasons in Cincinnati, he chose to announce his retirement. Ending his career with 1,246 points scored, 243 field goals in 340 attempts, and 517 extra points made in 539 attempts, Breech retired having successfully converted 71.5 percent of his field goal attempts and 95.9 percent of his extra points. During his time in Cincinnati, Breech kicked 225 field goals, scored a franchise-record 1,151 points, and connected on 71.9 percent of his field goal attempts. Occasionally called upon to punt as well, Breech punted the ball 14 times for 409 yards, giving him an average of 29.2 yards per kick.

Following his playing days, Breech remained in the Cincinnati area, where he became a sales executive for the Hauser Group, an insurance firm in the nearby suburb of Blue Ash. Breech also became the president of the Cincinnati chapter of the NFL Alumni and has spent many years serving on the board of directors for Kicks for Kids, an organization started by fellow former Bengals kicker Doug Pelfrey to help needy children.

BENGALS CAREER HIGHLIGHTS

Best Season

Although Breech successfully converted 85.7 percent of his field goal attempts in 1989, he scored just 73 points since he attempted only 14 field goals. Much more productive in 1985, Breech scored a career-high 120 points. But he connected on only 24 of 33 kicks, giving him a rather pedestrian field goal percentage of 72.7. On the other hand, when Breech finished third in the NFL with 97 points scored in 1987, he successfully converted 24 of his 30 field goal attempts, or 80 percent—a figure that placed him among the league leaders. All things considered, Breech had the finest season of his career in 1987.

Memorable Moments/Greatest Performances

Breech gave the Bengals a 34–33 win over the Baltimore Colts on December 7, 1980, by kicking a 21-yard field goal in the closing moments.

Breech provided further heroics the following week when he gave the Bengals a 17–14 victory over the Chicago Bears by splitting the uprights from 28 yards out in overtime.

Breech proved to be the difference in an 18–14 win over the Eagles on November 21, 1982, successfully converting all three of his field goal attempts, the longest of which came from 49 yards out.

Breech kicked four field goals against Cleveland on October 21, 1984, scoring in the process all the points the Bengals tallied during a 12–9 win over the Browns.

Breech again thwarted the Browns in the second meeting between the two teams on December 2, 1984, giving the Bengals a 20–17 overtime victory over their division rivals by kicking a game-winning 35-yard field goal 4:34 into the OT session.

After kicking a 51-yard field goal earlier in the contest, Breech gave the Bengals a 36–33 overtime win over the Bills on September 14, 1986, by splitting the uprights from 20 yards out, earning in the process NFL Special Teams Player of the Week honors.

Although the Bengals lost to the Houston Oilers, 31–29, on November 1, 1987, Breech kicked five field goals in one game for the only time in his career, with the longest of his three-pointers coming from 39 yards out.

Breech gave the Bengals a 30–27 overtime victory over the Jets on December 6, 1987, by driving the ball through the uprights from 32 yards out 9:44 into the OT session.

Although the Bengals ended up losing Super Bowl XXIII to the San Francisco 49ers, 20–16, Breech put them ahead by three points late in the fourth quarter when, after successfully converting field goals of 34 and 43 yards earlier in the contest, he connected from 40 yards out with just 3:20 left.

Breech came up big in the clutch again on October 7, 1990, when his 44-yard field goal 10:56 into overtime gave the Bengals a 34–31 win over the Los Angeles Rams.

Breech also delivered a pair of clutch kicks in 1992, giving the Bengals a 24–21 win over the Los Angeles Raiders on September 13 by splitting the uprights from 34 yards out just 1:10 into overtime, before giving them a 31–28 victory over the Bears on November 8 by successfully converting a 36-yard field goal attempt 8:39 into the overtime session.

Notable Achievements

- Scored more than 100 points four times.
- Converted at least 80 percent of field goal attempts three times.
- Finished second in NFL in field goals made once and field goal percentage once.
- Finished third in NFL in points scored twice.
- Holds Bengals career records for most points scored (1,151), field goals made (225), and extra points made (476).
- Ranks among Bengals career leaders with 181 games played (9th) and 13 seasons played (tied for 6th).
- Four-time division champion (1981, 1982, 1988, and 1990).

- Two-time AFC champion (1981 and 1988).
- 1986 Week 2 NFL Special Teams Player of the Week.
- Named to Bengals 50th Anniversary All-Time Team in 2017.

37

JOE MIXON

An extremely talented runner who led the Bengals in rushing in each of his seven seasons in Cincinnati, Joe Mixon proved to be one of the NFL's most productive running backs during his time in the Queen City. A one-time Pro Bowler who contributed significantly to teams that won two division titles and one AFC championship, Mixon gained more than 1,000 yards on the ground four times, amassed more than 1,000 yards from scrimmage five times, and scored more than 10 touchdowns twice, en route to establishing himself as one of the franchise's career leaders in all three categories. Nevertheless, Mixon sometimes found his outstanding play being overshadowed by his off-field troubles that caused many to question the quality of his character.

Born in Oakley, California, on July 24, 1996, Joseph Tyler Mixon grew up with his five older siblings some 50 miles northeast of San Francisco. Though raised by his mother, Alisa Smith, in a single-parent household, Mixon received constant support from his father, John Mixon, a Realtor and personal trainer who starred on the gridiron at Jefferson High School, in Daly City, California.

Developing into quite an athlete himself during his teenage years, the younger Mixon excelled in football and basketball at Freedom High School, performing especially well on the gridiron, where he rushed for 4,281 yards and 57 touchdowns in his three years on the varsity squad. Ranked as the top running back in the nation by Rivals.com as graduation neared, Mixon received almost 50 scholarship offers, before ultimately choosing the University of Oklahoma over Alabama, Wisconsin, Florida State, UCLA, and the University of California–Berkeley.

Prior to arriving on campus, though, Mixon faced charges of misdemeanor assault for having punched a female Oklahoma student in the face during an altercation in the summer of 2014. Caught on camera, the incident, which, according to Amelia Molitor, began when Mixon and some of his Oklahoma teammates followed her and her gay friend into a sandwich

Joe Mixon has led the Bengals in rushing in each of the last seven seasons.
Courtesy of Keith Allison and All-Pro Reels Photography

shop to continue their harassment of them, escalated when her companion used a racial slur toward Mixon. In response, Mixon issued an anti-gay slur, causing Molitor to push him away from her table. Mixon then lunged at her, prompting Molitor to slap him on the left side of his neck. An angry Mixon then punched Molitor, knocking her into the table and down onto the floor. After Mixon left the scene, Molitor, who had to undergo reconstructive surgery for four fractured bones in her face, staggered to her feet and remained in a chair until police arrived.

Subsequently suspended for the entire 2014 season, Mixon, who received a deferred sentence and was ordered to perform community service and undergo counseling, later issued a public apology, saying, "It really doesn't matter what she did, it's all on me. I take full responsibility for what I did. It's never OK to hit a woman. I would preach that to anybody. Hopefully people around the world will learn from my mistake."

Reinstated prior to the start of the ensuing campaign, Mixon starred for the Sooners at running back the next two seasons, rushing for 753 yards, amassing 1,109 yards from scrimmage, and scoring 11 touchdowns in 2015, before finishing second in the Big 12 with 1,274 yards rushing, 1,812 yards from scrimmage, and 16 TDs the following year, with the most memorable performance of his college career coming on October 22, 2016, when he gained 263 yards on the ground, accumulated 377 yards from scrimmage, and scored five touchdowns during a 66–59 win over Texas Tech. Yet, Mixon again experienced problems away from the playing field, suffering a one-game suspension in 2016 after he attempted to intimidate a parking attendant.

Choosing to forgo his two remaining years of college, Mixon declared himself eligible for the 2017 NFL Draft, which he entered as one of the most highly touted running backs in the nation. However, concerns over Mixon's character caused him to fall to the middle of the second round, where the Bengals selected him with the 48th overall pick.

Criticizing the Bengals for their selection of Mixon, New England Patriots owner Robert Kraft stated, "While I believe in second chances and giving players an opportunity for redemption, I also believe that playing in the NFL is a privilege, not a right. For me, personally, I believe that privilege is lost for men who have a history of abusing women."

With several other teams claiming that they also crossed Mixon's name off their draft board, Bengals owner Mike Brown defended his club's selection by telling the *Cincinnati Enquirer* that, while he considered it totally "unacceptable for a man to strike a woman," "the circumstances that led up to the incident remained unclear."

After adding that Mixon went on to "become a good citizen in Norman, a popular teammate, a player respected by his coaches, and one of the most talented players in college football," Brown stated, "We believe Joe has put this behind him and that he can turn into the player and community member that creates a plus for Cincinnati. We are going to do everything in our power to make this happen. Our hope is that time will prove that this opportunity is deserved, and perhaps—if given a chance—Joe can write a chapter in Cincinnati sports history that both he and Cincinnati can be proud of."

Following his arrival in Cincinnati, Mixon spent the first half of his rookie campaign assuming a backup role, before joining the starting unit at midseason. Performing well the rest of the year, Mixon ended up leading the Bengals with 626 yards rushing, while also making 30 receptions for 287 yards and scoring four touchdowns. Taking his game up a notch in 2018, Mixon gained 1,168 yards on the ground, made 43 receptions for 296 yards, amassed 1,464 yards from scrimmage, and scored nine TDs, despite missing two games with an injured knee. Mixon followed that up with another outstanding season, rushing for 1,137 yards, accumulating 1,424 yards from scrimmage, and scoring eight touchdowns for a Bengals team that won just two games.

A big, powerful runner, the 6'1", 220-pound Mixon explodes into the defensive line, often breaking tackles or dragging along defenders for additional yardage. Blessed with good speed, Mixon also has the ability to run outside, although he does most of his best work between the tackles. An excellent receiver out of the backfield as well, Mixon possesses soft hands and good moves once he gathers in the football, with his 60 receptions and 441 receiving yards in 2022 both placing him among the top running backs in the league.

Sidelined for much of 2020 with a foot injury, Mixon rushed for just 428 yards and scored only four touchdowns. But a return to full health the following year enabled Mixon to gain 1,205 yards on the ground, amass 1,519 yards from scrimmage, and score 16 touchdowns, with his outstanding performance earning him Pro Bowl honors. Though somewhat less productive in 2022, Mixon helped the Bengals capture their second straight division title by rushing for 814 yards, accumulating 1,255 yards from scrimmage, and scoring nine TDs.

Praising Mixon for the totality of his game following the conclusion of the campaign, former Bengals running back James Brooks stated, "You don't find that many guys that can run the ball, take the pounding, plus catch the ball and block, and he can do all that. . . . I think he's a heck of a back. I like his versatility. I told him, 'Keep doing what you're doing. Believe in yourself. Because I believe in you.'"

Bengals left tackle Orlando Brown Jr., who signed with the team as a free agent on March 17, 2023, also spoke highly of his former Oklahoma teammate, saying, "He's the best teammate I've had on all three levels. . . . Amazing guy. Dynamic runner. Very underrated when it comes to catching the ball. That's something that stuck out for him even when we were in school coming in together. Just how much energy he has daily. How much he loves the game. He has a real appreciation for life as well."

Unfortunately, Mixon again ran into trouble away from the playing field during the latter stages of the campaign, with a warrant being issued for his arrest for one count of aggravated menacing on February 2, 2023. Accused of pointing a gun at a woman in downtown Cincinnati one day before the Bengals faced the Buffalo Bills in the divisional round of the AFC playoffs, Mixon allegedly said, "You should be popped in the face. I should shoot you now. The police can't get me."

However, the Hamilton County Prosecutor's Office dismissed the charges against Mixon less than 24 hours later, reportedly telling county judge Curt Kissinger, "We need additional investigation before we would move forward with this case."

On April 7, 2023, the Cincinnati Police Department publicly announced the criminal charge against Mixon had been refiled. But following a four-day trial some four months later, Hamilton County Municipal Court found Mixon not guilty and acquitted him of the charges made against him.

Agreeing to restructure his contract to remain in Cincinnati just prior to the start of training camp in 2023, Mixon explained that his love for the city and the organization prompted him to accept less money, saying at the time, "I love the community here. I've been here since I was 20 years old. The city has embraced me. My teammates do the same. Same with ownership. If there's a place where I would want to stay for my whole career, it's here."

Mixon added, "I see the bigger picture. I see the task at hand and what we're trying to build, and, in order to keep other players here and pieces here, sometimes you have to sacrifice. I felt like this year was the year to sacrifice on the Super Bowl team we can potentially be. . . . That was my stance on it. We agreed on a number with great compensation this year with the incentives. Off my last deal, I feel like they allowed me to work to be able to make that money back. That's cool. I'll go to work for it."

Although the Bengals failed to advance to the playoffs for the first time in three years in 2023, Mixon had another excellent season, rushing for 1,034 yards, amassing 1,410 yards from scrimmage, and scoring 12 touchdowns. Nevertheless, the Bengals elected to part ways with him the following offseason, trading him to the Houston Texans for a seventh-round pick in the 2024 NFL Draft during the free agent signing period. Mixon, who left Cincinnati with career totals of 6,412 rushing yards, 283 receptions, 2,139 receiving yards, 8,551 yards from scrimmage, 49 rushing touchdowns, and 62 TDs, subsequently signed a three-year, $27 million contract extension with Houston that will expire at the end of 2026.

BENGALS CAREER HIGHLIGHTS

Best Season

Mixon performed extremely well for the Bengals in both 2018 and 2019, gaining more than 1,100 yards on the ground and amassing more than 1,400 yards from scrimmage in each of those campaigns. But Mixon posted slightly better overall numbers in 2021, when he earned his lone Pro Bowl nomination by ranking among the league leaders with 1,205 yards rushing, 1,519 yards from scrimmage, 13 rushing touchdowns, and 16 TDs.

Memorable Moments/Greatest Performances

In addition to scoring a touchdown and making three receptions for 51 yards during a 30–16 win over the Browns on November 26, 2017, Mixon went over 100 yards rushing for the first time in his career, gaining 114 yards on 23 carries.

Mixon helped lead the Bengals to a 37–34 victory over Tampa Bay on October 28, 2018, by rushing for 123 yards and two touchdowns.

Mixon helped the Bengals earn just their second win of the 2019 campaign by rushing for 162 yards and two TDs during a 33–32 victory over the Browns in the regular-season finale.

Mixon earned AFC Offensive Player of the Week honors by rushing for 151 yards and scoring three touchdowns during a 33–25 win over Jacksonville on October 4, 2020, scoring once on a 9-yard pass from Joe Burrow and twice on runs of 34 and 23 yards.

Mixon earned that distinction again by rushing for 165 yards and two touchdowns during a 41–10 blowout of the Steelers on November 28, 2021.

Mixon gained recognition as AFC Offensive Player of the Week for a third time by rushing for 153 yards, gaining another 58 yards on four pass receptions, and scoring a franchise-record five touchdowns during a 42–21 win over Carolina on November 6, 2022, with four of his TDs coming on runs and the other on a 12-yard pass from Joe Burrow.

Mixon helped lead the Bengals to a 31–14 victory over the Browns in the final game of the 2023 regular season by gaining 111 yards on just

14 carries and scoring twice, with one of his TDs coming on a short run and the other on a 6-yard pass from Jake Browning.

Notable Achievements

- Rushed for more than 1,000 yards four times.
- Amassed more than 1,000 yards from scrimmage five times, topping 1,500 yards once.
- Scored more than 10 touchdowns twice.
- Ranked among NFL leaders with 1,205 rushing yards (3rd) and 16 touchdowns (4th) in 2021.
- Led Bengals in rushing seven times.
- Ranks among Bengals career leaders with 1,571 rushing attempts (2nd), 6,412 rushing yards (3rd), 8,551 yards from scrimmage (5th), 8,551 all-purpose yards (5th), 49 rushing touchdowns (2nd), and 62 touchdowns (6th).
- Two-time division champion (2021 and 2022).
- 2021 AFC champion.
- Three-time AFC Offensive Player of the Week.
- 2021 Pro Bowl selection.

38

TEE HIGGINS

lthough Tee Higgins has spent most of his time in Cincinnati being overshadowed by Ja'Marr Chase, he has proven to be one of the NFL's finest number two receivers over the course of the past few seasons. A member of the Bengals since 2020, Higgins has combined with Chase the past three years to form an exceptional wide receiver tandem, joining his more celebrated teammate in surpassing 70 receptions and 1,000 receiving yards in both 2021 and 2022, after leading the team in yards gained through the air his first year in the league. A key contributor to teams that have won two division titles and one AFC championship, Higgins has given quarterback Joe Burrow another extremely talented receiver to target after being selected by the Bengals one round after they tabbed the star signal-caller with the first overall pick of the 2020 NFL Draft.

Born in Oak Ridge, Tennessee, on January 18, 1999, Tamaurice Higgins suffered through a difficult childhood, revealing years later that he often awoke in the middle of the night to find his mother missing, remembering, "When I'd wake up in the night, there'd be one of her friends there, just sitting on the couch. I'd burst out crying immediately. Then I'd take off running for Grandma's."

Claiming that she and her grandmother frequently tended to young Tamaurice in her mother's absence, Higgins's older sister, Shakia, who often lived with her grandmom, recalled, "I remember him coming down the street just crying, asking, 'Why my mama leaving?' And I couldn't really answer him at the time. I'd just tell him that she was sick, and we'd put him in the bed with us."

Unaware at the time that his mother's frequent late-night departures from home could be attributed to her dependence on drugs, Higgins finally learned of his mom's addiction in a horrific way at the age of six. Called to the school office in the middle of the day, Higgins learned from a weeping Shakia that their mother had been shot in the head by her drug-dealer boyfriend. Arriving home with his sister shortly thereafter, Higgins later

Tee Higgins has surpassed 70 receptions and 1,000 receiving yards twice each for the Bengals.
Courtesy of Keith Allison and All-Pro Reels Photography

described a scene that remains with him to this day: "I remember all these police cars and the ambulance, and all I wanted to do was see my mother, but no one would let me. I'm crying, and my sister's telling me she's going to be OK, and we'll see her later. I didn't want to hear any of that because I just wanted to see my mom."

While Higgins's mother, Camillia Stewart, survived the shooting, she spent the next few years battling her addiction, during which time she served multiple prison sentences for possession, before finally overcoming her dependence on drugs in 2008 following nearly a year of treatment at a rehabilitation center.

Drawing inspiration from his mother, Higgins says, "Whatever issue I'm having, it'll never compare to what my mom went through, by overcoming drugs, getting shot, and being sober for all these years. If I ever have a problem, I just look at how she's overcome, and I keep moving."

After getting his start in football in the local pee-wee leagues, Higgins eventually developed into a star in multiple sports at Oak Ridge High School, excelling in both football and basketball. Named a finalist for Mr. Basketball in Tennessee his junior year, Higgins proved to be even more outstanding on the gridiron, making 68 receptions for 1,044 yards and 18 touchdowns as a senior, with his exceptional play earning him Tennessee Mr. Football honors at the AAAAA level for the second straight year.

Recruited by several colleges for both basketball and football as graduation neared, Higgins ultimately accepted a football scholarship to Clemson University, after initially committing to the University of Tennessee. Higgins subsequently spent three seasons playing wideout for the Tigers, making 17 receptions for 345 yards and two touchdowns in a part-time role as a freshman in 2017, before helping Clemson win the National Championship the following year by catching 59 passes, amassing 936 receiving yards, and scoring 12 TDs. Although Clemson failed to repeat as national champions in 2019, losing to LSU by a score of 42–25 in the final game of the College Football Playoffs, Higgins had another outstanding season, making 59 receptions, finishing third in the ACC with 1,167 receiving yards, and leading the conference with 13 touchdown receptions.

Praising his team's star wideout for his exceptional play at the end of the year, Tigers head coach Dabo Swinney proclaimed, "Tee Higgins is as complete a receiver as we've had come out of Clemson. I think he's in the same category as Mike Williams when it comes to being a complete receiver, and you're talking about size, speed, athleticism, catch radius, ball skills, ability to lean on people, body control, and all of those type of things. He's as complete a receiver as we've had come out of here. Tee is a great kid and a Day One starter [in the NFL]."

Choosing to forgo his final year of college, Higgins declared himself eligible for the 2020 NFL Draft, where the Bengals selected him with the first pick of the second round (33rd overall). Joining the starting unit following a strong showing during the preseason, Higgins performed well in his first year as a pro, making 67 receptions and leading the team with 908 receiving yards and six TD receptions, with his 67 catches tying a then-franchise record for rookies previously set by Cris Collinsworth in 1981. Meanwhile,

Higgins's 908 receiving yards placed him third in the league among all first-year players.

Improving upon those numbers in 2021, Higgins gathered in 74 passes, amassed 1,091 receiving yards, and made six touchdown receptions, in helping the Bengals post a regular-season record of 10–6 that earned them their first division title in six years. Continuing to excel during the postseason, Higgins totaled 18 receptions, 309 receiving yards, and two touchdowns for a Bengals team that ended up suffering a narrow 23–20 defeat at the hands of the Los Angeles Rams in Super Bowl LVI. Particularly outstanding in the final two contests, Higgins caught six passes and amassed a team-high 103 receiving yards against Kansas City in the AFC Championship Game, before making four receptions for 100 yards and two touchdowns against Los Angeles in the Super Bowl.

A matchup nightmare for opposing defenses, the 6'4", 220-pound Higgins possesses the size, strength, and catch radius to ward off defenders for the football on contested catches, the speed to beat his man deep, and the agility to outmaneuver would-be tacklers in the open field. Too big and strong for most cornerbacks to guard, and too fast for most safeties to cover one-on-one, Higgins presents problems to virtually every defensive secondary in the league, with his ability to stretch the field and make catches in traffic making him the perfect complement to Ja'Marr Chase at wideout. Add Tyler Boyd to the mix and the Bengals have arguably the finest trio of receivers in the league.

Although Higgins had another excellent year in 2022, helping the Bengals capture their second straight division title by making 74 receptions for 1,029 yards and seven touchdowns, his involvement in a near-tragic incident that occurred during a late-season meeting with the Buffalo Bills tempered his enthusiasm over his outstanding individual performance. Tackled by Damar Hamlin after making a catch near midfield, Higgins drove his shoulder into the defensive back's chest, causing him to go into cardiac arrest. Fortunately, first responders got to the fallen Hamlin quickly and saved his life by initiating CPR and administering defibrillation on the field. Distraught and guilt-ridden by his involvement in the play, Higgins kept in close contact with Hamlin and his family as he recovered and has since forged a close relationship with them.

Limited to only 12 games in 2023 by injuries to his rib and hamstring, Higgins made just 42 receptions for 656 yards and five touchdowns, giving him career totals of 257 receptions, 3,684 receiving yards, and 24 TD catches. Assigned the franchise tag by the Bengals at the end of the year,

Higgins subsequently requested a trade, putting his future status as a member of the team very much into question as of this writing.

CAREER HIGHLIGHTS

Best Season

Higgins posted extremely comparable numbers in 2021 and 2022, making 74 receptions and surpassing 1,000 receiving yards in each of those campaigns. But with Higgins dropping three fewer passes (5) and the Bengals advancing to the Super Bowl in 2021, we'll identify that as his finest season.

Memorable Moments/Greatest Performances

Higgins helped lead the Bengals to a 41–21 win over the Baltimore Ravens on December 26, 2021, by making 12 receptions for 194 yards and two touchdowns.

Although the Bengals lost Super Bowl LVI to the Los Angeles Rams, 23–20, Higgins made four receptions for 100 yards and two touchdowns, one of which came on a 75-yard connection with Joe Burrow.

Higgins contributed to a 27–15 victory over the Miami Dolphins on September 29, 2022, by making seven receptions for 124 yards and one touchdown, which covered 59 yards.

Higgins made seven receptions for 114 yards and one touchdown during a 20–16 win over the Tennessee Titans on November 27, 2022, with his 27-yard TD catch early in the fourth quarter providing the margin of victory.

Higgins helped the Bengals earn their seventh straight win by making eight receptions for 128 yards and one touchdown during a 22–18 victory over the Patriots on December 24, 2022.

Higgins gathered in four passes for 61 yards and two touchdowns during a 27–24 overtime win over the Minnesota Vikings on December 16, 2023, with his 21-yard TD grab with just 39 seconds left in regulation sending the game into OT.

Higgins starred in defeat the following week, making five receptions for 140 yards and one touchdown during a 34–11 loss to Pittsburgh on December 23, scoring his TD on a career-long 80-yard catch-and-run.

Notable Achievements

- Has surpassed 70 receptions and 1,000 receiving yards twice each.
- Led Bengals with 908 receiving yards in 2020.
- Two-time division champion (2021 and 2022).
- 2021 AFC champion.

39

RUFUS MAYES

cquired from the Chicago Bears in a trade that ranks among the best in franchise history, Rufus Mayes spent nine seasons in Cincinnati giving the Bengals consistently excellent play on the left side of their offensive line. Playing mostly left tackle from 1970 to 1978, Mayes contributed greatly to teams that made three playoff appearances and won two division titles by providing ample blindside pass protection for quarterbacks Virgil Carter and Ken Anderson, while also creating huge holes for running backs Paul Robinson, Jess Phillips, Essex Johnson, Boobie Clark, Archie Griffin, and Pete Johnson. Yet, despite his outstanding play, Mayes is largely forgotten today because arguably the greatest left tackle in NFL history, Anthony Muñoz, laid claim to the starting left tackle job almost as soon as he left Cincinnati.

Born in Clarksdale, Arizona, on December 5, 1947, Rufus Lee Mayes grew up in Toledo, Ohio, where he starred in football while attending Macomber-Whitney High School, helping to lead his team to the 1964 City League championship. Offered an athletic scholarship to Ohio State University, Mayes began his college career as a tight end, before transitioning to offensive tackle prior to the start of his senior year. A three-year starter at OSU, Mayes appeared in a total of 28 games for the Buckeyes, who, after compiling a perfect 10–0 record during the 1968 campaign, captured the National Championship by defeating the University of Southern California (USC) in the 1969 Rose Bowl.

Accorded Second-Team All-America honors following his senior year, Mayes later received high praise from legendary Buckeyes head coach Woody Hayes, who called him one of the best offensive tackles he ever coached, and added, "He was quicker than most of them, and, of course, very powerful."

Impressed with Mayes's exceptional play at the collegiate level, the Chicago Bears made him the 14th overall pick of the 1969 NFL Draft when they selected him in the first round. Mayes subsequently spent his

Rufus Mayes spent nine seasons in Cincinnati excelling for the Bengals on the left side of their offensive line.

first pro season starting at right tackle for the Bears, before packing his bags and heading for Cincinnati when the Bengals acquired him for defensive linemen Bill Staley and Harry Gunner in January 1970, in what the *Chicago Tribune* ranked in 2004 as the sixth-worst trade in Bears history.

While neither Staley nor Gunner ended up making much of an impact in Chicago, Mayes helped solidify the Bengals' offensive line. After spending his first season in Cincinnati at left guard, Mayes moved to the outside the following year. He subsequently started every game at left tackle for the Bengals in four of the next eight seasons, at one point starting 67 of

70 contests. And, with Mayes anchoring the left side of the line, the Bengals offense finished in the top half of the NFL in points scored seven times, total offense and passing offense six times, and rushing offense on four separate occasions.

Extremely quick and very strong, the 6'5", 262-pound Mayes proved to be equally effective as a pass-protector and run-blocker. After Ken Anderson took over as the Bengals' primary signal-caller in 1972, Mayes helped limit the opposition to 24 sacks in each of the next two seasons. Meanwhile, running backs Essex Johnson and Boobie Clark both had the finest seasons of their respective careers running behind Mayes.

With Mayes playing out his option in 1978, he became a free agent, after which he signed with the Philadelphia Eagles. Mayes subsequently spent one year in Philadelphia assuming a backup role, before announcing his retirement following the conclusion of the 1979 campaign. Over 11 NFL seasons, Mayes appeared in a total of 139 games, 111 of which he started. In his nine years with the Bengals, he started 98 of the 110 games in which he appeared.

Following his playing days, Mayes moved with his wife and young son to the Seattle suburb of Redmond, Washington, where he became a marketing representative for Hewlett-Packard in nearby Bellevue. Mayes lived until January 9, 1990, when he died at only 42 years of age of complications from bacterial meningitis. Following his passing, his former coach at Macomber High School, Steve Contos, called him "a great guy, a very bright, very concerned, happy, easy to get along with type of guy."

BENGALS CAREER HIGHLIGHTS

Best Season

Although Mayes never gained Pro Bowl or All-Pro recognition, he performed well enough from 1974 to 1976 to earn either of those honors. Playing his best ball for the Bengals over the course of those three seasons, Mayes perhaps made his greatest overall impact in 1976, when he helped Bengals running backs average a robust 4.4 yards per carry.

Memorable Moments/Greatest Performances

Mayes helped the Bengals amass 452 yards of total offense during a 34–24 win over the Browns on October 13, 1974, with 189 of those yards coming on the ground and the other 263 through the air.

Mayes's superior blocking at the point of attack helped the Bengals gain a season-high total of 441 yards through the air and amass 553 yards of total offense during a 33–24 win over the Bills on November 17, 1975.

Notable Achievements

- Two-time division champion (1970 and 1973).

40

ROSS BROWNER

A significant contributor to Bengals teams that won two division titles and one AFC championship, Ross Browner spent nine of his 10 NFL seasons in Cincinnati, recording the fifth most sacks in franchise history during that time. The team leader in sacks on three separate occasions, Browner did an excellent job of applying pressure to opposing quarterbacks from his right defensive end position, while also tracking down opposing ball-carriers. Displaying a nose for the football throughout his career, Browner ranks extremely high in team annals in fumble recoveries as well, with his strong all-around play earning him team MVP honors once and a spot on the Bengals 40th Anniversary All-Time Team.

Born in Warren, Ohio, on March 22, 1954, Ross Dean Browner grew up in that small rural town with his sister and six younger brothers, three of whom followed him into the NFL. Displaying more of an interest in sports other than football during his early years, Browner recalled, "I practically grew up at the Warren YMCA. I competed as a swimmer and a diver. I put a lot of time into the sport."

Beginning to focus more on football as a teenager, Browner remembered, "It was like this. All my brothers and friends were playing football in our side yard. I didn't want to get left behind. Plus, I was noticing that the girls were going for the football players."

Developing into a standout on the gridiron at Warren Western Reserve High School, Browner helped lead his team to the State Football Championship his senior year, earning in the process First-Team Ohio AAA All-State honors as a defensive end.

Recruited by more than 30 Division I colleges as graduation neared, Browner, who also played tight end in high school, eventually narrowed his choices down to Notre Dame and Ohio State, whose head coach Woody Hayes urged him to stay home and play for the Buckeyes. But Browner, who grew up watching Fighting Irish football games on television, had been greatly impressed by head coach Ara Parseghian and the size of the

Ross Browner ranks among the Bengals career leaders in both sacks and fumble recoveries.

Notre Dame campus when he visited South Bend, later recounting in the book, *What It Means to Be Fighting Irish*, "Ohio State has a very impressive campus, but eighty-six thousand students, or whatever, it really concerned me, compared to just six thousand at Notre Dame."

Ultimately choosing to enroll at Notre Dame, Browner, whom Parseghian recruited as a tight end, moved to the defensive side of the ball prior to the start of his freshman year. After helping to lead the Fighting Irish to the National Championship for the first of two times as a freshman in 1973, Browner suffered a one-year suspension for violating the school's dormitory code, which forbids after-hour visits by women. Returning to action in 1975, Browner spent the next three seasons garnering numerous individual accolades, including gaining unanimous All-America recognition twice, winning the Outland Trophy as the nation's best interior lineman as a junior, and being named the winner of the Lombardi Trophy as the nation's top lineman and the Maxwell Award as the nation's best player the following year.

Recalling the elite level at which Browner performed, former Notre Dame offensive coordinator Tom Pagna said, "Ross had all the tools—size, agility, speed, and toughness. He was a prototype defensive end."

Meanwhile, longtime Notre Dame Football observer and senior editor of IrishIllustrated.com Tim Prister wrote, "Ross Browner was the most dominant defensive player in the history of Notre Dame Football. He was a man-child as a freshman, a Heisman Trophy like presence on the '77 national championship team, a proud representative of his alma mater, and a great NFL player. There are not enough superlatives to describe his prowess on the football field."

However, while at Notre Dame, Browner suffered a great loss when his father, Jimmie Browner Sr., passed away in 1976. With his dad imploring him with his final words to "take care of the family," the 22-year-old Browner had a huge responsibility thrust upon him and subsequently dedicated the rest of his career to his father's memory.

Selected by the Bengals in the first round of the 1978 NFL Draft, with the eighth overall pick, Browner welcomed going to Cincinnati, later saying, "I was so happy to be picked by the Bengals and Paul Brown. He was a wonderful owner. He followed me through my high school days. I admired him as a coach and owner."

Browner continued, "It's funny. I first met Paul at the high school All-Star game. He came and spoke to me and said, 'Hey, young man. You can really play. I'm going to keep my eye on you!' He asked where I was going to college, and I told him Notre Dame. I thought he was playing when he said he'd keep his eye on me, but he did. . . . He told me he watched me play and I was the only guy he didn't want to have to play against in the draft!"

Also given the opportunity to compete north of the border, Browner recalled, "The CFL was big then—a lot of guys were going to play in Canada for American dollars. Forrest Gregg happened to be coaching the Toronto team, and they made an offer to me. My attorney talked to me—I wanted my family to be able to see me play, and back then there were only three networks that showed games. If I wanted them to see me play, I'd have to play in the United States. So, I signed a four-year deal with the Bengals."

Performing extremely well in his first pro season, Browner earned team MVP honors, a spot on the NFL All-Rookie Team, and a runner-up finish to Detroit's Al "Bubba" Baker in the NFL Defensive Rookie of the Year voting by registering eight sacks and recovering three fumbles. Browner followed that up with another solid season, recording six sacks in 1979, before assuming a somewhat different role after Forrest Gregg took over as head coach the following year.

Used as a rover along the defensive front his first two seasons in Cincinnati, Browner remembered, "They played me as a swing lineman then—over the right, left, and middle. A lot like Lawrence Taylor."

Explaining how his role changed following the hiring of Gregg, Browner said, "He changed our defense to a 3–4—it hindered me but made our defense more effective. I had to take on more blockers—I had to adapt to that. Hank Bullough ran a lot of blitz schemes and showed us some different things. He had us slant right and left as linemen to be more disruptive, so we didn't have to pound down the middle of the line all the time. We moved to the 4–3 when we really needed a good pass rush."

Playing under Gregg from 1980 to 1983, Browner recorded a total of 24 sacks, 10 of which came during the AFC championship campaign of 1981. Suspended by the league for the first four games of the 1983 season after testing positive for cocaine, Browner saw his string of 40 consecutive starts come to an end. However, he subsequently began a new streak, starting the next 60 games the Bengals played.

Although Browner never developed into the dominant player he had been in college, he gave the Bengals consistently excellent play from his post at right defensive end. Standing 6'3" and weighing 262 pounds, Browner possessed the size and strength to drive opposing linemen into the offensive backfield. Extremely quick as well, Browner did an outstanding job of pursuing opposing ball-carriers from sideline to sideline. Browner, who boxed during his youth and eventually won the 1979 NFL heavyweight boxing championship, also knew how to use his pugilistic background to his advantage, saying, "You do a lot of boxing on the field! It helps when you try to beat a lineman's hands and knock them down and get underneath them. You use a lot of similar techniques. I had to learn how to bull rush, but once you go into a lineman you used some of those techniques—swim moves and uppercuts and jabs!"

Browner added, "I always watched the snap of the ball. It was something that helped me get a jump and get on the offensive linemen faster.

It helped me to knock their hands down faster so I could disrupt plays in the backfield."

In discussing his former Bengals teammate, Louis Breeden stated, "Ross was a unique player in the sense you didn't just see that kind of athleticism on the defensive line. He wasn't the biggest guy weight-wise. But Ross was quick off the ball, extremely athletic, and used his hands well."

Although Browner jumped to the Houston Gamblers of the USFL in 1985, he returned to the Bengals when the league folded at the end of the year. Browner remained in Cincinnati until the end of 1986, when he signed with the Packers. After one year in Green Bay, Browner announced his retirement, ending his career with 62 1/2 sacks, 10 fumble recoveries, and one interception, with all but one of his sacks coming as a member of the Bengals.

Following his playing days, Browner spent several years living in Mason, Ohio, where he worked in real estate. Moving with his family to Atlanta, Georgia, in 1992, Browner subsequently created his own sports entertainment company and sold life insurance, before relocating again in 2005, this time to Nashville, Tennessee, where he worked for Backfield in Motion, a nonprofit organization that supports inner-city boys. Browner later worked as vice president for the U.S. Community Credit Union and spent eight years serving as president of the Nashville Chapter of the NFL Players Association for retired players.

Plagued by health issues in retirement, Browner was diagnosed with diabetes in 1994 and underwent 22 operations after being bitten by a brown recluse spider. After having his foot amputated in 2012, Browner told ESPN one year later, "After my last infection in March, my doctor gave me two choices. 'You can keep your foot, be sick all the time, and possibly die, or we can do an amputation and you can have a better quality of life.' I wanted a better quality of life and the chance to be around my wife and my sons. I feel better than I have in a very long time. I was tired of being in and out of the hospital."

Browner lived another 10 years, passing away from complications of COVID-19 at the age of 67 on January 4, 2022.

Remembering his former teammate upon learning of his passing, Isaac Curtis said, "That big laugh. Heh, heh, heh. You could hear it all over the place. He brought sunshine into the locker room. He just had that energy that was contagious."

Louis Breeden added, "He was always upbeat. If he was ever down because of a loss, he wasn't down for very long and picking up everybody else."

BENGALS CAREER HIGHLIGHTS

Best Season

Brown made his greatest overall impact in 1981, when he helped lead the Bengals to the division title and their first AFC championship by recording a career-high 10 sacks.

Memorable Moments/Greatest Performances

Although the Bengals suffered a 26–21 defeat at the hands of the San Francisco 49ers in Super Bowl XVI, Browner performed exceptionally well, sacking Joe Montana once and setting a Super Bowl record for most stops by a defensive lineman by making 10 tackles, including eight of the solo variety.

Browner contributed to a 23–10 win over the Browns on December 12, 1982, by recording the only interception of his career, which he subsequently returned 29 yards.

Browner helped the Bengals earn their first win of the season by sacking Warren Moon twice during a 13–3 victory over the Houston Oilers on October 7, 1984.

Browner recorded another two sacks during a 35–30 win over the Giants on October 13, 1985, bringing down Phil Simms behind the line of scrimmage twice.

Browner registered the first two points of a convincing 50–24 victory over the Cowboys on December 8, 1985, when he sacked Danny White in the end zone for a safety.

Notable Achievements

- Recorded 10 sacks in 1981.
- Led Bengals in sacks three times.
- Ranks among Bengals career leaders with 61 1/2 sacks (5th) and 10 fumble recoveries (tied for 6th).
- Two-time division champion (1981 and 1982).
- 1981 AFC champion.
- Member of 1978 NFL All-Rookie Team.
- 1978 Bengals team MVP.
- Named to Bengals 40th Anniversary All-Time Team in 2007.

41

DAVE LAPHAM

A part of the Bengals family for nearly half a century, Dave Lapham spent 10 seasons establishing himself as the most versatile offensive lineman in franchise history, before beginning an extremely successful stint in the broadcast booth that has lasted 38 years. Manning every position along the offensive front at one time or another, Lapham spent most of his time on the interior of the line, starting at right guard on Paul Brown's best and last team in 1975 and at left guard on the Bengals' first Super Bowl team in 1981. Missing just five games his entire career, Lapham proved to be an invaluable member of teams that won two division titles and one conference championship, with his total body of work earning him a spot on the Bengals 50th Anniversary All-Time Team.

Born in Melrose, Massachusetts, on June 24, 1952, David Allan Lapham grew up with his three siblings in the nearby Boston suburb of Wakefield, where he starred in football, basketball, and track at Wakefield Memorial High School. A three-year letterman and captain in both football and basketball, and a four-year letterman and captain in track and field, Lapham proved to be especially proficient on the gridiron, where his superior blocking at tackle earned him All–Middlesex League and Agganis All-Star honors. An outstanding student as well, Lapham also earned All-Scholastic honors in football and praise from former Wakefield head coach, Whip Halliday, who called him "one of the top linemen to come out of Wakefield High."

Lapham's excellence in the classroom gained him acceptance to several Ivy League schools, including Yale and Harvard. Recalling his aspirations at the time, Lapham said, "I was interested in law. I was going to be Perry Mason."

However, Lapham also had a strong desire to play professional football, prompting him to ultimately accept an athletic scholarship to Syracuse University, where he became a three-year starter and a team captain. Aided immensely by upperclassman Joe Ehrmann his first year at Syracuse,

Dave Lapham manned every position on the Bengals' offensive line at one time or another during his 10 seasons in Cincinnati.

Lapham remembered, "Joe was an All-American defensive tackle who went on to be drafted by the Colts. I was on the freshman team, he was on the varsity, and we went head-to-head in scrimmages. He took the time to show me what you need to do to be successful. That was really big for me."

After Lapham established himself as a top pro prospect during his time at Syracuse, the Bengals selected him in the third round of the 1974 NFL Draft, with the 61st overall pick. Lapham subsequently spent his rookie season assuming the role of a backup, before displacing veteran Pat Matson as the starter at right guard in 1975. Lapham manned that post exclusively in each of the next three seasons as well, before also seeing some action at center in 1979 and tackle in 1980. Meanwhile, with Lapham providing strong interior blocking for quarterback Ken Anderson and running backs Boobie Clark, Archie Griffin, and Pete Johnson, the Bengals' offense gradually emerged as one of the more potent ones in the AFC, finishing in the league's top 10 in scoring in both 1975 and 1976, while also ranking second in total yards gained in the first of those campaigns.

Standing 6'4" and weighing close to 260 pounds, Lapham possessed good size and strength for an offensive lineman of his era. He also had quick feet and good mobility. But Lapham's greatest assets proved to be his analytical mind, knowledge of the offense, and tremendous versatility, which surfaced again when he moved to left guard in 1981. Starting all but three games at that post over the course of the next three seasons, Lapham continued to perform well, while also serving as a mentor to future Hall of Fame left tackle Anthony Muñoz.

However, Lapham's time as a player in Cincinnati came to an end early in 1984, when he signed a 10-year guaranteed personal services contract with Donald Trump, the majority owner of the United States Football League's (USFL) New Jersey Generals. Upon informing the media of his impending departure, Lapham called it a "business decision for my family."

Lapham ended up playing just two seasons with the Generals, before announcing his retirement when the USFL folded following the conclusion of the 1985 campaign. Choosing to return to Cincinnati, Lapham, who always held an offseason job—as a substitute teacher and in the marketing department of a savings and loan company—made good use of the degree he obtained while attending Syracuse University's Newhouse School of Communications by becoming a Bengals broadcaster. The team's radio color analyst since 1986, Lapham has worked with play-by-play announcers Phil Samp, Brad Johansen, Ken Broo, Paul Keels, Pete Arbogast, and Dan Hoard at different times over the course of the past 38 years, during which time he has become known for urging on the Bengals with exhortations such as "come on!" and "get him!" and further displaying his partiality by calling players by their first names. Lapham also co-hosts, with Dan Hoard and Zac Taylor, *Bengals Weekly*, works on Fox Sports Net's broadcasts of Big 12 Conference games, and occasionally appears as a panelist on *Sports Rock*, a local sports commentary program. A philanthropist at heart, Lapham, who resides in Cincinnati with his wife, Lynne, remains active in the community, serving as president of the charitable foundation Charities M.D., which awards scholarships to students hoping to pursue a career in health care.

CAREER HIGHLIGHTS

Best Season

Although Lapham never gained Pro Bowl or All-Pro recognition, he remained a consistently excellent performer throughout his career, having arguably his finest season in 1982, when Pro Football Reference assigned him an "Approximate Value" of 10 that represented his highest grade after he helped the Bengals finish fourth in the NFL in points scored and second in total yardage gained on offense.

Memorable Moments/Greatest Performances

Lapham helped the Bengals amass 258 yards on the ground and 484 yards of total offense during a 31–0 manhandling of the Philadelphia Eagles on December 7, 1975.

Lapham's strong blocking at the point of attack helped the Bengals gain a season-high 269 yards on the ground during a 27–24 win over the Kansas City Chiefs on November 21, 1976.

Lapham's superior blocking up front helped the Bengals rush for 245 yards and amass 494 yards of total offense during a lopsided 48–16 win over the Browns in the 1978 regular-season finale.

Notable Achievements

- Missed just five games in 10 seasons.
- Two-time division champion (1981 and 1982).
- 1981 AFC champion.
- 1980 Bengals Man of the Year.
- Named to Bengals 40th Anniversary All-Time Team in 2007.
- Named to Bengals 50th Anniversary All-Time Team in 2017.

42

EDDIE BROWN

An explosive wide receiver who possessed exceptional speed and tremendous open field running ability, Eddie Brown spent seven seasons in Cincinnati, leading the Bengals in receptions in four of those, while also finishing first on the team in receiving yards on three separate occasions. The 1985 NFL Offensive Rookie of the Year, Brown amassed more than 1,000 yards from scrimmage for the first of two times, before setting a single-season franchise record for most receiving yards three years later that remained the highest mark in team annals for the next 15 seasons. A member of Bengals teams that won two division titles and one AFC championship, Brown earned one Pro Bowl selection and one All-Pro nomination, before retiring at only 30 years of age after sustaining a severe neck injury.

Born in Miami, Florida, on December 17, 1962, Eddie Lee Brown starred on the gridiron at Miami Senior High School, where he excelled on both sides of the ball for the Stingarees. After attending a junior college for one year, Brown transferred to the University of Miami, which recruited him as a defensive back. However, prior to suiting up for the Hurricanes, Brown moved to wide receiver, where he spent the next two seasons catching passes from Bernie Kosar, while also returning punts.

Following a solid junior year in which he helped Miami win its first National Championship by making 30 receptions for 640 yards and five touchdowns, Brown emerged as one of the nation's top wideouts under new head coach Jimmy Johnson in 1984, gaining consensus First-Team All-America recognition by catching 59 passes, amassing 1,114 receiving yards, and scoring nine TDs, with his 1,114 yards through the air setting a new school record.

Recalling his former college teammate, Hurricanes offensive lineman Dave Heffernan stated, "One of the things Eddie did so well was, after catching the ball, Eddie had a great ability to run a pattern and, instead of going up to get the ball, really just sort of shoot his hands up and never

Eddie Brown earned NFL Offensive Rookie of the Year honors in 1985 by amassing more than 1,000 yards from scrimmage.

break stride and pull it down. He did some wonderful things after he caught the ball."

Miami running back Todd Stanish also marveled at his former team-mate's run-after-catch ability, saying, "He was the type of receiver that would break a game open. I mean, he'd catch a five-yard slant and turn it into 60 yards. His ability to cut, stop, juke, make the defenders miss him was one of his greatest attributes."

Meanwhile, Jimmy Johnson stated, "Eddie Brown was such an electri-fying type of player. He had fantastic speed and such great athletic ability.

He could touch the football and, all of a sudden, everybody's gonna be on the edge of their seat because you knew that he had a chance to score. He had such great running ability after he caught the football."

Impressed with Brown's outstanding play at Miami, the Bengals made him the second receiver selected in the 1985 NFL Draft when they claimed him in the first round, with the 13th overall pick, three spots ahead of Jerry Rice. Outperforming both Rice and Al Toon, whom the Jets selected with the 10th overall pick, Brown earned NFL Offensive Rookie of the Year honors in 1985 by making 53 receptions for 942 yards and eight touchdowns, while also gaining another 129 yards on 14 carries. Brown followed that up with two more solid seasons, catching 58 passes, amassing 964 receiving yards, and scoring four touchdowns in 1986, before making 44 receptions for 608 yards and three TDs during the strike-shortened 1987 campaign. Brown then reached the apex of his career in 1988, when he earned his lone Pro Bowl, All-Pro, and All-AFC nominations by catching 53 passes, accumulating 1,273 receiving yards, and scoring nine touchdowns for the AFC champion Bengals, with his average of 24 yards per catch setting an NFL single-season record that still stands for receivers with at least 50 receptions.

Combining with tight end Rodney Holman and fellow wideouts Cris Collinsworth and Tim McGee to give quarterback Boomer Esiason an extremely talented group of pass-catchers, the speedy Brown, who stood 6-foot and weighed 185 pounds, did an outstanding job of stretching the field, thereby creating openings for the other members of Cincinnati's receiving corps. And, once he got his hands on the football, Brown proved to be just as elusive as he was in college, using his great speed to run away from defenders and his tremendous moves to evade would-be tacklers.

Although somewhat less productive in 1989, Brown had another excellent year for the Bengals, making 52 receptions for 814 yards and six touchdowns, before helping them win the division title the following season by catching 44 passes, amassing 706 receiving yards, and finishing third in the league with nine TD catches. But, after leading the Bengals with 59 receptions and 827 receiving yards in 1991, Brown suffered a serious neck injury during the following preseason that effectively ended his playing career. Unable to mount a comeback after sitting out the entire 1992 campaign, Brown announced his retirement with career totals of 363 receptions, 6,134 receiving yards, 6,298 yards from scrimmage, 6,352 all-purpose yards, and 41 touchdowns, all of which came through the air.

Since retiring from football, Brown, who resides in Miami, Florida, has remained out of the spotlight, keeping to himself most of the time. However, shortly after leaving the game, Brown appeared in an episode of the *NFL on CBS* television show that presented the highlights of his playing career.

In discussing Brown's legacy, Jimmy Johnson said, "He really was a great player and was an outstanding professional player, and had he not been injured, he would have been a great player for all-time."

CAREER HIGHLIGHTS

Best Season

Although Brown performed exceptionally well as a rookie, he had his most productive season for the Bengals in 1988, when he helped lead them to the AFC championship by making 53 receptions, finishing third in the league with a career-high 1,273 receiving yards, and placing fifth in the circuit with nine TD catches, with his 1,273 yards gained through the air remaining the highest single-season total in team annals until 2003, when Chad Johnson amassed 1,355 receiving yards.

Memorable Moments/Greatest Performances

Although the Bengals lost to the St. Louis Cardinals, 41–27, on September 15, 1985, Brown excelled in his second game as a pro, making five receptions for 106 yards, and scoring the first touchdown of his career when he gathered in a 44-yard pass from Ken Anderson.

Brown contributed to a 21–14 victory over the Phoenix Cardinals in the 1988 regular-season opener by making six receptions for 143 yards and one touchdown, which came on a 61-yard connection with Boomer Esiason.

Brown earned AFC Offensive Player of the Week honors by making seven receptions for a career-high 216 yards and two touchdowns during a 42–7 rout of the Steelers on November 6, 1988, scoring one of his TDs on a career-long 86-yard hookup with Boomer Esiason.

Brown earned that distinction again by making 10 receptions for 178 yards and two touchdowns during a 21–16 win over the San Diego Chargers on September 16, 1990.

Notable Achievements

- Finished third in NFL with 1,273 receiving yards in 1988.

- Surpassed 900 receiving yards two other times.
- Amassed more than 1,000 yards from scrimmage twice.
- Holds NFL single-season record for receivers with at least 50 receptions for most yards per catch (24.0 in 1988).
- Led Bengals in receptions four times and receiving yards three times.
- Ranks among Bengals career leaders with 363 receptions (9th), 6,134 receiving yards (6th), 41 touchdown receptions (5th), and 41 touchdowns (10th).
- Two-time division champion (1988 and 1990).
- 1988 AFC champion.
- Member of 1985 NFL All-Rookie Team.
- 1985 NFL Offensive Rookie of the Year.
- 1985 *Sporting News* NFL Rookie of the Year.
- Two-time AFC Offensive Player of the Week.
- 1988 Pro Bowl selection.
- 1988 Second-Team All-Pro selection.
- 1988 First-Team All-AFC selection.

43

RICH BRAHAM

I n discussing Rich Braham, longtime Bengals placekicker Shayne Graham called his former teammate "one of the toughest, smartest, coolest dudes I ever played with. An amazing player, and an even better person. In my opinion, one of the most underappreciated players during my tenure!"

A staple of the Bengals offensive line for more than a decade, Braham spent parts of 12 seasons in Cincinnati, starting at either left guard or center in 10 of those. The glue that held the unit together, Braham became known for his intelligence and toughness, playing through injuries that would have felled a lesser man. Unfortunately, the failure of the Bengals to perform at the same level as a team much of the time prevented Braham from ever gaining Pro Bowl or All-Pro recognition. But the men who competed alongside him knew just how much he contributed to any success the team experienced.

Born in Morgantown, West Virginia, on November 6, 1970, Richard Lee Braham Jr. attended University High School, where he lettered in both football and basketball. Proving to be especially proficient on the court, Braham earned Second-Team Prep All-State honors his final two seasons, remembering, "Basketball is actually the sport I liked the most before I went into high school in the 10th grade. West Virginia actually recruited me more off the basketball court than they did off football film because of the level of competition compared to many other states. We were in Division 2A. I was a center in basketball. Small school, and I was one of the largest guys there. At the time of my senior year, I was 6–4, 210 pounds. Made All-State a couple of times."

Choosing to remain close to home, Braham enrolled at West Virginia University on a partial athletic scholarship that turned into a full scholarship after he added more than 100 pounds onto his frame while redshirting his freshman year. Initially a tight end, Braham transitioned to offensive tackle while at WVU, performing well enough at that post as a junior to be named the winner of the Whitey Gwynne award as the Mountaineers'

Rich Braham started for the Bengals at either left guard or center for 10 seasons.

unsung hero on offense. Even better his senior year, Braham anchored a line that helped pave the way for running back Robert Walker to rush for a then–school record 1,250 yards, earning in the process team MVP, All–Big East, and Second-Team All-America honors. An outstanding student as well, Braham received the Ira E. Rodgers Award for maintaining the highest academic grade-point average on the team.

Selected by the Arizona Cardinals in the third round of the 1994 NFL Draft, with the 76th overall pick, Braham spent the first half of his rookie campaign serving as a member of the team's practice squad, before being released. Braham subsequently became a member of the Bengals when they claimed him off waivers on the recommendation of offensive line coach Paul Alexander, who recalled, "When I worked him out at West Virginia, the first rep he went easy on me. Then I told him to block me hard. The next rep, he drove me five yards and pancaked me into the ground. When I got up, I told him, 'You gotta play for me.' He did. Thirteen years as the Bengals center. One tough man."

After garnering very little playing time the rest of the year as a backup offensive tackle, Braham missed the entire 1995 season after he seriously injured his ankle during the preseason. Upon his return to the Bengals in 1996, Braham moved inside to left guard, where he performed so well that the Patriots offered him an incentive-laden three-year deal when he became a restricted free agent at the end of the year. However, Braham elected to remain in Cincinnati when the Bengals matched New England's offer.

After two more years at guard, Braham moved to center prior to the start of the 1999 campaign. He subsequently spent the next seven seasons anchoring the Bengals offensive line from that position, starting every game they played four times, despite undergoing four arthroscopic knee surgeries and a similar procedure on his elbow, suffering two sprained ankles and a broken toe, and sustaining a herniated disk in his neck.

Although the 6'4", 305-pound Braham developed a reputation for his mental and physical toughness, he also became known for his intelligence and leadership ability, with longtime line-mate Willie Anderson saying at one point during the 2003 campaign, "The biggest decision they made was inserting Richie into the lineup because we probably wouldn't be anywhere without him. His direction, his leadership, his toughness. He's definitely the smartest offensive lineman, and he's one of the smartest on the team. He's a finance major. He has to know basically the same things (quarterback Jon) Kitna has to know. You have to play smart football to win, and I think one of the reasons we can do so many things offensively is because Jon and Richie are two smart guys at crucial positions."

The unquestioned leader of the Bengals offensive line, Braham had the responsibility of calling out the line assignments before each play. Meanwhile, he did an outstanding job of picking up blitzing linebackers and creating holes for Bengals runners, with both Corey Dillon and Rudi Johnson having most of their finest seasons running behind him.

After starting every game in each of the three previous seasons, Braham missed six contests in 2004 due to a pair of knee injuries. Returning to action full-time the following year, Braham helped lead the Bengals to their first division title in 15 seasons with his consistently excellent play up front.

However, he suffered a season-ending tibia plateau fracture in Week 2 of the 2006 campaign that prompted him to announce his retirement at the end of the year. Appearing in a total of 146 games with the Bengals, Braham started all but four of those, with 98 of his starts coming at center and the other 44 at left guard.

After retiring from football, Braham returned to his hometown of Morgantown, West Virginia, where he watched his oldest son, Noah, begin to follow in his footsteps in 2022 by accepting a football scholarship to WVU.

CAREER HIGHLIGHTS

Best Season

Braham performed extremely well at left guard in 1997, earning a career-best "Approximate Value" of 10 from Pro Football Reference by helping Bengals runners average a robust 4.3 yards per carry. But the team finished well out of contention in the AFC Central with a record of just 7–9. On the other hand, with Braham starting for them at center in 2005, the Bengals won the division title. Furthermore, Cincinnati runners averaged 4.2 yards per carry, the Bengals allowed just 21 sacks as a team, and Braham received a rating of 9 from Pro Football Reference. All things considered, the 2005 campaign proved to be the most impactful of Braham's career.

Memorable Moments/Greatest Performances

Braham's superior work up front helped the Bengals amass 515 yards of total offense during a lopsided 41–14 victory over the Tennessee Oilers on December 4, 1997.

Braham's strong blocking at the point of attack helped the Bengals rush for a season-high 279 yards during a 44–28 win over the Browns on December 12, 1999.

Braham helped the Bengals amass 398 yards of total offense during a 24–13 win over the Arizona Cardinals on December 3, 2000, with 292 of those yards coming on the ground.

Notable Achievements

- Tied for eighth in franchise history in seasons played (12).
- 2005 division champion.
- Named to Bengals 40th Anniversary All-Time Team in 2007.

44

BRIAN SIMMONS

A versatile linebacker who had the misfortune of playing for some of the worst teams in franchise history, Brian Simmons spent nine of his 10 NFL seasons in Cincinnati, excelling on defense for Bengals squads that posted just one winning record. Combining with Takeo Spikes much of that time to give the Bengals a formidable linebacker tandem, Simmons recorded the fourth-most tackles and third-most forced fumbles of any player in team annals. Yet Simmons, who manned multiple linebacker positions during his nine-year stint in the Queen City, perhaps made his greatest impact on the organization with his quiet leadership, which helped the Bengals gradually emerge from the depths of the NFL to win their first division title in 15 years.

Born in New Bern, North Carolina, on June 21, 1975, Brian Eugene Simmons starred in multiple sports at New Bern High School, earning letters in football, baseball, basketball, and track. An excellent student who also conducted himself extremely well off the playing field, Simmons received the school's Outstanding Citizenship Award, with former New Bern assistant principal Terry Fuhrman recalling, "We had a lot of student-athletes who were on the edge of going the wrong way. . . . He was never in my office (for discipline). It's not that he wasn't ever around bad situations, it was that he knew when to get up and leave if something bad was happening."

After excelling on the gridiron for New Bern at outside linebacker, Simmons received a football scholarship to the University of North Carolina at Chapel Hill, where he spent four seasons playing for head coach Mack Brown. A three-year starter for the Tar Heels, Simmons helped North Carolina earn two straight top-10 rankings in the final AP poll by recording career totals of 340 tackles, 36 tackles for loss, 11 sacks, and six interceptions. A two-time semifinalist for the Butkus Award as the nation's most outstanding linebacker, Simmons earned First-Team All-ACC honors twice, Second-Team All-America honors as a junior in 1996, and consensus

First-Team All-America honors his senior year, when he served as a Tar Heels co-captain.

In discussing his prize linebacker on one occasion, Mack Brown said, "We weren't sure how he'd handle the transition from high school to college. He's so soft-spoken, you weren't sure if he got it at first. He did."

Selected by the Bengals in the first round of the 1998 NFL Draft, with the 17th overall pick, Simmons immediately laid claim to the team's starting left-inside linebacker job upon his arrival in Cincinnati. Performing well as a rookie, Simmons recorded 78 tackles and three sacks, picked off

Brian Simmons ranks among the Bengals career leaders in tackles and forced fumbles.

one pass, forced two fumbles, and recovered another for a Bengals team that finished the season with a record of just 3–13. Although the Bengals posted just four victories the following year, Simmons had another very solid season, recording a team-high 114 tackles, while also registering three sacks and recovering one fumble.

Simmons subsequently missed all but one game in 2000 after tearing cartilage in his right knee during the regular-season opener against Cleveland. But he showed no signs of rust when he returned to action in 2001, recording 84 tackles and a career-high 6 1/2 sacks, while also forcing two fumbles and scoring the first of his three career touchdowns after being shifted to middle linebacker in the Bengals' new 4–3 defensive scheme. After one more year in the middle, Simmons displayed his versatility by moving to right-outside linebacker in 2003. Performing extremely well at that post over the course of the next three seasons, Simmons registered more than 100 tackles twice. Meanwhile, after posting identical 8–8 records in 2003 and 2004, the Bengals won the division title in 2005 by compiling a regular-season mark of 11–5.

Blessed with outstanding physical tools, the 6'3", 240-pound Simmons possessed the size and strength to ward off blockers near the line of scrimmage and bring down opposing ball-carriers before they broke into the open field, the quickness and dexterity to apply pressure to opposing quarterbacks, and the speed and athleticism to pursue runners from sideline to sideline. Although quiet, both on and off the field, Simmons also proved to be an exceptional leader, earning the respect of his teammates with his calm demeanor and cerebral nature.

Revealing the influence that his fellow linebacker had on him, Takeo Spikes said, "Some of the things that I'm quick to go off on, he's kind of like the mild-mannered guy where he's able to sit back and keep his cool about certain things and keeps me complacent. There's a lot of stuff that burns you up, but he sits back and thoroughly thinks through a lot of stuff. It's just the mental aspect on the field and off the field. . . . He's a good guy as a person. You don't meet too many people like him, that are men."

Extremely down-to-earth, Simmons maintained the same quiet, unassuming lifestyle he led prior to becoming a pro football player, once saying, "Football is what I do and not what I am. I come to work, and I play football. I love the game, but it's not my life. It's a big part of my life, but it's not who I am. You have to separate them. Football is part of the reason that I live my life and the way that I'm able to live it. But I'm going to be who I'm going to be regardless of what I'm doing. I think when you get caught up and let football and how you live get combined, that's when guys get into trouble."

Exhibiting that being true to himself always remained his top priority after he signed a six-year contract extension with the Bengals prior to the start of the 2001 season, Simmons said at the time, "Maybe I could have gotten more in free agency, but I know I could have gotten a whole lot less also. That's the way I look at it. I could've gotten a little more, maybe, but it wasn't a given. On the other hand, if something happens, you've got to look at what you're losing. The two weren't even close."

Simmons spent one more season in Cincinnati, recording 61 tackles, two interceptions, and one forced fumble in 2006, before being released by the Bengals at the end of the year. Simmons, who, during his time in Cincinnati, recorded 726 tackles (512 solo), 23 sacks, and 11 interceptions, amassed 169 interception-return yards, forced 13 fumbles, recovered eight others, and scored three touchdowns, subsequently signed with the New Orleans Saints, for whom he assumed a backup role in 2007, before announcing his retirement.

Since retiring as an active player, Simmons has remained close to the game. After spending seven years serving as Northeast regional scout for the Jacksonville Jaguars, Simmons became the color analyst for the Tar Heel Sports Network football broadcasts in 2016. Since 2018, he has also been a member of the Windermere Prep Lakers coaching staff, assuming the role of head coach in 2022. While serving in that capacity, Simmons led the school to its first ever trip to the Florida High School Athletic Association playoffs.

BENGALS CAREER HIGHLIGHTS

Best Season

Simmons had an excellent year for the Bengals in 1999, when, in addition to recording three sacks and recovering one fumble, he established career-high marks with 114 combined tackles and 17 tackles for loss. However, he performed slightly better two years later, concluding the 2001 campaign with 84 combined tackles, 6 1/2 sacks, two forced fumbles, one interception, and one touchdown.

Memorable Moments/Greatest Performances

Simmons contributed to a 21–10 win over the defending Super Bowl champion Baltimore Ravens on September 23, 2001, by recording an interception, a sack, and two tackles for loss.

Simmons scored the first touchdown of his career when he ran 56 yards to pay dirt after recovering a fumble during a 26–23 overtime win over the Steelers on December 30, 2001.

Simmons lit the scoreboard again when he returned his interception of a Brad Johnson pass 51 yards for a touchdown during a 35–7 loss to Tampa Bay on September 29, 2002.

Simmons earned AFC Defensive Player of the Week honors by forcing a fumble, which he recovered, and recording an interception, two pass deflections, and six tackles during a 27–24 win over the Seattle Seahawks on October 26, 2003.

Simmons contributed to a 41–38 victory over the 49ers on December 14, 2003, by making nine tackles and recovering two fumbles.

Simmons helped lead the Bengals to a 16–13 win over the Dolphins on September 19, 2004, by returning his interception of an A. J. Feeley pass 50 yards for a touchdown.

Simmons earned his second AFC Defensive Player of the Week nomination by forcing a fumble and recording a sack and eight tackles during a 21–9 win over the Ravens on November 6, 2005.

Notable Achievements

- Scored three defensive touchdowns.
- Recorded more than 100 tackles three times.
- Recorded 6½ sacks in 2001.
- Finished fourth in NFL with four fumble recoveries in 2003.
- Led Bengals in tackles three times.
- Ranks among Bengals career leaders with 726 tackles (4th) and 13 forced fumbles (3rd).
- 2005 division champion.
- Two-time AFC Defensive Player of the Week.
- Named to Bengals 40th Anniversary All-Time Team in 2007.

45

LEON HALL

A versatile cornerback who performed well both on the perimeter and in the slot, Leon Hall gave the Bengals consistently excellent play on the right side of their defense for nearly a decade. The team's primary starter at right cornerback from 2007 to 2015, Hall led the Bengals in interceptions four times, en route to recording the fourth-most picks of any player in team annals. Also one of the franchise's all-time leaders in interception-return yards and interceptions returned for touchdown, Hall proved to be a key contributor to teams that won three division titles. Yet even though Hall earned one All-Pro nomination, he likely would have accomplished a good deal more had he not been hampered by injuries much of his time in Cincinnati.

Born in Oceanside, California, on December 9, 1984, Leon Lastarza Hall grew up in nearby Vista, where he excelled both on the gridiron and in the classroom at Vista High School, starring as a wide receiver and defensive back in football, while also winning the *San Diego Union-Tribune* Scholar-Athlete award his senior year. Offered an athletic scholarship to the University of Michigan, Hall spent his college career playing for head coach Lloyd Carr, under whom he recorded 12 interceptions and scored two touchdowns in his four seasons on the varsity squad.

Having gained consensus First-Team All-America recognition as a senior in 2006, Hall entered the 2007 NFL Draft as one of the nation's most highly touted prospects, often drawing comparisons to future Hall of Fame cornerback Ronde Barber. Selected by the Bengals in the first round, with the 18th overall pick, after posting an impressive time of 4.38 seconds in the 40-yard dash at the NFL Combine, Hall arrived in Cincinnati with huge expectations surrounding him.

After spending the first half of the 2007 campaign serving the Bengals as a third cornerback and nickelback, Hall laid claim to the starting right cornerback job in Week 10, displacing in the process Deltha O'Neal as the starter at that post. Performing extremely well in his first pro season, Hall

Leon Hall excelled at cornerback for Bengals teams that won three division titles.
Courtesy of Navin Rajagopalan

earned a spot on the NFL All-Rookie Team by picking off five passes and recording 70 tackles, including 56 of the solo variety. Hall followed that up by recording three interceptions, registering 75 tackles, and scoring one touchdown in 2008, before earning Second-Team All-Pro honors in 2009 by picking off six passes, forcing two fumbles, and making 71 tackles, in helping the Bengals capture the division title. Although the Bengals failed to repeat as division champions the following year, finishing the regular season with a record of just 4–12, Hall turned in another solid performance, recording four interceptions, two forced fumbles, and 44 tackles.

Combining with Johnathan Joseph his first four years in the league to give the Bengals one of the NFL's better cornerback tandems, the 5'11", 195-pound Hall proved to be a sure tackler and an excellent one-on-one defender who had the ability to play either outside or inside. Particularly effective in the slot, Hall used the knowledge he gained from studying the tendencies of his opponents on film to mirror them all over the field.

Praising Hall for his ability to play inside, Bengals defensive coordinator Paul Guenther said, "He's a real smart player. He understands splits, motions, stems of receivers. It's a different position in there. Some can go in and do it, some can't. . . . I think he's one of the best in the league at it."

Guenther also spoke of Hall's leadership skills and strong sense of responsibility, saying, "He's a quiet leader. He leads by example. . . . He understands all the ins and outs. I just have to look at Leon. If he makes a little mistake in practice, he goes, 'I got you.' I don't even have to tell him, so it's good to have a guy like that around."

Hall also made a strong impression on Guenther's predecessor in Cincinnati, Mike Zimmer, who stated, "Leon is one of the best competitors I've ever had, that I've ever coached. He's a great competitor. He's a tough guy. He's smart. He wants to go out and challenge people all the time. . . . His mentality helps a lot of the younger guys. I know that a lot of the other guys, when he's out there they feel like, 'Hey, this guy's got him. We don't have to worry about him.'"

Rewarded by the Bengals for his outstanding play and superior leadership with a $39 million contract extension prior to the start of the 2011 campaign, Hall unfortunately suffered a torn Achilles tendon against the Steelers in Week 9 that forced him to miss the rest of the season. Although Hall returned to action the following year, he failed to regain his earlier form, picking off just two passes and registering only 38 tackles for a Bengals team that earned a spot in the playoffs as a wild card. Hall sustained another serious injury that limited him to just five games and one interception in 2013 when he tore his other Achilles tendon during a 27–24 win over Detroit in mid-October. Rejoining the Bengals in 2014, Hall started all but one contest at his familiar position of right cornerback. But, having lost some of his earlier speed and quickness, he recorded just one interception, although he managed to register 67 tackles, which represented his highest single-season total since 2009.

Reduced to a part-time role in 2015, Hall picked off just two passes and recorded 55 tackles. Yet, even in somewhat limited duty, Hall continued to positively impact the other players around him, providing veteran leadership to the team's young defensive backs, while also serving as a calming influence for temperamental cornerback Adam "Pac-Man" Jones. Nevertheless, with Hall no longer able to compete at an elite level, the Bengals chose not to re-sign him when he became an unrestricted free agent at the end of 2015, prompting him to eventually sign a one-year deal with the Giants.

In discussing the team's decision not to actively pursue Hall, Bengals head coach Marvin Lewis said during a conference call, "We have drafted some young players over the last three or four seasons and at some point, you are trying to clear opportunity and space. We spoke with Leon a number of times, and Leon was hesitant to commit to coming back because he was unsure what his role was going to be at that point. We thought that we moved on from Leon and Leon moved a little bit away from us as well."

Hall, who left Cincinnati with career totals of 26 interceptions, 261 interception-return yards, 472 tackles (367 solo), five forced fumbles, two fumble recoveries, and three touchdowns, ended up spending just one year in New York, before splitting the next two seasons between the San Francisco 49ers and Oakland Raiders. After serving all three teams as a backup, Hall chose to announce his retirement following the conclusion of the 2018 campaign, ending his career with 27 interceptions, 290 interception-return yards, 544 tackles, six forced fumbles, two fumble recoveries, two sacks, and three touchdowns.

Since retiring as an active player, Hall has remained close to the game by coaching middle school football at Cincinnati Country Day School, a Division VI school that has 30 players in its varsity program. At different times, Hall has served as wide receivers and defensive backs coach, defensive coordinator, and assistant defensive coordinator.

BENGALS CAREER HIGHLIGHTS

Best Season

Although Hall registered a career-high 75 tackles, picked off three passes, and led the NFL with 24 passes defended in 2008, he performed slightly better the following year, when he earned his lone All-Pro nomination by recording six interceptions, making 71 tackles, forcing two fumbles, and again successfully defending 24 passes.

Memorable Moments/Greatest Performances

Hall earned AFC Defensive Player of the Week honors by recording three interceptions, one of which he returned 50 yards for a touchdown, during a 14–0 shutout of the Browns on December 21, 2008.

Hall lit the scoreboard again when he returned his interception of a Ben Roethlisberger pass 17 yards for a touchdown during a 13–10 win over the Steelers on December 23, 2012.

Hall scored the only touchdown the Bengals registered during a 19–13 loss to the Houston Texans in the 2012 AFC wild card game when he ran 21 yards to pay dirt after picking off a Matt Schaub pass.

Hall garnered AFC Defensive Player of the Week honors for the second and final time by returning his interception of a Nick Foles pass 19 yards for a touchdown during a 31–7 win over the St. Louis Rams on November 29, 2015.

Notable Achievements

- Scored three defensive touchdowns.
- Recorded at least five interceptions twice.
- Led NFL with 24 passes defended in 2008.
- Led Bengals in interceptions four times.
- Ranks among Bengals career leaders with 26 interceptions (4th), 261 interception-return yards (8th), and three touchdown interceptions (tied for 3rd).
- Three-time division champion (2009, 2013, and 2015).
- Member of 2007 NFL All-Rookie Team.
- Two-time AFC Defensive Player of the Week.
- 2009 Second-Team All-Pro selection.

46

DARNAY SCOTT

An extremely consistent player who averaged 55 receptions and 854 receiving yards during his seven seasons in Cincinnati, Darnay Scott combined with Carl Pickens for much of the 1990s to give the Bengals one of the NFL's most potent wide receiver tandems. The team leader in receptions twice and receiving yards three times, Scott caught more than 60 passes once, amassed more than 1,000 receiving yards once, and made at least five touchdown receptions in six straight seasons, en route to establishing himself as one of the franchise's career leaders in all three categories. Yet, the fact that Scott spent his entire time in Cincinnati playing for losing teams often prevents him from being included among the finest wideouts in team annals.

Born in St. Louis, Missouri, on July 7, 1992, Darnay Scott grew up in a St. Louis housing project, before moving to San Diego, California, in 1988 to live with his aunt and uncle. A troubled youth, Scott briefly attended Summer High School, where he struggled both in and out of the classroom, suffering from poor grades, while also spending a week in a juvenile detention center after being arrested and expelled from the junior varsity football team for fighting.

Transferring to Kearny High School after his sophomore year, Scott found a sanctuary on the football field, excelling as both a wide receiver and defensive back for the Komets for two seasons. Performing especially well as a senior, Scott recorded 38 receptions, amassed 790 receiving yards, caught 19 touchdown passes, and registered 11 interceptions, one of which he returned 70 yards for a TD. An outstanding all-around athlete, Scott also served as a member of the school's basketball and track teams, winning the 100- and 200-meter events at the CIF San Diego Section track and field championships in 1990.

Continuing to excel on the gridiron after accepting an athletic scholarship to San Diego State University, Scott made 35 receptions for 727 yards and six touchdowns as a freshman, breaking the NCAA single-game record

Darnay Scott led the Bengals in receptions twice and receiving yards three times.
Courtesy of George A. Kitrinos

for first-year players by amassing 243 receiving yards during a 52–52 tie with Brigham Young University on November 16, 1991. Scott followed that up with two more outstanding seasons, recording 68 receptions, amassing 1,150 receiving yards, and scoring nine touchdowns his sophomore year, before making 75 receptions for 1,262 yards and 10 TDs as a junior.

Choosing to forgo his senior year of college after posting three-year totals of 178 receptions, 3,139 receiving yards, 1,397 kickoff-return yards, and 25 touchdowns for the Aztecs, Scott entered the 1994 NFL Draft, where the Bengals selected him in the second round, with the 30th overall pick. Making an immediate impact his first year in the league, Scott earned a spot on the NFL All-Rookie Team by making 46 receptions for 866 yards and five touchdowns, while also gaining 106 yards on the ground and accumulating another 342 yards on special teams, giving him a total of 1,314 all-purpose yards. Scott followed that up with another solid season, catching 52 passes, amassing 821 receiving yards, and scoring five touchdowns in 1995. However, he ran into trouble with the law prior to the start of the ensuing campaign, when police arrested him on four firearms charges after they found two loaded guns in his car during a May 12, 1996, traffic stop. Forced to pay a $2,000 fine after initially pleading innocent to all charges, Scott did not miss any playing time in 1996, finishing the season with 58 receptions for 833 yards and five TDs, before making 54 receptions for 797 yards and five touchdowns the following year.

Combining with quarterback Jeff Blake and fellow wideout Carl Pickens to form one of the more exciting passing attacks in the NFL, Scott helped make the Bengals a fun watch, even though they consistently finished well out of contention in the AFC Central. Blessed with good size and outstanding speed, the 6'1", 200-pound Scott did an excellent job of catching the ball in traffic, stretching the field, and beating his man deep, making 12 touchdown receptions of 50 or more yards over the course of his career. Meanwhile, from 1994 to 1999, Scott and Pickens combined to catch 788 passes, amass 11,131 receiving yards, and score 80 touchdowns.

Performing well once again in 1998, Scott made 51 receptions for 817 yards and seven touchdowns, before posting the most impressive numbers of his career the following year, when he caught 68 passes, amassed 1,022 receiving yards, and scored seven TDs. However, Scott subsequently missed the entire 2000 campaign after fracturing his left tibia and fibula during a morning practice on August 1. Fully recovered by the start of the 2001 season, Scott made 57 receptions and accumulated a team-high 819 receiving yards. But after the Bengals signed free agent wideout Michael Westbrook the following offseason, they released Scott in a salary cap move.

Scott, who left Cincinnati with career totals of 386 receptions, 5,975 receiving yards, 36 touchdown catches, 6,112 yards from scrimmage, and 6,454 all-purpose yards, subsequently signed with the Jacksonville Jaguars, who released him after he injured his shoulder during training camp. Scott then signed with the Dallas Cowboys, with whom he spent his final NFL season assuming a backup role, making just 22 receptions for 218 yards and one touchdown in 2002, before announcing his retirement at the end of the year.

Unfortunately, Scott, who spent one night in jail after police arrested him a second time in July 2000 on a charge of theft by deception for allegedly writing a bad check to a motorcycle shop, has continued to run afoul of the law since he retired from football. Indicted twice on charges of failing to pay child support, Scott reportedly owed more than $10,000 in arrears prior to his second indictment in April 2009. Scott, who is 52 years old as of this writing, currently lives in San Diego, where he coaches football at Mesa College and mentors students at Lincoln High School.

BENGALS CAREER HIGHLIGHTS

Best Season

Scott performed exceptionally well as a rookie in 1994, when his work on special teams enabled him to amass a career-high 1,314 all-purpose yards. But he made his greatest impact as a receiver in 1999, when he established career-high marks in receptions (68), receiving yards (1,022), yards from scrimmage (1,022), and touchdown catches (7).

Memorable Moments/Greatest Performances

Scott starred in defeat on October 30, 1994, making four receptions for 155 yards and two touchdowns during a 23–20 loss to the Cowboys, with his TDs coming on connections of 67 and 55 yards with Jeff Blake.

Scott followed that up by making seven receptions for 157 yards during a 20–17 overtime win over Seattle one week later.

Although the Bengals lost to the Seahawks, 24–21, on September 17, 1995, Scott connected with Jeff Blake on a career-long 88-yard touchdown reception.

Scott contributed to a 31–24 win over the Cowboys on December 14, 1997, by making four receptions for 112 yards and one TD, which came on a 48-yard pass from Boomer Esiason.

Scott proved to be a key factor in a 16–14 win over the Baltimore Ravens in the final game of the 1997 season, making six receptions for 129 yards and one touchdown, which came on a 77-yard hookup with Boomer Esiason late in the fourth quarter that provided the margin of victory.

Scott helped lead the Bengals to a 34–28 overtime win over Detroit on September 13, 1998, by making five receptions for 130 yards and two TDs, the longest of which covered 70 yards.

Scott starred during a 25–24 victory over the Steelers on December 20, 1998, making seven receptions for 152 yards and one touchdown, which came on a 61-yard hookup with Jeff Blake.

Scott contributed to a 23–21 win over the Tennessee Titans in the final game of the 2001 regular season by making nine receptions for 152 yards.

Notable Achievements

- Surpassed 1,000 receiving yards once.
- Amassed more than 1,000 all-purpose yards twice.
- Led Bengals in receptions twice and receiving yards three times.
- Ranks among Bengals career leaders with 386 receptions (8th), 5,975 receiving yards (8th), and 36 touchdown receptions (tied for 7th).
- Member of 1994 NFL All-Rookie Team.

47

JEFF BLAKE

A talented quarterback who created excitement in Cincinnati briefly during the darkest period in franchise history, Jeff Blake spent parts of six seasons starting behind center for the Bengals. The team's primary signal-caller from 1994 to 1999, Blake, who became known for his ability to deliver the deep ball, passed for more than 3,500 yards and 20 touchdowns twice each, in helping the Bengals compile two of the three best regular-season records they posted from 1991 to 2002. A one-time Pro Bowler, Blake ranks among the franchise's all-time leaders in every major statistical category for quarterbacks. Nevertheless, Blake left Cincinnati believing that he could have accomplished a good deal more had the organization put more faith in him.

Born in Daytona Beach, Florida, on December 4, 1970, Jeffrey Bertrand Coleman Blake grew up in a single-parent household after his mother, Peggy, died in 1976 while saving her younger sister from drowning. Raised by his father, Emory Blake, a former running back in the Canadian Football League, young Jeff began his own career on the gridiron at the age of 10 in the Orlando suburb of Sanford, Florida, where he played quarterback in the local Pop Warner League. Acquiring an intricate knowledge of the game from his dad, who often quizzed him on offensive formations and defensive schemes, Blake recalled, "My dad never wanted anybody to be able to say I wasn't smart enough to be a quarterback."

Coached by his father in high school, Blake developed into a star QB at Seminole High, garnering interest from several major colleges as graduation neared. However, prior to that, Blake suffered a serious injury in the 10th grade when a drunk driver struck him as he rode a motor scooter. In addition to having his throwing arm broken, Blake had his right fibula shattered so severely that it required the insertion of a 12-inch steel rod, 47 stitches, a month of traction, and a year off from football to fully heal. Telling his father afterward while recuperating in the hospital that his mother must have been looking out for him since he survived the accident,

Jeff Blake became known during his time in Cincinnati for his ability to deliver the deep ball.
Courtesy of George A. Kitrinos

Blake promised his dad, "Whatever I do from now on, I'm going to do it to honor her."

With the backward thinking of the time often forcing Black quarterbacks to move to other positions once they reached college or the pros, Blake received offers to play defensive back at Florida and wide receiver at both Miami and Florida State. Rejecting all three schools, Blake later said, "I was one of the top-ranked quarterbacks in high school during my senior year, and I had never played any other position. I wasn't going to sacrifice my hard work and my destiny to satisfy someone's limitations on me."

Ultimately accepting an athletic scholarship to East Carolina University because, in his own words, "They were used to having black quarterbacks there. So, in their eyes, I was simply a quarterback," Blake barely played as a freshman and experienced just a moderate amount of success in each of the next two seasons. But he established himself as one of the nation's top signal-callers as a senior in 1991, when he earned Second-Team All-America honors and a seventh-place finish in the Heisman Trophy voting by leading East Carolina to a record of 11–1 and a number nine ranking in the nation. Guiding the Pirates to nine fourth-quarter comebacks and a victory over North Carolina State in the Peach Bowl in his final season, Blake threw for 28 touchdowns and 3,073 yards, ending his time at East Carolina with 32 school records. Yet, despite Blake's superb performance, questions about his size and the ability of Black quarterbacks to succeed in the NFL caused him to fall to the sixth round of the 1992 NFL Draft, where the New York Jets finally selected him with the 166th overall pick.

Looking back at his later-than-expected selection, Blake said, "I took a team that was not on anybody's radar to a top-10 ranking and put up some good numbers, and I would have matched my stats and our record against anyone. There were guys drafted in front of me that I was better than, and one guy got drafted that I had never heard of. A couple of those guys taken before me never took a snap in the NFL. It was crazy."

Following his arrival in New York, Blake spent two seasons assuming the role of third-string quarterback, completing just four passes in nine attempts in three game appearances, before being waived by the Jets following the conclusion of the 1993 campaign. But during his time in New York, Blake formed a bond with head coach Bruce Coslet, who, after being fired by the Jets and accepting the position of offensive coordinator in Cincinnati, urged his new team to sign the free agent signal-caller.

After joining the Bengals, Blake spent the first part of the 1994 season backing up former first-round draft pick David Klingler, who failed to win any of his seven starts. Replacing Klingler behind center in Week

8, Blake nearly led the Bengals to a win over the heavily favored Dallas Cowboys by throwing a pair of long touchdown passes to Darnay Scott, although the two-time defending Super Bowl champions ultimately prevailed, 23–20. Remaining the starter for the rest of the year, Blake led the Bengals to victories in three of their final eight games, finishing the season with 2,154 passing yards, 14 TD passes, nine interceptions, a 51.0 pass-completion percentage, and a quarterback rating of 76.9.

Although the Bengals posted a losing record during the season's second half, Blake inspired confidence in his teammates, with second-year tight end Tony McGee saying, "He's so confident. He acts like a 10-year veteran out there."

Center Derrick Brilz added, "We all know that, if we can just keep blocking, he'll make something happen back there. He's also raised the play of a lot of individuals on this team. Look at our offensive production since he's been the starter."

The team's full-time starter the following year, Blake emerged as one of the league's better signal-callers, earning Pro Bowl honors by throwing for 3,822 yards and 28 touchdowns, completing 57.5 percent of his passes, and posting a quarterback rating of 82.1, while also running for 309 yards and two scores. Meanwhile, the Bengals finished the season with a respectable 7–9 record, which represented their best mark in five years. Continuing to perform well in 1996, Blake led the Bengals to a record of 8–8 by finishing fifth in the league with 3,624 yards passing and 24 TD passes, completing 56.1 percent of his passes, compiling a QBR of 80.3, and running for 317 yards and two TDs.

Nicknamed "Shake n' Blake" for his ability to connect with his receivers downfield after evading opposing pass-rushers, the 6-foot, 223-pound Blake generated a tremendous amount of excitement among Bengals fans, with Tony McGee recalling, "At that time, we were so starved for excitement within the stadium, within the team, within the organization, that that gave us that spark. They started the promotion 'Shake n' Blake' and all that. It was just perfect timing and something that was well-needed throughout the organization from the players and the fans. It was a wonderful thing. It really was."

Blessed with an uncanny ability to sense pressure, Blake often took flight from the pocket, doing so mostly out of necessity. Also blessed with a very strong throwing arm, Blake, whose high release point helped negate his height disadvantage, proved to be particularly adept at throwing the deep ball, often hooking up with speedy wideouts Carl Pickens and Darnay Scott on long scoring plays.

In discussing his ability to deliver the long ball effectively, Blake said, "It has nothing to do with your height. . . . I mean, you can be 5–5 and throw the ball 60 yards. . . . It's got more to do with arm strength and having that skill set and understanding what you're doing. . . . It has to do with trajectory because the deep ball is not a hard throw. It's a finesse throw."

Blake continued, "I felt like I needed something, a niche, or something that was going to separate me from everybody else. I honed in on it once I realized we were capable of doing that on a consistent basis and hitting it."

Claiming that Blake did indeed separate himself from others with his high-arching deep spirals, Tony McGee stated, "He had something that was very unique. He had the strength in his release point. A lot of quarterbacks, they're so tall that their trajectory and their arm, the flow of their arm, is going totally different. When you look at Jeff releasing the ball, you'll see his elbow pointing to the sky. Now, if he was coming out of college, he wouldn't get drafted with that type of throw. He wouldn't get drafted with those mechanics. However, he had a special talent that he could deliver that ball with that type of timing with those type of receivers that worked well."

Despite the success that Blake experienced the previous two seasons, Bengals management decided that he no longer represented their best option when the team won only three of its first 11 games in 1997. After Boomer Esiason (then in his second tour of duty with the club) replaced Blake behind center for the final five games of the 1997 season, veteran signal-caller Neil O'Donnell spent most of the ensuing campaign starting for the Bengals at quarterback. With O'Donnell failing to turn things around, the Bengals turned to Blake once again in 1999. But after Blake threw for 2,670 yards and 16 touchdowns in his 12 starts for a Bengals team that finished the season with a record of just 4–12, his dissatisfaction with the organization's inability to fully commit to him prompted him to sign with the New Orleans Saints as a free agent at the end of the year.

In explaining his decision years later, Blake said, "I just think, the whole time I was in Cincinnati, I never really got the feeling that they were going to fully build a team around me, because I wasn't supposed to be there. . . . They kept bringing more and more guys in. I only had one year with the Bengals where I didn't have to fight for my job."

Blake, who left the Bengals having passed for 15,134 yards and 93 touchdowns, thrown 62 interceptions, completed 55.8 percent of his passes, posted a QBR of 79.3, and run for 1,499 yards and 10 touchdowns as a member of the team, ended up spending two seasons in New Orleans, starting for the Saints in one of those. He then split his final four seasons between the Baltimore Ravens, Arizona Cardinals, Philadelphia Eagles, and Chicago Bears, serving as the primary starter in both Baltimore and Arizona. Choosing to announce his retirement following the conclusion of the 2005 campaign, Blake ended his career with 21,711 passing yards, 134 touchdown passes, 99 interceptions, a pass-completion percentage of 56.4, a QBR of 78.0, 2,027 yards gained on the ground, and 14 rushing touchdowns.

After initially settling down in Austin, Texas, following his playing days, Blake later moved to the city of Houston, where he became a coach for aspiring quarterbacks and a personal trainer. Working mostly with amateur athletes, Blake helps prepare them for life outside of football by building their character so that they may avoid many of the pitfalls that often derail the careers of pro athletes. Named the head coach and offensive coordinator at Valley Sports Academy in Lake Hallie, Wisconsin, in 2023, Blake spent this past season assuming both roles for the facility's new 7-on-7 football team.

Looking back on his own playing career, Blake said, "I wish I could have, at some point in my career, gone to a team that was more loyal, a team that gave me a chance to be the guy. I was never in a position where the team said, 'Jeff Blake is our quarterback, and we're going to draft around what he needs to succeed.'"

BENGALS CAREER HIGHLIGHTS

Best Season

Although Blake also performed well the following year, he posted the best overall numbers of his career in 1995, when he gained Pro Bowl recognition for the only time by passing for 3,822 yards and 28 touchdowns, throwing 17 interceptions, completing 57.5 percent of his passes, compiling a QBR of 82.1, and running for 309 yards and two TDs.

Memorable Moments/Greatest Performances

Blake led the Bengals to their first win of the 1994 season by completing 31 of 43 passes for 387 yards during a 20–17 overtime victory over Seattle on November 6, 1994, earning in the process AFC Offensive Player of the Week honors.

Blake followed that up with another strong outing, throwing for 354 yards and four touchdowns during a 34–31 win over the Houston Oilers, with three of his TD tosses going to Carl Pickens.

Although the Bengals lost to Houston, 38–28, on September 24, 1995, Blake had another big game against the Oilers, passing for 356 yards and three touchdowns.

Blake led the Bengals to a 41–31 win over Atlanta on November 24, 1996, by throwing for 349 yards and four touchdowns, connecting with Carl Pickens three times and Darnay Scott once.

Blake gave the Bengals a dramatic 31–24 victory over the Indianapolis Colts in the 1996 regular-season finale when he hit Tony McGee with a 9-yard TD pass as time expired in regulation.

Blake helped lead the Bengals to a 25–24 win over the Steelers on December 20, 1998, by throwing for 367 yards and one touchdown.

Blake starred during a 44–30 win over San Francisco on December 5, 1999, throwing for 334 yards and four touchdowns, the longest of which went 58 yards to Darnay Scott.

Notable Achievements

- Passed for more than 3,500 yards and 20 touchdowns twice each.
- Ranks among Bengals career leaders with 2,221 pass attempts (5th), 1,240 pass completions (6th), 15,134 passing yards (5th), and 93 touchdown passes (6th).
- Three-time AFC Offensive Player of the Week.
- 1996 Week 17 Pro Football Writers NFL Offensive Player of the Week.
- November 1994 AFC Offensive Player of the Month.
- 1995 Pro Bowl selection.

48

ESSEX JOHNSON

An outstanding all-around back who starred for the Bengals during their formative years, Essex Johnson spent eight seasons in Cincinnati, proving to be the team's most potent offensive weapon much of that time. Known affectionately to his teammates as "The Essex Express," Johnson excelled as both a runner and a receiver out of the backfield, gaining more than 800 yards on the ground and amassing more than 1,200 yards from scrimmage twice each, in helping the Bengals capture two division titles. Yet, had Johnson not sustained a serious knee injury while still in his prime, he likely would have accomplished a good deal more.

Born in Shreveport, Louisiana, on October 15, 1946, Essex L. Johnson received his introduction to organized football at Shreveport High School, where he starred on the gridiron on both sides of the ball. Offered an athletic scholarship to Grambling State University, Johnson spent his college career playing defensive back/wingback for teams that won three straight Southwestern Athletic Conference (SWAC) titles under legendary head coach Eddie Robinson.

Selected by Cincinnati in the sixth round of the 1968 NFL Common Draft, with the 156th overall pick, Johnson joined the Bengals in their inaugural season, two years prior to the NFL/AFL merger. Shifted from defensive back to halfback upon his arrival in Cincinnati, Johnson subsequently spent his first two pro seasons returning punts and kickoffs, while seeing very little action on offense as a backup to starting running backs Paul Robinson and Jess Phillips. Although Robinson and Phillips remained the primary starters in 1970, Johnson began to garner significantly more playing time, rushing for 273 yards, amassing 463 yards from scrimmage, accumulating 603 all-purpose yards, and scoring four touchdowns for the AFC Central Division champions.

Shouldering an even greater part of the offensive burden in 1971, Johnson finished second on the team with 522 yards rushing, 780 yards from scrimmage, and six touchdowns, before emerging as the Bengals'

Essex Johnson helped lead the Bengals to their first two division titles.

primary offensive weapon the following year, when he gained 825 yards on the ground, made 29 receptions for 420 yards, finished eighth in the NFL with 1,245 yards from scrimmage, and scored six touchdowns. Turning in another exceptional performance in 1973, Johnson helped lead the Bengals to a 10–4 record and their second division title by establishing career-high marks with 997 yards rushing, 1,353 yards from scrimmage, and seven touchdowns.

Standing 5'9" and weighing just over 200 pounds, Johnson possessed great speed and outstanding strength, enabling him to either run away from defenders or bounce off them once he broke into the open field.

Also blessed with superb moves and exceptional balance, Johnson had the ability to turn short gains into long runs, making him one of the league's most dangerous runners once he got his hands on the football. An excellent receiver out of the backfield as well, Johnson ranked among the league's finest all-purpose backs, making him a foundational piece upon which head coach Paul Brown and his assistant, Bill Walsh, built what essentially served as a precursor to the West Coast offense that became popular more than a decade later.

In discussing his former teammate, Ken Anderson said, "When you think of the great Bengals running backs, No. 19 was one of them. A tough, stocky guy that could run."

Bengals radio analyst, Dave Lapham, who spent two seasons blocking for Johnson, described his former teammate as: "Fast as hell. He could go from zero to eighty in three full steps. . . . I'm not saying he was (Christian) McCaffrey, but a much earlier version of a back that could catch coming out of the backfield. . . . He could have played slot receiver. He had that kind of talent."

Expressing his admiration for Johnson after he amassed 237 yards from scrimmage and scored two touchdowns during a September 30, 1973, win over his team, San Diego Chargers defensive end Deacon Jones stated, "He's the second-best runner in football. I'd say O. J. is the best, but he's a tough kid. We really laid some leather to him, but he kept on plugging."

Bengals teammate Mike Reid took things one step further, saying, "He's the best. The very best. [Washington's] Larry Brown can do nothing that Essex can't do. And I don't think O. J. is as fast as Essex."

Unfortunately, Johnson badly injured his knee during the early stages of a 34–16 loss to Miami in the divisional round of the 1973 playoffs, prompting Ken Anderson to later say, "That was one of the critical things in our playoff game with the Dolphins. When he got hurt in the first quarter, that really took away a lot of our stuff."

Still suffering from the after-effects of his injury in 1974, Johnson appeared in only five games, finishing the season with just 44 yards rushing, 129 yards from scrimmage, and one TD. After undergoing a second surgery on his knee the following offseason, Johnson appeared in every game the Bengals played in 1975. But, unable to regain his earlier form, he gained just 177 yards on the ground, amassed only 373 yards from scrimmage, and scored just two touchdowns, before being waived prior to the start of the ensuing campaign.

Johnson, who left Cincinnati having rushed for 3,070 yards and 18 touchdowns, made 121 receptions for 1,541 yards and 11 TDs, amassed

4,611 yards from scrimmage and 5,671 all-purpose yards, and averaged 4.5 yards per carry, subsequently spent one season in Tampa Bay, accumulating 367 more yards from scrimmage and scoring another two touchdowns for the Buccaneers after being selected by them in the 1976 NFL Expansion Draft, before announcing his retirement at the end of the year.

Although little is known about Johnson's post-football life, he lived until October 29, 2020, when he passed away just two weeks after celebrating his 74th birthday. Paying tribute to Johnson upon learning of his passing, Bengals owner Mike Brown, who, as the son of then-Bengals head coach Paul Brown, saw him perform at every stage of his career, said, "He wasn't a polished player when he got here. A lot of stuff was new to him. He caught up quickly enough and became our bell-cow running back. Really, probably the star of the team. He had exceptional speed, good quickness, and he could catch the ball. Kenny [Anderson] can attest to that."

Meanwhile, Dave Lapham recalled his former teammate as "One of those good guys. Great guy. A welcoming sort of guy. . . . He wouldn't shun a rookie. When I made the team, he was all about it. He told me, 'Glad you made the team. Help us win.' It was easy to like Essex Johnson."

BENGALS CAREER HIGHLIGHTS

Best Season

Although Johnson also performed extremely well the previous season, he played his best ball for the Bengals in 1973, when, in addition to gaining 356 yards on 28 pass receptions and scoring seven touchdowns, he ranked among the league leaders with 997 yards rushing, 1,353 yards from scrimmage, and an average of 5.1 yards per carry.

Memorable Moments/Greatest Performances

Johnson scored his first career touchdown on a 35-yard run during the fourth quarter of a 24–10 win over Denver on September 15, 1968.

Johnson helped lead the Bengals to a 30–20 victory over the Houston Oilers on December 13, 1970, by rushing for 58 yards, gaining another 59 yards on two pass receptions, and scoring a pair of touchdowns, one of which came on a 49-yard pass from Virgil Carter.

Johnson went over 100 yards rushing for the first time as a pro in the 1971 regular-season opener, when he carried the ball eight times for 113 yards and one touchdown, which came on a 68-yard touchdown run.

Although the Bengals lost to the Browns, 31–27, on December 5, 1971, Johnson recorded a career-long 86-yard touchdown run, finishing the game with 109 yards on just four carries.

Johnson led the Bengals to a convincing 30–7 victory over the Oilers on October 29, 1972, by rushing for 103 yards and one TD, while gaining another 54 yards on three pass receptions.

Johnson proved to be a thorn in the side of the Oilers again on September 23, 1973, rushing for 131 yards, amassing 180 yards from scrimmage, and scoring a touchdown during a 24–10 win.

Johnson followed that up by amassing a career-high 237 yards from scrimmage during a 20–13 victory over the San Diego Chargers on September 30, 1973, gaining 121 yards on the ground, another 116 yards through the air, and scoring two touchdowns, the longest of which came on a 78-yard catch-and-run.

Notable Achievements

- Rushed for 997 yards in 1973.
- Amassed more than 1,000 yards from scrimmage twice.
- Averaged more than 6 yards per carry twice.
- Recorded longest run in NFL in 1971 (86 yards).
- Led Bengals in rushing twice.
- Ranks among Bengals career leaders with 3,070 yards rushing (9th).
- Two-time division champion (1970 and 1973).

49

COY BACON

Although Coy Bacon spent just two seasons in Cincinnati, the dominance he displayed during his relatively brief stay in Ohio earned him a spot on this list. An elite pass-rusher who recorded an unofficial total of 130 1/2 sacks over the course of his career, Bacon gained Pro Bowl recognition in each of his two years with the Bengals, setting a single-season franchise record in sacks in one of those. Named Second-Team All-Pro once and First-Team All-AFC twice during his time in Cincinnati, Bacon later received the additional honor of being named to the Bengals 50th Anniversary All-Time Team, even though he donned the team's colors in only 1976 and 1977.

Born in Cadiz, Kentucky, on August 30, 1942, Lander McCoy Bacon grew up some 350 miles northeast, in Ironton, Ohio, where he played football and basketball at Ironton High School. Offered a football scholarship to Jackson State University, in Jackson, Mississippi, McCoy spent three seasons excelling for the Tigers at linebacker and defensive end, before leaving school after his junior year.

After one year away from the game, Bacon tried out for the American Football League's Houston Oilers, who chose not to offer him a contract when they learned that he had not graduated from college. Ultimately forced to sign with the Charleston Rockets of the Continental Football League, Bacon spent two years competing semi-professionally, earning All-Star honors in 1966, before serving on the taxi squad of the Dallas Cowboys in 1967 after signing with them as an undrafted free agent.

Dealt to the Los Angeles Rams prior to the start of the 1968 campaign, Bacon spent his first year on the West Coast assuming a backup role, before displacing veteran Roger Brown as the starter at right defensive tackle the following season. Performing well in his first year as a full-time starter, Bacon recorded eight sacks for a Rams team that finished first in the NFL Coastal Division with a record of 11–3. Continuing to excel the next three seasons after moving to right defensive end, Bacon registered a total of 32

Coy Bacon's unofficial total of 21 1/2 sacks in 1976 remains the highest single-season mark in franchise history.

1/2 sacks for the Rams from 1970 to 1972, earning the first of his three Pro Bowl nominations in the last of those campaigns. Meanwhile, despite playing alongside Pro Football Hall of Famers Deacon Jones and Merlin Olsen, Bacon received the honor of being named the team's defensive lineman of the year by the Rams Alumni Organization in both 1971 and 1972.

With the Rams seeking an upgrade at quarterback, they traded Bacon and running back Bob Thomas to the San Diego Chargers for star signal-caller John Hadl in January 1973. Bacon spent the next three years in San Diego playing for losing Charger teams, collecting a total of 23 1/2 sacks, before being dealt to the Bengals for wide receiver Charlie Joiner on January 25, 1976.

While Joiner went on to establish himself as one of the finest receivers in the game and a Hall of Fame caliber player in San Diego, the Bengals benefited from the trade as well the next two seasons, especially in 1976, when Bacon set a single-season franchise record that still stands by recording an unofficial total of 21 1/2 sacks (as calculated by pro football researchers years later).

Commenting on his extraordinary 1976 campaign, Bacon later said, "Couldn't anybody stop me. They just double-teamed me, because I had confidence one man couldn't stop me on a pass rush. That was a good year."

Employing tactics he learned from Deacon Jones during his time in Los Angeles, the 6'4", 270-pound Bacon used the head-slap to his advantage and often feinted one way before heading in the other direction. And, like Jones, Bacon possessed a flamboyant personality and enjoyed talking to his opponent.

In discussing his former teammate, longtime Bengals radio analyst, Dave Lapham, told the *Cincinnati Enquirer*, "He was the best pass-rusher I ever saw. He always gained ground . . . never wasted any steps. He could make you miss. He had a very nimble body for a guy his size."

Former Bengals defensive lineman Ken Johnson added, "Coy was an excellent pass-rusher. He had a couple moves that he used to use on offensive tackles that they couldn't handle. It was sort of like deception. He would make them think he was going one way, and then he would go inside or go outside. That was the key."

Not nearly as effective against the run, Bacon sometimes took plays off, preferring to save his energy for applying pressure to opposing quarterbacks. As a result, while Paul Zimmerman of *Sports Illustrated* included Bacon on his 2000 list of the 10 greatest pass-rushers of all time, Hall of Fame NFL executive Gil Brandt placed him at number 23 when he named his best-ever all-around defensive ends four years later.

Bacon spent one more year in Cincinnati, recording 5 1/2 sacks and recovering two fumbles for the Bengals in 1977, before his dissatisfaction with management and the team's conversion to a 3–4 defense prompted him to request a trade. Subsequently dealt to the Washington Redskins, along with Lemar Parrish, for a first-round draft pick on June 26, 1978, Bacon left the Bengals having registered a total of 27 sacks as a member of the team.

Remaining one of the league's top pass-rushers for three more years, Bacon finished in double digits in sacks three straight times for the Redskins, before assuming a backup role in 1981. Released by Washington at the end of the year, Bacon signed with the Washington Federals of the

USFL, with whom he spent the next two seasons, before announcing his retirement. In addition to recording an unofficial total of 130 1/2 sacks over the course of 14 NFL seasons, Bacon intercepted two passes, recovered 15 fumbles, scored two touchdowns, and recorded one safety.

Eventually returning to Ironton, Ohio, Bacon became heavily involved with drugs, before becoming a born-again Christian. Bacon subsequently began traveling as a motivational speaker and working with troubled youth at the Ohio River Valley Juvenile Correctional Facility, where he continued to counsel youngsters on the evils of drug addiction until December 22, 2008, when he died at the age of 66.

Upon learning of Bacon's passing, Bengals owner Mike Brown issued a statement that read: "Coy was a tremendous player for the Bengals, the greatest pass-rusher our team has ever had. After he left the team, he worked hard to make life better for youths in the Ironton area. What he did was admirable, something all of us respect. We are saddened by his passing."

BENGALS CAREER HIGHLIGHTS

Best Season

Bacon had easily the finest season of his career in 1976, when he earned Pro Bowl, Second-Team All-Pro, and First-Team All-AFC honors by leading the NFL with 21 1/2 sacks, while also recording 59 tackles, forcing three fumbles, and recovering two others.

Memorable Moments/Greatest Performances

Bacon began his banner year of 1976 in fine fashion, recording three of the six sacks the Bengals registered during a 17–7 win over the Denver Broncos in the regular-season opener.

Two weeks later, on September 26, 1976, Bacon led a Bengals defense that recorded six sacks, created four turnovers, and allowed just 36 yards of total offense during a 28–7 victory over the Green Bay Packers.

Bacon proved to be the driving force behind a 27–7 victory over the Houston Oilers in Week 7, leading a defense that registered another six sacks.

Bacon put the finishing touches on a 42–3 rout of the Jets in the final game of the 1976 regular season when he sacked quarterback Richard Todd in the end zone for a safety late in the fourth quarter.

Notable Achievements

- Led NFL with 21 1/2 sacks in 1976.
- Holds Bengals single-season record for most sacks (21 1/2).
- Two-time Pro Bowl selection.
- 1976 Bengals team MVP.
- 1976 Second-Team All-Pro selection.
- Two-time First-Team All-AFC selection.
- Named to Bengals 50th Anniversary All-Time Team in 2017.

50

TYLER BOYD

One of the more unheralded players in team annals, Tyler Boyd persevered through several losing seasons in Cincinnati to become a major contributor to teams that won two division titles and one AFC championship. Despite spending much of his time in the Queen City being overshadowed by fellow wideouts Ja'Marr Chase and Tee Higgins, Boyd did an excellent job for the Bengals out of the slot, surpassing 75 receptions three times and 1,000 receiving yards twice. A totally selfless player, Boyd proved to be an outstanding team leader as well, with his strong on-field performance and veteran leadership making him a key figure in the Bengals' recent resurgence.

Born in Clairton, Pennsylvania, on November 15, 1994, Tyler Boyd grew up some 15 miles southeast of Pittsburgh, in a poverty-stricken, crime-infested area. In describing his hometown, Boyd said, "It's very small. It's nothing positive coming out of Clairton, only guns and violence and football usually. Nobody ever made it in any sport other than football. We had a few people make it to college, but no one really got to the league but me. It's just tough living, man. It's nothing but violence and gun crime. It's kind of no other positive way of making it out other than football. . . . It looks like an abandoned city. It's tough to see it. It's better to *see* it than *say* it because once you see it, you really understand. There's nothing there. It's like a black hole."

While Boyd and his circle of close friends managed to stay out of trouble, his father ended up spending eight years in prison after being indicted, along with 41 others, as part of a major drug dealing network. In attempting to explain his dad's illicit behavior, Boyd said, "Our fathers didn't have diplomas to show for, so that was the quickest way to help provide for the family. I wasn't particularly accepting of it but, at the time, that's what we needed to get done and have a life to at least get the things we wanted and do the things we wanted. I always supported him because he made sure he did whatever he had to do to sustain us."

Tyler Boyd has proven to be one of the NFL's best slot receivers during his time in Cincinnati.
Courtesy of Alexander Jonesi

Raised mostly by his mother, who remarried shortly after he entered the seventh grade, Boyd began playing midget football at the age of six, before developing into a star in multiple sports at Clairton High School, where he excelled in football, baseball, and basketball. Particularly outstanding on the gridiron, Boyd rushed for 5,755 yards and set a Western Pennsylvania Interscholastic Athletic League (WPIAL) record by scoring 117 touchdowns as a combination running back, wide receiver, quarterback, defensive back, and punt returner, in leading his school to four WPIAL titles and an overall record of 63–1.

Yet, even though Rivals.com rated him as the number six overall prospect in the state of Pennsylvania after he gained 2,584 yards on the ground and led the WPIAL with 51 touchdowns and 345 points his senior year, Boyd felt unfulfilled, later saying, "I graduated with 30 people; nobody believed in me despite all the accolades and everything I accomplished; just never got the respect, and never felt that I was working my way to the top."

All that began to change, though, after Boyd received an athletic scholarship to the University of Pittsburgh. Named All-ACC and a Freshman All-American after making 85 receptions, amassing 1,174 receiving yards, and scoring eight touchdowns his first year with the Panthers, Boyd followed that up by totaling 2,187 receiving yards, 2,599 yards from scrimmage, and 14 TDs over the course of the next two seasons, before choosing to forgo his final year of college and declaring himself eligible for the 2016 NFL Draft.

Selected by the Bengals in the second round, with the 55th overall pick, Boyd entered the professional ranks with questions surrounding his speed after he posted a time of 4.58 seconds in the 40-yard dash at the NFL Scouting Combine. Remaining undeterred, Boyd posted solid numbers his first year in the league, catching 54 passes, amassing 603 receiving yards and 661 yards from scrimmage, and scoring one touchdown, while serving as the third option behind veteran wideouts A. J. Green and Brandon LaFell.

Limited to just 10 games in 2017 by a knee injury he sustained during a 20–16 win over the Buffalo Bills on October 8, Boyd made only 22 receptions for 225 yards and two touchdowns. But after joining the starting unit the following year, Boyd emerged as the Bengals' most reliable receiver, leading the team with 76 receptions, 1,028 receiving yards, and seven TD catches despite missing the final two games of the campaign with a sprained MCL. Equally productive in 2019, Tate scored five touchdowns and established career-high marks with 90 receptions, 1,046 receiving yards, and 1,069 yards from scrimmage. After spending the previous two seasons working primarily on the outside, Boyd moved to the slot in 2020 following the arrival of Tee Higgins. Excelling at his new post, Boyd made a team-high 79 receptions, accumulated 841 receiving yards, and scored four touchdowns for a Bengals team that posted its fifth consecutive losing record.

Unusually large for a slot receiver, the 6'2", 203-pound Boyd possesses the size and strength to outmuscle his defender for the football, as well as the intelligence and instincts to find the "soft spot" in the zone. In discussing the problems that Boyd presents to opposing defensive backs, Bengals slot cornerback Mike Hilton, who previously competed against him as a member of the Pittsburgh Steelers, said, "If you turn on his film, the way he's able to find holes in the zone and beat man coverage, and his yards after the catch, there's not too many like him."

A sure-handed, precise route-runner who does much of the "dirty work" between the 20s, Boyd plays the game without fear, with former Bengals wide receivers coach Bob Bicknell saying, "He's not afraid. If he makes a mistake, he makes a mistake. Which he rarely does. He's just not afraid of that. I love him. He's one of my favorite players of all-time."

Perhaps Boyd's greatest attribute, though, is his selfless attitude, which became quite evident after Ja'Marr Chase joined the Bengals' receiving corps in 2021. Although Boyd continued to receive his fair share of targets, catching 67 passes, amassing 828 receiving yards, and scoring five touchdowns for the eventual AFC champions, he could have displayed resentment toward one of the most highly touted wideouts to enter the NFL in years. Instead, Boyd welcomed Chase with open arms, working with him on further honing his skills, while never expressing dissatisfaction over his somewhat diminished role.

Praising Boyd for the tone he set, Bengals wide receivers coach Troy Walters stated, "You see the contracts they are giving out now, and guys are making a lot of money, and never once have I heard him complain or gripe about his contract. He just loves ball, and I think they could pay him $200, and he would get out here and play and have a smile on his face and have a great attitude. He loves the game, and he loves his teammates, and he loves the Cincinnati Bengals organization."

Bengals head coach Zac Taylor also expressed his affection for Boyd when he said, "TB has always been a guy I've loved being around. No ego to that guy whatsoever. There've been games certainly over the course of his career since I've been here where he maybe was targeted two or three times. And I've had regret leaving a game where 'Here's one of our best players that we didn't target.' It's always me telling him 'I didn't forget about ya. I need to get you more involved.' And it's always 'Whatever, coach. I understand. That's just the way the game went.' Never once have I heard him complaining about not getting targeted. He just goes out there and works, leads. He's always positive."

Continuing to perform well for the Bengals the past two seasons, Boyd caught 58 passes, amassed 762 receiving yards, and scored five touchdowns in 2022, before making 67 receptions for 667 yards and two touchdowns in 2023. Heading into the 2024 campaign, Boyd boasts career totals of 513 receptions, 6,000 receiving yards, 6,166 yards from scrimmage, and 31 TD catches, with his figures in the first two categories placing him among the franchise's all-time leaders. But with Boyd inking a one-year, free-agent deal with Tennessee this past offseason, he will be adding to those totals as a member of the Titans.

CAREER HIGHLIGHTS

Best Season

Boyd had an outstanding year for the Bengals in 2018, making 76 receptions for 1,028 yards and a career-high seven touchdowns. But he missed two games, enabling him to post slightly better overall numbers in 2019, when he caught 90 passes, amassed 1,046 receiving yards and 1,069 yards from scrimmage, and scored five TDs.

Memorable Moments/Greatest Performances

Boyd scored what proved to be the game-winning touchdown of a 31–27 victory over Baltimore in the 2017 regular-season finale when he gathered in a 49-yard pass from Andy Dalton with just 44 seconds left in regulation.

Boyd helped lead the Bengals to a 37–34 win over Tampa Bay on October 28, 2018, by making nine receptions for 138 yards and one touchdown.

Boyd played a huge role in a 15–10 win over Denver on December 19, 2021, making five catches for 96 yards and one touchdown, which came on a 56-yard pass from Joe Burrow late in the third quarter that gave the Bengals their only TD of the game.

Boyd contributed to a 35–17 victory over Atlanta on October 23, 2022, by making eight receptions for 155 yards and one touchdown, which came on a 60-yard connection with Burrow.

Notable Achievements

- Surpassed 75 receptions three times.
- Amassed more than 1,000 receiving yards twice.
- Led Bengals in receptions and receiving yards three times each.
- Ranks among Bengals career leaders in receptions (4th), receiving yards (7th), and touchdown receptions (11th).
- Two-time division champion (2021 and 2022).
- 2021 AFC champion.

SUMMARY
AND HONORABLE MENTIONS

(THE NEXT 25)

Having identified the 50 greatest players in Cincinnati Bengals history, the time has come to select the best of the best. Based on the rankings contained in this book, the members of the Bengals' all-time offensive and defensive teams are listed below. Our squads include the top player at each position, with the offense featuring the three best wide receivers, two best running backs, tackles, and guards, and the top quarterback, tight end, and center. Meanwhile, the defense features two ends, two tackles, three linebackers, two cornerbacks, and a pair of safeties. Special teams have been accounted for as well, with a placekicker, punter, kickoff returner, and punt returner also being included, some of whom were taken from the list of honorable mentions that will soon follow.

OFFENSE:		DEFENSE:	
Player:	Position:	Player:	Position:
Ken Anderson	QB	Carlos Dunlap	LE
Corey Dillon	RB	Tim Krumrie	LT
James Brooks	RB	Geno Atkins	RT
Bob Trumpy	TE	Ross Browner	RE
Chad Johnson	WR	Reggie Williams	LB
A. J. Green	WR	Bill Bergey	LB
Isaac Curtis	WR	Jim LeClair	LB
Anthony Muñoz	LT	Lemar Parrish	LCB
Dave Lapham	LG	David Fulcher	SS
Bob Johnson	C	Tommy Casanova	FS
Max Montoya	RG	Ken Riley	RCB

Willie Anderson	RT	Kevin Huber	P
Jim Breech	PK	Brandon Tate	PR
Brandon Tate	KR		

Although I limited my earlier rankings to the top 50 players in Bengals history, many other fine players have donned the team's colors through the years, some of whom narrowly missed making the final cut. Following is a list of those players deserving of an honorable mention. These are the men I deemed worthy of being slotted into positions 51 to 75 in the overall rankings. Where applicable and available, the statistics they compiled during their time in Cincinnati are included, along with their most notable achievements while playing for the Bengals.

51 - REGGIE NELSON (DB; 2010-2015)

Bengals Numbers: 23 Interceptions, 333 Interception-Return Yards, 462 Tackles, 5 1/2 Sacks, 5 Forced Fumbles, 4 Fumble Recoveries, 1 TD.

Notable Achievements

- Missed just three games in six seasons, appearing in 93 of 96 contests.
- Recorded at least four interceptions three times.
- Amassed more than 100 interception-return yards twice.
- Led NFL with eight interceptions in 2015.
- Led Bengals in interceptions four times and tackles once.
- Ranks among Bengals career leaders in interceptions (6th) and interception-return yards (4th).
- Two-time division champion (2013 and 2015).
- 2015 Pro Bowl selection.
- 2015 Second-Team All-Pro selection.
- 2015 First-Team All-AFC selection.

52 - KEVIN HUBER (P; 2009-2022)

Career Numbers: 45,766 Total Punt Yards, 45.3 Yards Punting Average.

Notable Achievements

- Missed just two games from 2009 to 2021, appearing in 207 of 209 contests.
- Averaged more than 45 yards per punt nine times.
- Recorded five punts of more than 70 yards.
- Recorded longest punt in NFL twice.
- Holds Bengals record for longest punt (75 yards).
- Holds Bengals single-season record for most total punt yards (4,101 in 2017).
- Holds Bengals career records for most total punt yards, highest punting average, and most games played (216).
- Five-time division champion (2009, 2013, 2015, 2021, and 2022).
- 2021 AFC champion.
- 2013 Week 13 AFC Special Teams Player of the Week.
- 2014 Pro Bowl selection.
- 2014 *Sporting News* First-Team All-Pro selection.

53 - RODNEY HOLMAN (TE; 1982-1992)

Bengals Numbers: 318 Receptions, 4,329 Receiving Yards, 34 Touchdown Receptions.

Notable Achievements

- Made 50 receptions, amassed 736 receiving yards, and scored nine touchdowns in 1989.
- Ranks among Bengals career leaders in receptions (11th), receiving yards (12th), and touchdown receptions (10th).
- Three-time division champion (1982, 1988, and 1990).
- 1988 AFC champion.
- Three-time Pro Bowl selection (1988, 1989, and 1990).
- Two-time Second-Team All-Pro selection (1989 and 1990).
- Two-time First-Team All-AFC selection (1989 and 1990).
- 1988 Second-Team All-AFC selection.

54 - JUSTIN SMITH (DE; 2001-2007)

Bengals Numbers: 43 1/2 Sacks, 470 Tackles, 6 Forced Fumbles, 5 Fumble Recoveries, 2 Interceptions.

Notable Achievements

- Missed just one game in seven seasons, appearing in 111 of 112 contests, 107 of which he started.
- Led Bengals in sacks four times.
- Led Bengals defensive linemen in tackles six times.
- Ranks eighth in Bengals history in sacks.
- 2005 division champion.
- Member of 2001 NFL All-Rookie Team.
- Named to Bengals 40th Anniversary All-Time Team in 2007.

55 - TAKEO SPIKES (LB; 1998-2002)

Bengals Numbers: 571 Tackles, 14 1/2 Sacks, 5 Interceptions, 85 Interception-Return Yards, 5 Forced Fumbles, 12 Fumble Recoveries, 2 TDs.

Notable Achievements

- Missed just one game in five seasons, starting 79 of 80 contests.
- Recorded more than 100 tackles five times.
- Led Bengals in tackles four times.
- Ranks among Bengals career leaders in tackles (7th) and fumble recoveries (5th).
- Member of 1998 NFL All-Rookie Team.
- 2001 Week 2 AFC Defensive Player of the Week.
- Named to Bengals 40th Anniversary All-Time Team in 2007.

56 - VONTAZE BURFICT (LB; 2012-2018)

Bengals Numbers: 604 Tackles, 8 1/2 Sacks, 5 Interceptions, 82 Interception-Return Yards, 4 Forced Fumbles, 5 Fumble Recoveries, 1 TD.

Notable Achievements

- Recorded more than 100 tackles three times.
- Led NFL with 171 combined tackles in 2013.
- Led Bengals in tackles twice.
- Holds Bengals single-season record for most tackles (171 in 2013).

- Ranks fifth in Bengals history in tackles.
- Two-time division champion (2013 and 2015).
- 2013 Week 11 AFC Defensive Player of the Week.
- 2013 Pro Bowl selection.
- 2013 Second-Team All-Pro selection.
- 2013 First-Team All-AFC selection.

57 - CEDRIC BENSON (RB; 2008-2011)

Bengals Numbers: 4,176 Rushing Yards, 80 Receptions, 556 Receiving Yards, 4,732 Yards from Scrimmage, 21 Rushing TDs, 1 TD Reception, 22 TDs, 3.8 Rushing Average.

Notable Achievements

- Rushed for more than 1,000 yards three times.
- Led Bengals in rushing four times.
- Ranks among Bengals career leaders with 1,109 rushing attempts (6th) and 4,176 yards rushing (6th).
- 2009 division champion.

58 - JESSIE BATES III (DB; 2018-2022)

Bengals Numbers: 14 Interceptions, 180 Interception-Return Yards, 1 Touchdown-Interception, 479 Tackles, 3 Forced Fumbles, 2 Fumble Recoveries.

Notable Achievements

- Recorded more than 100 tackles three times.
- Led Bengals in interceptions twice and combined tackles once.
- Two-time division champion (2021 and 2022).
- 2021 AFC champion.
- Member of 2018 NFL All-Rookie Team.
- 2020 Second-Team All-Pro selection.

59 - DAN ROSS (TE; 1979-1983 AND 1985)

Bengals Numbers: 263 Receptions, 3,204 Receiving Yards, 16 Touchdown Receptions.

Notable Achievements

- Surpassed 50 receptions twice, catching 71 passes in 1981.
- Led Bengals in receptions twice and receiving yards once.
- Holds Bengals single-season records for most receptions (71) and most receiving yards (910) by a tight end (both in 1981).
- Made 11 receptions for 104 yards and two touchdowns vs. 49ers in Super Bowl XVI.
- Two-time division champion (1981 and 1982).
- 1981 AFC champion.
- Member of 1979 NFL All-Rookie Team.
- 1982 Pro Bowl selection.
- 1982 Second-Team All-Pro selection.
- Two-time Second-Team All-AFC selection (1981 and 1982).
- Named to Bengals 40th Anniversary All-Time Team in 2007.

60- JOE WALTER (OT; 1985-1997)

Notable Achievements

- Two-time division champion (1988 and 1990).
- 1988 AFC champion.

61 - BRANDON TATE (WR/PR/KR; 2011-2015)

Bengals Numbers: 33 Receptions, 469 Receiving Yards, 3 TD Receptions, 21 Rushing Yards, 490 Yards from Scrimmage, 1,411 Punt-Return Yards, 3,517 Kickoff-Return Yards, 5,418 All-Purpose Yards, 1 Punt-Return TD, 4 TDs.

Notable Achievements

- Finished second in NFL with 543 punt-return yards in 2011.
- Holds Bengals single-season record for most punt-return yards (543 in 2011).
- Holds Bengals career record for most punt-return yards.
- Ranks second in franchise history in career kickoff-return yards.
- Two-time division champion (2013 and 2015).
- 2011 Week 8 AFC Special Teams Player of the Week.

62 - GIOVANI BERNARD (RB; 2013-2020)

Bengals Numbers: 3,697 Rushing Yards, 342 Receptions, 2,867 Receiving Yards, 6,564 Yards from Scrimmage, 22 Rushing TDs, 11 TD Receptions, 33 TDs, 4.0 Rushing Average.

Notable Achievements

- Amassed more than 1,000 yards from scrimmage three times.
- Ranks among Bengals career leaders in rushing yards (8th), yards from scrimmage (10th), receptions (10th), and rushing TDs (tied for 10th).
- Two-time division champion (2013 and 2015).
- Member of 2013 NFL All-Rookie Team.
- Finished third in 2013 NFL Offensive Rookie of the Year voting.

63 - AL BEAUCHAMP (LB; 1968-1975)

Bengals Numbers: 8 1/2 Sacks, 15 Interceptions, 144 Interception-Return Yards, 7 Fumble Recoveries, 3 TDs.

Notable Achievements

- Missed just one game in eight seasons, appearing in 111 of 112 contests.
- Recorded six interceptions in 1971.
- Ranks among Bengals career leaders in interceptions (tied for 11th).
- Two-time division champion (1970 and 1973).

64 - SHAYNE GRAHAM (K; 2003-2009)

Bengals Numbers: 177 Field Goals, 248 Extra Points, 779 Points, 86.8 Field Goal Percentage.

Notable Achievements

- Scored more than 100 points five times, topping 120 points three times.
- Converted more than 85 percent of field goal attempts five times, surpassing 90 percent once.
- Kicked seven field goals vs. Baltimore Ravens on November 11, 2007.
- Finished second in NFL with 31 field goals made in 2007.

- Ranks second in Bengals history in points scored, field goals made, and extra points made.
- Two-time division champion (2005 and 2009).
- 2004 Week 2 NFL Special Teams Player of the Week.
- 2005 Pro Bowl selection.
- 2005 Second-Team All-Pro selection.
- 2005 First-Team All-AFC selection.
- Named to Bengals 40th Anniversary All-Time Team in 2007.

65 - RON CARPENTER (DT/DE; 1970-1976)

Career Numbers: 45 1/2 Sacks, 10 Fumble Recoveries, 1 Safety.

Notable Achievements

- Missed just one game in seven seasons, appearing in 97 of 98 contests.
- Finished in double digits in sacks twice.
- Finished third in NFL with 13 sacks in 1974.
- Ranks among Bengals career leaders in sacks (7th) and fumble recoveries (tied for 6th).
- Two-time division champion (1970 and 1973).

66 - PAUL ROBINSON (RB/KR; 1968-1972)

Bengals Numbers: 2,441 Rushing Yards, 69 Receptions, 454 Receiving Yards, 2,895 Yards from Scrimmage, 924 Kickoff-Return Yards, 3,820 All-Purpose Yards, 19 Rushing TDs, 2 TD Receptions, 21 TDs, 4.0 Rushing Average.

Notable Achievements

- Amassed more than 1,000 yards from scrimmage once.
- Amassed more than 1,000 all-purpose yards twice.
- Led AFL with 1,023 yards rushing and eight rushing touchdowns in 1968.
- 1970 division champion.
- 1968 Week 11 AFL Offensive Player of the Week.
- 1968 Bengals team MVP.
- 1968 AFL Offensive Rookie of the Year.
- 1968 UPI and *Sporting News* AFL Rookie of the Year.

- Two-time Pro Bowl selection (1968 and 1969).
- 1968 First-Team All-AFL selection.
- 1968 Second-Team All-NFL/AFL selection.

67 – PAT MCINALLY (P/WR; 1976–1985)

Career Numbers: 29,307 Total Punt Yards, 41.9 Yards Punting Average, 57 Receptions, 808 Receiving Yards, 5 Touchdown Receptions.

Notable Achievements

- Never missed a game, appearing in 149 consecutive contests.
- Averaged more than 45 yards per punt once.
- Led NFL in punting average twice.
- Ranks third in Bengals history in total punt yards.
- Two-time division champion (1981 and 1982).
- 1981 AFC champion.
- 1981 Pro Bowl selection.
- 1981 First-Team All-Pro selection.
- 1981 First-Team All-AFC selection.
- Two-time Second-Team All-AFC selection (1977 and 1978).
- Named to Bengals 50th Anniversary All-Time Team in 2017.

68- TREY HENDRICKSON (DE; 2021-2023)

Bengals Numbers: 39 1/2 Sacks, 109 Tackles, 9 Forced Fumbles.

Notable Achievements

- Has finished in double digits in sacks twice.
- Finished second in NFL with 17 1/2 sacks in 2023.
- Has led Bengals in sacks three times.
- Ranks among Bengals career leaders in sacks (10th) and forced fumbles (7th).
- Two-time division champion (2021 and 2022).
- 2021 AFC champion.
- 2022 Week 3 AFC Defensive Player of the Week.
- Three-time Pro Bowl selection (2021, 2022, and 2023).

69 - TIM MCGEE (WR/KR; 1986-1992, 1994)

Bengals Numbers: 282 Receptions, 4,703 Receiving Yards, 4,721 Yards from Scrimmage, 1,249 Kickoff-Return Yards, 5,991 All-Purpose Yards, 25 Touchdown Receptions, 25 TDs.

Notable Achievements

- Made 65 receptions and amassed 1,211 receiving yards in 1989.
- Amassed more than 1,000 all-purpose yards twice.
- Led NFL with 1,007 kickoff-return yards in 1986.
- Led Bengals in receptions once and receiving yards three times.
- Ranks among Bengals career leaders in receiving yards (10th).
- Two-time division champion (1988 and 1990).
- 1988 AFC champion.
- 1989 Week 11 AFC Offensive Player of the Week.
- 1986 First-Team All-AFC selection.

70 - BOOBIE CLARK (RB; 1973-1978)

Bengals Numbers: 2,978 Rushing Yards, 151 Receptions, 1,139 Receiving Yards, 4,117 Yards from Scrimmage, 25 Rushing TDs, 27 TDs, 3.8 Rushing Average.

Notable Achievements

- Rushed for 988 yards and eight touchdowns in 1973.
- Amassed 1,335 yards from scrimmage in 1973.
- Led Bengals in rushing yards twice and receptions once.
- Ranks among Bengals career leaders in rushing yards (10th) and rushing touchdowns (9th).
- 1973 division champion.
- 1973 UPI and *Sporting News* AFC Rookie of the Year.
- 1973 Bengals team MVP.

71 - JEREMY HILL (RB; 2014-2017)

Bengals Numbers: 2,873 Rushing Yards, 67 Receptions, 484 Receiving Yards, 3,357 Yards from Scrimmage, 29 Rushing TDs, 30 TDs, 4.1 Rushing Average.

Notable Achievements

- Amassed more than 1,000 yards from scrimmage twice.
- Averaged 5.1 yards per carry in 2014.
- Led all NFL rookies with 1,124 rushing yards in 2014.
- Led NFL with 11 rushing touchdowns in 2015.
- Finished third in NFL with nine rushing touchdowns in 2014.
- Ranks among Bengals career leaders in rushing touchdowns (7th).
- 2015 division champion.
- 2014 Week 15 AFC Offensive Player of the Week.
- Member of 2014 NFL All-Rookie Team.

72 - DAN WILKINSON (DT/DE; 1994-1997)

Bengals Numbers: 25 Sacks, 162 Tackles, 2 Forced Fumbles, 1 Fumble Recovery, 1 Interception.

Notable Achievements

- Led all AFC defensive interior linemen with eight sacks in 1995.
- Led Bengals with 6 1/2 sacks in 1996.

73 - ICKEY WOODS (RB; 1988-1991)

Career Numbers: 1,525 Rushing Yards, 47 Receptions, 397 Receiving Yards, 1,922 Yards from Scrimmage, 27 Rushing TDs, 27 TDs, 4.6 Rushing Average.

Notable Achievements

- Rushed for 1,066 yards and 15 touchdowns in 1988.
- Led NFL with average of 5.3 yards per carry in 1988.
- Finished second in NFL with 15 touchdowns in 1988.
- Holds Bengals single-season record for most rushing touchdowns (15).
- Ranks among Bengals career leaders in rushing touchdowns (8th).
- Two-time division champion (1988 and 1990).
- 1988 AFC champion.
- 1988 Week 6 AFC Offensive Player of the Week.
- 1988 Week 13 NFL Offensive Player of the Week.
- Member of 1988 NFL All-Rookie Team.

- Finished third in 1988 NFL Offensive Rookie of the Year voting.
- 1988 Second-Team All-Pro selection.
- 1988 Second-Team All-AFC selection.
- Named to Bengals 40th Anniversary All-Time Team in 2007.

74 - JERMAINE GRESHAM (TE; 2010-2014)

Bengals Numbers: 280 Receptions, 2,722 Receiving Yards, 24 Touchdown Receptions.

Notable Achievements

- Surpassed 50 receptions four times and 700 receiving yards once.
- 2013 division champion.
- Two-time Pro Bowl selection (2011 and 2012).

75 - VONN BELL (DB; 2020-2022)

Bengals Numbers: 5 Interceptions, 71 Interception-Return Yards, 288 Tackles, 1 1/2 Sacks, 8 Forced Fumbles, 4 Fumble Recoveries.

Notable Achievements

- Led Bengals with 114 combined tackles in 2020.
- Tied for Bengals team lead with four interceptions in 2022.
- Ranks among Bengals career leaders in forced fumbles (tied for 7th).
- Two-time division champion (2021 and 2022).
- 2021 AFC champion.

GLOSSARY

ABBREVIATIONS AND STATISTICAL TERMS

C. Center.

COMP %. Completion percentage. The number of successfully completed passes divided by the number of passes attempted.

DB. Defensive Back.

FS. Free Safety.

INTS. Interceptions. Passes thrown by the quarterback that are caught by a member of the opposing team's defense.

KR. Kickoff returner.

LCB. Left cornerback.

LE. Left end.

LG. Left guard.

LOLB. Left-outside linebacker.

LT. Left tackle.

MLB. Middle linebacker.

NT. Nose tackle.

P. Punter.

PASS YDS. Passing yards.

PK. Placekicker.

PR. Punt returner.

QB. Quarterback.

QBR. Quarterback rating.

RB. Running back.

RCB. Right cornerback.

RE. Right end.

RECS. Receptions.

REC YDS. Receiving yards.

RG. Right guard.

ROLB. Right-outside linebacker.

RT. Right tackle.

SS. Strong safety.

ST. Special teams.

TD PASSES. Touchdown passes.

TD RECS. Touchdown receptions.

TDS. Touchdowns.

TE. Tight end.

WR. Wide receiver.

YDS FROM SCRIMMAGE. Yards from scrimmage (running and receiving combined).

YDS RUSHING. Rushing yards.

BIBLIOGRAPHY

BOOKS

Felser, Larry. *The Birth of the New NFL: How the 1966 NFL/AFL Merger Transformed Pro Football.* Guilford, CT: Lyons Press, 2008.

Jones, Danny. *More Distant Memories: Pro Football's Best Ever Players of the 50's, 60's, and 70's.* Bloomington, IN: AuthorHouse, 2006.

Powell, Mark, *Legends of the Jungle: Introducing the Initial Candidates for a Possible Cincinnati Bengals Hall of Fame.* iUniverse, 2017.

Prister, Tim, *What It Means to Be Fighting Irish: Ara Parseghian and Notre Dame's Greatest Players.* Chicago: Triumph Books, 2004.

Silverman, Steve. *Who's Better, Who's Best in Football?: Setting the Record Straight on the Top 60 NFL Players of the Past 60 Years.* New York: Skyhorse Publishing, 2009.

WEBSITES

Cincinnati Bengals
(www.bengals.com)
Cincinnati Enquirer
(www.cincinnati.com)
ESPN.com
(https://sports.espn.go.com)
Newsday.com
(www.newsday.com)
NYDailyNews.com
(www.nydailynews.com/new-york)
NYTimes.com
(www.nytimes.com)
Pro Football Talk from *nbcsports.com*
(https://profootballtalk.nbcsports.com)

StarLedger.com
(www.starledger.com)
SunSentinel.com
(https://articles.sun-sentinel.com)
The Players, online at Profootballreference.com
(www.pro-football-reference.com/players)